BEACON
BIBLE
EXPOSITIONS

BEACON BIBLE EXPOSITIONS

BEACON BIBLE EXPOSITIONS

VOLUME **1**

MATTHEW

by

WILLIAM E. McCUMBER

Editors
WILLIAM M. GREATHOUSE
WILLARD H. TAYLOR

BEACON HILL PRESS OF KANSAS CITY
Kansas City, Missouri

Permissions to quote from the following copyrighted versions of the Bible
are acknowledged with appreciation:

Revised Standard Version of the Bible (RSV), copyrighted 1946 and 1952.

The New English Bible (NEB), © the Delegates of the Oxford University
    Press and the Syndics of the Cambridge University Press, 1961, 1970.

The Holy Bible, New International Version (NIV), copyright © 1973 by
    New York Bible Society International.

Contents

7191

Editors' Preface

No Christian preacher or teacher has been more aware of the creating and sustaining power of the Word of God than the Apostle Paul. As a stratagem in his missionary endeavors, he sought out synagogues in the major cities where he knew Jews would gather to hear the Old Testament. No doubt he calculated that he would be invited to expound the Scriptures and so he would have a golden opportunity to preach Christ. That peripatetic preacher was confident that valid Christian experience and living could not be enjoyed apart from the Word of God, whether preached or written. To the Thessalonians he wrote: "And we also thank God constantly for this, that when you received the word of God which you heard from us, you accepted it not as the word of men but as what it really is, the word of God, which is at work in you believers" (1 Thess. 2:13, RSV). Strong Christians, and more broadly, strong churches, are born of, and nurtured on, authentic and winsome exposition of the Bible.

Beacon Bible Expositions provide a systematic, devotional Bible study program for laymen and a fresh, homiletical resource for preachers. All the benefits of the best biblical scholarship are found in them, but nontechnical language is used in the composition. A determined effort is made to relate the clarified truth to life today. The writers, Wesleyan in theological perspective, seek to interpret the gospel, pointing to the Living Word, Christ, who is the primary Subject of all scripture, the Mediator of redemption, and the Norm of Christian living.

The publication of this series is a prayerful invitation to both laymen and ministers to set out on a lifelong, systematic study of the Bible. Hopefully these studies will supply the initial impetus.

—WILLIAM M. GREATHOUSE AND
WILLARD H. TAYLOR, *Editors*

Topical Outline of Matthew

First Narrative Section: Genealogy, Infancy, Preparation
 The "Begats" (1:1-17)
 The "Beholds" (1:18-25)
 The Wise Men (2:1-12)
 The Unwise Men (2:13-23)
 The Voice in the Wilderness (3:1-12)
 The Voice from Heaven (3:13-17)
 The Voice of the Tempter (4:1-11)
 The Voice of the Saviour (4:12-25)

First Teaching Section: The Sermon on the Mount
 The "Blesseds" (5:1-16)
 The "Buts" (5.17-48)
 Catching God's Eye (6:1-18)
 Trusting God's Love (6:19-34)
 Don't Judge Your Brother (7:1-6)
 Don't Misjudge Your Father (7:7-12)
 The Two Ways (7:13-23)
 The Two Destinies (7:24-29)

Second Narrative Section: Ministry in Galilee
 Authority over Illness (8:1-17)
 Authority over Nature (8:18-27)
 Authority over Demons (8:28-34)
 Putting Men on Their Feet (9:1-9)
 Putting Critics in Their Place (9:10-17)
 The Unintimidated Christ (9:18-26)
 The Incomparable Christ (9:27-34)
 Help Wanted (9:35-38)

Second Teaching Section: The Charge to the Twelve
 The Mission of the Twelve (10:1-15)
 Sheep in a Wolf Pack (10:16-33)
 The Great Divider (10:34—11:1)

Third Narrative Section: Conflict and Rejection
 Rebuke and Tribute for John (11:2-19)
 Cities That Failed (11:20-24)
 Revelation and Invitation (11:25-30)
 Lord of the Sabbath (12:1-8)
 Withered Hands, Withered Hearts (12:9-21)
 The Kingdom of God Has Come (12:22-37)
 The Sign of Jonah (12:38-45)
 The Family of Jesus (12:46-50)

Introduction

1. *Authorship*

Tradition which reaches back to the first half of the second century names the Apostle Matthew as the author of this Gospel. While a majority of scholars have abandoned this view, some still find no cogent reasons for denying authorship to Matthew.

The subject matter, methodology, vocabulary, and style of the Gospel point to a Jewish-Christian author, versed in the Old Testament, conversant with Pharisaic Judaism, sharing a vision of world evangelism, and concerned for the instruction of converts to the faith. He is interested in case-law commentary, and aware of a near total split between Church and synagogue. He is precise and orderly in arranging and combining his materials. Matthew seems eminently qualified, and this book is content to accept him as the author of the first Gospel.

At the same time, the anonymity of the text and the ambiguity of the tradition are respected. One can reject Matthew as the writer without rejecting the Christ to whom the Gospel witnesses. The gospel message is not "Believe that the Apostle Matthew wrote the Gospel which has traditionally borne his name, and you will be saved."

If Matthew wrote it, the brief autobiography of his conversion in 9:9 is intriguing for what it omits. In Luke's account the tax collector "left everything" (RSV) to follow Jesus. When we recall the insistence of the first Gospel upon the high cost of discipleship, the lack of reference to his sacrifice of everything suggests a becoming humility and modesty in Matthew.

When and where the Gospel was written is uncertain, also. A date lying between A.D. 60 and 70 would satisfy our present knowledge of its background and text. The internal indicators point to a Jewish-Christian milieu with a definite interest in the evangelization of Gentiles. A Palestinian or near-Palestinian location is very probable. Antioch in Syria is a strong candidate as the place of origin.

Since this book is neither introduction nor commentary, detailed arguments, pro and con, for Matthean authorship are not presented. The reader is urged to examine them in a number of works on the subject.

2. *Structure*

The structural joints in the Gospel are highly visible. Dominant are the five blocks of teaching material, interspersed with narrative. Each of these sections closes with the formula "When Jesus had finished . . ." (RSV), with slight variations in the words following the formula. These are found at 7:28; 11:1; 13:53; 19:1; and 26:1. The five blocks of teaching are (1) the Sermon on the Mount (cc. 5—7); (2) the charge to the Twelve (c. 10); (3) the parables of the Kingdom (c. 13); (4) the discipline of the Church (c. 18); and (5) the eschatological discourse (cc. 24—25).

The ministry of Jesus is structured into two main periods, each introduced by the phrase "From that time . . ." The first is at 4:17, "From that time Jesus began to preach . . . ," and introduces the public ministry in Galilee. The second is at 16:21, "From that time Jesus began to show his disciples that he must . . . suffer" (RSV), and introduces a ministry which concentrates upon the Twelve as Jesus moves toward the Cross. The hinge of the movement is Peter's confession to Jesus' messiahship at Caesarea Philippi.

Matthew also uses the Rabbinic method of teaching by numbers. The numbers *2, 3, 7,* and *10* are employed, with *3* dominating. Random samples are: 2 demoniacs (8:28), 3 temptations (4:1-11), 3 "sowing" parables (13:1-32), 7 woes (23:13-30), and 10 miracles grouped in chapters 8 and 9. This was a common device for aiding teaching and learning.

Throughout Matthew's Gospel are Old Testament quotations prefaced with "introductory formulas" such as "All this was done, that it might be fulfilled which was spoken of the Lord by the prophet, saying" (1:22). Some scholars believe that these quotations are significantly structural, with the subject matter of Matthew serving as commentary (after the *pēsher* model) upon them.

3. *Content*

The middle of Matthew's Gospel is understood from its ends. It opens with a genealogy of Jesus and closes with the Great Commission to the disciples. The genealogy relates Jesus to Abraham and David, for Matthew intends to proclaim Him as the One in whom God's covenants with Abraham and David are fulfilled. He is the Seed of Abraham in whom all nations are blessed. He is the Son of David who rules over the people of God. The closing paragraph, therefore, discloses the risen Lord with greater authority than David possessed—indeed, with all authority—who sends His disciples to all nations with the gospel.

The dominant concept in Matthew is the kingdom of heaven, which is both present and future. The eschatological Kingdom, which was coming to shatter evil and establish a perfect human society of the righteous at the end of history, is already present, operative in the healing, judging, and saving ministry of Jesus. In its present hidden form the Kingdom is unrecognized, persecuted, and rejected by those who will not repent and believe the gospel. Those who would inherit the kingdom of the Father in the end must follow Jesus now, though the cost of discipleship is high, since the kingdom of God is opposed by the evil one. Discipleship means radical obedience to Jesus, a love that fulfills the law. The Kingdom is not opposed to law, but it does collide with legalism. The Messiah is in constant conflict with scribes and Pharisees, whose traditions He repudiates. The Kingdom is the rule of God and not the rules of men. The conflict climaxes in the Cross, which is not Jesus' defeat but His victory, as the Resurrection demonstrates.

This truth of the kingdom of heaven as present and future, rejected of men but vindicated by God, is set forth in alternating sections of instruction and action, all marked by a unique divine authority which astonishes the crowds. Miracles and parables abound in witness to One whose birth, life, and death were unlike all others. He is the Lord, the Son of Man, the Son of God, who is also Rabbi, Prophet, and Christ; and who will be Judge of all men and nations; truly the divine-human One. No developed Christology is found in the Gospel, of course, but the highest Christology is implicitly there.

The Messiah creates a messianic community, His *ecclesia,* in which He will be present until the end of the age, and through which His suffering-servant ministry is to be continued until the consummation. Instruction is given by which the Church can order and discipline its life as it serves the Kingdom in this world.

Matthew writes as a scribe trained for the kingdom of heaven, who from the treasure of his Jewish heritage and Christian faith brings forth old and new to supply the needs of his household, the Church. His Gospel reveals how effectively he has succeeded in the mission to make disciples and teach them to observe all that Christ commanded.

4. *Nature*

The Gospel of Matthew, like the other Synoptics, is essentially proclamation. It not only records Christ's preaching; it preaches Christ. It not only describes the ministry of Jesus as a proleptic form of the kingdom of God; it continues that ministry by setting Him forth, compelling men to settle their destinies by their responses to Him.

Within the Church of Matthew's day, and in ours, it functions pedagogically. It is *didache* and *kerygma.* It is a teaching manual and, therefore, a learning tool, replete with urgent lessons and mnemonic aids. Instruction in "the kingdom of God, and his righteousness" is supplied to us as we read and study Matthew. We learn what to believe and how to behave as disciples of Jesus Christ.

History is there, and elements of biography. But essentially Matthew is confession, witness, proclamation, instruction, which mediates the presence and instruments the power of the Lord Jesus Christ.

A final word: The text of Matthew is more valuable than any exposition or commentary. Don't neglect the text itself, and read it in a modern English text as well as in the King James Version.

First Narrative Section:
Genealogy, Infancy, Preparation
Matthew 1:1—4:25

MATTHEW 1

The "Begats"

Matthew 1:1-17

1 The book of the generation of Jesus Christ, the son of David, the son of Abraham.

2 Abraham begat Isaac; and Isaac begat Jacob; and Jacob begat Judas and his brethren;

3 And Judas begat Phares and Zara of Thamar; and Phares begat Esrom, and Esrom begat Aram;

4 And Aram begat Aminadab; and Aminadab begat Naasson; and Naasson begat Salmon;

5 And Salmon begat Booz of Rachab; and Booz begat Obed of Ruth; and Obed begat Jesse;

6 And Jesse begat David the king; and David the king begat Solomon of her that had been the wife of Urias;

7 And Solomon begat Roboam; and Roboam begat Abia; and Abia begat Asa;

8 And Asa begat Josaphat; and Josaphat begat Joram; and Joram begat Ozias;

9 And Ozias begat Joatham; and Joatham begat Achaz; and Achaz begat Ezekias;

10 And Ezekias begat Manasses; and Manasses begat Amon; and Amon begat Josias;

11 And Josias begat Jechonias and his brethren, about the time they were carried away to Babylon:

12 And after they were brought to Babylon, Jechonias begat Salathiel; and Salathiel begat Zorobabel;

13 And Zorobabel begat Abiud; and Abiud begat Eliakim; and Eliakim begat Azor;

14 And Azor begat Sadoc; and Sadoc begat Achim; and Achim begat Eliud;

15 And Eliud begat Eleazar; and Eleazar begat Matthan; and Matthan begat Jacob;

16 And Jacob begat Joseph the husband of Mary, of whom was born Jesus, who is called Christ.

17 So all the generations from Abraham to David are fourteen generations; and from David until the carrying away into Babylon are fourteen generations; and from the carrying away into Babylon unto Christ are fourteen generations.

The Gospel of Matthew begins with a list of names which the average modern reader finds dull to read and hard to pronounce. But this ancestry list serves a vital role in Matthew's purpose and will reward patient attention.

1. The primary purpose of the genealogy is *to link Jesus to Abraham and David.* The "credentials" of Jesus as the Messiah would be suspect to all Jews unless He was *the son of David, the son of Abraham.*

Matthew writes to affirm Jesus as the One in whom ancient covenants with Abraham and David are fulfilled. The covenant which God made with Abraham promised blessing upon all families of the earth (Gen. 12:1-3). David was promised an Offspring who would establish his throne forever (2 Sam. 7:12-16). Matthew opens with the genealogy which traces Jesus back to both illustrious ancestors, and closes with the risen Lord, in possession of *all authority,* sending His gospel to *all* nations.

2. There are valuable *secondary lessons in the genealogy.* One is that God works in history. In the world of Matthew's day many thought God was aloof from human events, at best an absentee landlord, at worst an indifferent spectator. But the living God of Israel had involved himself in the sweaty and bloody arena of history as a Deliverer and Judge of His people. Jesus is the Son of God, in whose career among men the Almighty's work was being continued. The 42 generations, broken into three groups of 14, may be an arbitrary scheme; but they say clearly that (1) God works in human events, and (2) Jesus is the meaning of all history, both that which was before His day and that since.

Another secondary lesson is that God loves all people. Messiah's ancestry is not pure Jewish. A Moabitess is there. Neither are Jesus' ancestors the morally elite. Some sordid sins are recalled by such entries as Rahab, Bathsheba, and Manasseh; a harlot, an adulteress, an idolater! The inclusion of Gentiles and rascals in the ancestry list bears implicit reminder that God loves sinning humanity, and Jesus comes to redeem them from guilt and bondage.

Still another indirect lesson of the genealogy is that

God keeps His word. Patient centuries filled with impatient people may elapse between promise and fulfillment, but God does not default those promises. Between Abraham, with whom covenant was made, and Jesus, in whom the covenant-promise is realized, are 42 generations of checkered events. Throughout them sin-weary people keep raising an anguished cry, "How long, O Lord, how long?" Now at last the answer is given in Jesus Christ! God keeps faith with those to whom He makes promise.

We who follow Jesus are recipients of the *better promises* of the *better covenant,* to use the language of the Epistle to the Hebrews. Our own trial of faith is created by two millennia of baffling and bloodied history since Jesus was born. But we may be assured that what God has begun in Jesus will be brought to its pledged glorious consummation. Maranatha!

The "Beholds"

Matthew 1:18-25

18 Now the birth of Jesus Christ was on this wise: When as his mother Mary was espoused to Joseph, before they came together, she was found with child of the Holy Ghost.
19 Then Joseph her husband, being a just man, and not willing to make her a publick example, was minded to put her away privily.
20 But while he thought on these things, behold, the angel of the Lord appeared unto him in a dream, saying, Joseph, thou son of David, fear not to take unto thee Mary thy wife: for that which is conceived in her is of the Holy Ghost.
21 And she shall bring forth a son, and thou shalt call his name JESUS: for he shall save his people from their sins.
22 Now all this was done, that it might be fulfilled which was spoken of the Lord by the prophet, saying,
23 Behold, a virgin shall be with child, and shall bring forth a son, and they shall call his name Emmanuel, which being interpreted is, God with us.
24 Then Joseph being raised from sleep did as the angel of the Lord had bidden him, and took unto him his wife:
25 And knew her not till she had brought forth her firstborn son: and he called his name JESUS.

Jesus' birth, writes Matthew, *took place in this way* (18, RSV). Some have charged Matthew with inventing or repeating a legend, but others are content to accept the biblical account. His birth might reasonably be unique whose life and death were!

1. *"In this way" points to a surprising way.* The wonder of the birth is expressed in the two "behold" phrases. *Behold,*

the angel . . . (20). Joseph, resolved to quietly "break the engagement," is approached *in a dream* by *the angel of the Lord,* a special messenger of God to assure him that Mary's unborn Child was supernaturally conceived through the creative power of the Holy Spirit.

The errands of angels are as privileged as their natures are mysterious. They were heralds of the resurrection of Jesus (28:5-6) and of His second advent (Acts 1:10-11). Here the angel proclaims the Incarnation. These messages became the privileged task of all Jesus' followers. We share with angels the joy of announcing a Saviour to needy men.

Behold, a virgin . . . (23). The chosen vessel for Jesus' coming to the world was a humble, faithful Jewish maiden. God uses the humblest of persons in service to the highest of purposes. In the wonder of grace Mary's Son will be Mary's Saviour. How unsearchable is the wisdom of God!

2. *"In this way" points to a scriptural way.* "All this took place to fulfil what the Lord had spoken by the prophet" (22, RSV). This is the first of nine significant quotations from the Old Testament which Matthew introduces with a "fulfillment formula" (Gk., *hina plērothē*). They are not mere proof texts, but intended to call attention to their contexts in the Old Testament.

Matthew views Jesus as the Fulfillment of the Old Testament. The Messiah relives in His own career the decisive events of Israel's experience. A strong case can be made for seeing these quotations with introductory formulas as a basic structure in Matthew, interspersed with material which forms a commentary *(pēsher)* upon them.

The passage cited here from Isaiah underscores the action of God who comes sovereignly to save when the nation is helpless to save itself.

3. *"In this way," therefore, points to a saving way.* "He shall save his people from their sins" (21). The saving mission of Jesus is summed up in the names given to Him. By the prophet, He is called *Emmanuel.* By the parents, He is called *Jesus.*

Emmanuel means *"God with us."* In the person of Jesus, the living God was present with men on a saving mission. The God of Israel revealed himself as One who judged and delivered by intervening personally on behalf of His oppressed people (cf. Exod. 3:7-10). Broadus observes that the power of the gospel "does not reside in propositions, but in a person." Men are not saved by their ideas of God, but by God's actions for them.

Jesus is that action. The most probable translation of the name Jesus is a prayer, "O Lord, save!" Jesus is God's answer to man's cry for salvation. He is the redeeming action by which God extricates helpless man from the predicament of sin and guilt.

The Virgin Birth is thus a sign of grace. It is enacted gospel. The holy God, at His gracious initiative, does for man what man cannot do—provides a Saviour, who is none other than God with us and for us.

MATTHEW 2

The Wise Men

Matthew 2:1-12

1 Now when Jesus was born in Bethlehem of Judaea in the days of Herod the king, behold, there came wise men from the east to Jerusalem,

2 Saying, Where is he that is born King of the Jews? for we have seen his star in the east, and are come to worship him.

3 When Herod the king had heard these things, he was troubled, and all Jerusalem with him.

4 And when he had gathered all the chief priests and scribes of the people together, he demanded of them where Christ should be born.

5 And they said unto him, In Bethlehem of Judaea: for thus it is written by the prophet,

6 And thou Bethlehem, in the land of Juda, art not the least among the princes of Juda: for out of thee shall come a Governor, that shall rule my people Israel.

7 Then Herod, when he had privily called the wise men, enquired of them diligently what time the star appeared.

8 And he sent them to Bethlehem, and said, Go and search diligently for the young child; and when ye have found him, bring me word again, that I may come and worship him also.

9 When they had heard the king, they departed; and, lo, the star, which they saw in the east, went before them, till it came and stood over where the young child was.

10 When they saw the star, they rejoiced with exceeding great joy.

11 And when they were come into the house, they saw the young child with Mary his mother, and fell down, and worshipped him: and when

they had opened their treasures, they presented unto him gifts; gold, and frankincense, and myrrh.
12   And being warned of God in a dream that they should not return to Herod, they departed into their own country another way.

Wise men do not dogmatize about the *wise men*, for they are shrouded in mystery. Unhappy traditions have made them three in number and kings in office, with no supporting evidence whatever. *From the east* is very ambiguous, so that *their own country* cannot be positively identified. We can learn more from them than we can learn about them.

1. *Wise men follow God's guidance.* From *their own country* they made a lengthy and hazardous journey guided unerringly by divine means.

An unusual means of guidance occurred, called *the star* and *his star*. This star, of which so much is conjectured, so little known, led them first to Jerusalem and then on to Bethlehem.

God's usual means of guidance was also involved, the Scriptures. The precise place of birth was identified from a passage in Micah.

Both means of guidance pointed the way to the Saviour. We cannot mourn the absence of a star who yet have the Scriptures. They are given to lead us to Christ (cf. John 20:31).

2. *Wise men worship God's Son.* Reaching the house where the Holy Family were residing, they *fell down* and *worshipped him*. We cannot read into their act of homage theological and liturgical significance of later Christian worship. But if ours is more fully informed, it should be more faithfully rendered!

They presented gifts to the infant King of *gold, and frankincense, and myrrh.* From early centuries the gifts have been allegorized to the point of absurdity. They gave what they had and it was fitting to the occasion.

Recent researches have suggested that these items were commonly used by magi as "tools of the trade." If so, offering them could attest "a declaration of dissociation from former practices." Matthew may have intended the account, in part, as a blow at astrology.

A final comment on their worship: Matthew says they saw both Mary and the baby Jesus, and worshipped *him*, not them! How tragic that in the course of church history millions would kneel and pray to Mary who never prayed to her Son. Wise men worship *Him!*

3. *Wise men heed God's warning.* *"Warned of God in a dream,"* they returned home without reporting the infant Messiah's location to designing Herod. They spared themselves the tragedy of becoming accomplices in crime against Jesus, and became laborers with God in protecting the endangered Child.

Later Pilate will have the Messiah before him to free or to kill. How fateful for the Roman procurator that he did not heed a dream-warning (27:19)!

For the magi, Herod became a kind of Christ-alternative, as Barabbas was for the mob in Pilate's court. They could honor the puppet king or the true King. They wisely chose the latter.

The Unwise Men

Matthew 2:13-23

13 And when they were departed, behold, the angel of the Lord appeareth to Joseph in a dream, saying, Arise, and take the young child and his mother, and flee into Egypt, and be thou there until I bring thee word: for Herod will seek the young child to destroy him.

14 When he arose, he took the young child and his mother by night, and departed into Egypt:

15 And was there until the death of Herod: that it might be fulfilled which was spoken of the Lord by the prophet, saying, Out of Egypt have I called my son.

16 Then Herod, when he saw that he was mocked of the wise men, was exceeding wroth, and sent forth, and slew all the children that were in Bethlehem, and in all the coasts thereof, from two years old and under, according to the time which he had diligently enquired of the wise men.

17 Then was fulfilled that which was spoken by Jeremy the prophet, saying,

18 In Rama was there a voice heard, lamentation, and weeping, and great mourning. Rachel weeping for her children, and would not be comforted, because they are not.

19 But when Herod was dead, behold, an angel of the Lord appeareth in a dream to Joseph in Egypt,

20 Saying, Arise, and take the young child and his mother, and go into the land of Israel: for they are dead which sought the young child's life.

21 And he arose, and took the young child and his mother, and came into the land of Israel.

22 But when he heard that Archelaus did reign in Judaea in the room of his father Herod, he was afraid to go thither: notwithstanding, being

warned of God in a dream, he turned aside into the parts of Galilee:
23 And he came and dwelt in a city called Nazareth: that it might be
fulfilled which was spoken by the prophets, He shall be called a Naza-
rene.

In Matthew's infancy narrative some men appear as villains. They go as far as an attempt to murder the infant Messiah. The plot miscarries, for *the angel of the Lord* warns Joseph to flee with the mother and Child into Egypt. Probably the magi's gifts were put to practical use, helping to finance the saving flight.

(Matthew sees the flight and return as fulfillment of Hosea's words, *Out of Egypt have I called my son* [Hos. 6:1]. The son, in Hosea's passage, is Israel. Jesus is living through the experience of His people, a Matthean motif.)

These who oppose the Messiah are the unwise men, opposites of the magi who worshipped Him.

1. The infancy narrative *mentions some unwise theologians* (4-6). They are designated *the chief priests and scribes of the people,* and were assembled at Herod's orders to tell him where the Messiah's birth would occur. And they were ready with the answer: *In Bethlehem . . . for thus it is written.* Here are men who knew the Scriptures but did not know the Saviour!

How pathetic they are in contrast to the magi who hastened to find the newborn King! These custodians of the Bible and hope of Israel did not even get excited enough by the report of the star and the journey of the magi to travel to Bethlehem and investigate. They merely rolled their scrolls and settled back in dull religious routines. They were so truly the prisoners of Rome's puppet they would not seek God's Ruler.

2. The infancy narrative also *exposes some unwise politicians,* the murderous *Herod* and the menacing *Archelaus.*

Herod's "slaughter of the innocents" did not surprise his contemporaries. Paranoid fears of being assassinated or deposed had driven him to butcher every suspected rival to his throne, including his favorite wife and several sons. One who would murder his own family without blinking would think nothing of having a few baby boys put to the sword.

Archelaus was "a chip off the old block," the worst of Herod's heirs. He "celebrated" his inauguration by the massacre of 3,000 people.

The words of the angel, *They are dead which sought the child's life* (20), is a fitting epitaph for all who opposed Jesus! Even those who took His life when He had grown to manhood only finally succeeded in destroying themselves. He is risen and He reigns, while all their crowns have fallen and their thrones have crumbled. Men are fools who set themselves against God's purposes in Christ (cf. Psalm 2).

3. The infancy narrative also *mentions some unwise soldiers,* those who carried out the odious command of Herod to kill the babies.

Their conduct is as inexcusable as it is reprehensible. Guilt is not assuaged by pleading, "We were only obeying orders." What we do through others we do ourselves. Herod was a murderer without drawing a sword. But the obverse is true: What we do for others, we do ourselves. The soldiers were as guilty as if the massacre-plot had been their own devising.

The *furious rage* (16, RSV) of Herod intimidated them, but does not vindicate them. Better to suffer the wrath of Herod than of God (cf. 10:28).

MATTHEW 3

The Voice in the Wilderness

Matthew 3:1-12

> 1 In those days came John the Baptist, preaching in the wilderness of Judaea,
> 2 And saying, Repent ye: for the kingdom of heaven is at hand.
> 3 For this is he that was spoken of by the prophet Esaias, saying, The voice of one crying in the wilderness, Prepare ye the way of the Lord, make his paths straight.
> 4 And the same John had his raiment of camel's hair, and a leathern girdle about his loins; and his meat was locusts and wild honey.
> 5 Then went out to him Jerusalem, and all Judaea, and all the region round about Jordan,
> 6 And were baptized of him in Jordan, confessing their sins.
> 7 But when he saw many of the Pharisees and Sadducees come to his baptism, he said unto them, O generation of vipers, who hath warned you to flee from the wrath to come?

8 Bring forth therefore fruits meet for repentance:
9 And think not to say within yourselves, We have Abraham to our father: for I say unto you, that God is able of these stones to raise up children unto Abraham.
10 And now also the axe is laid unto the root of the trees: therefore every tree which bringeth not forth good fruit is hewn down, and cast into the fire.
11 I indeed baptize you with water unto repentance: but he that cometh after me is mightier than I, whose shoes I am not worthy to bear: he shall baptize you with the Holy Ghost, and with fire:
12 Whose fan is in his hand, and he will throughly purge his floor, and gather his wheat into the garner; but he will burn up the chaff with unquenchable fire.

In those days came John the Baptist, preaching (1). In earlier days the prophets came, in later days the apostles. In our days God still sends men to herald His word to a dying world. And every messenger worth his salt must be, like John the Baptist, a *voice,* not a mere echo of popular and palatable thought.

1. *John's voice broke a silence* (1-6). Some four centuries had elapsed since an authentic prophet's voice had sounded the word of the Lord to Israel. The uncompromising voices that had challenged king, priest, and commoner alike; that had rebuked sin, threatened judgment, and promised salvation, were abruptly stilled. Israel waited, with deferred hopes and postponed decisions, to hear again the living words of God from the lips of man. The wait had ended, the prophet had appeared, and once again the nation was on trial.

God's silences are hard to understand, harder to endure, but they are always broken in decisive victory. At first Jesus answers not a word to the pleading mother of a sick girl, but when He does speak the demon is exorcised and the girl is delivered (15:22-28). *There was silence in heaven,* while on the earth the beasts raged and the saints bled. But when God does break the silence evil is judged, the saints are vindicated, and the triumph of the Lamb is consummated (Rev. 8:1 f.). So now, God ends the "intertestamental" period of silence, and Messiah's healing, judging, saving ministry is announced. *The kingdom of heaven is at hand* (2)!

2. *John's voice challenged an axiom* (7-10). Many in Israel were convinced that election purchased immunity from

ultimate judgment and guaranteed final salvation. Perhaps no groups more smugly assumed their acceptance with God than did the *Pharisees,* custodians of the Torah, and the *Sadducees,* controllers of the Temple. In preaching reminiscent of Jeremiah's famous "Temple Sermon" (Jer. 7:1 f.), John staggered these religious leaders, branding them a *generation of vipers,* warning them that physical descent from Abraham was no shelter from *the wrath to come.* The Lord would not travel crooked paths. Repentance, evidenced in honest confession and changed behavior, was the condition of entrance into *the kingdom of heaven.*

John's baptisms marked him as more than a prophet. They must probably be understood in the light of the proliferating "baptist movement" of those days. But he sounded the ancient and authentic note of prophecy in his rugged denunciation of sin and firm insistence upon repentance as an indispensable ingredient of righteousness. Neither the legalism of the Pharisees nor the ritualism of the Sadducees constituted genuine righteousness. Men must break with sin, and publicly identify themselves with the coming Messiah.

3. *John's voice heralded the Messiah.* Not as a distant and vague hope, but as the Coming One whose ministry would follow closely upon John's. Of this Coming One the forerunner posits three truths.

He is superior to prophets. So much mightier than John will the Messiah be that John feels unworthy to serve Him as a sandal-bearer.

He is a Separator of men. The message of John points to a division within Israel, to be effected by the Messiah, and already suggested by those who receive the baptism of John. Under the figures of fruitful and unfruitful trees, of wheat and chaff, the messianic community (the true Israel, the remnant) is marked off from the nation at large. The people of the Messiah will be baptized with the Holy Spirit, the promised eschatological gift of life, power, and cleansing (Joel 2:28-32; Ezek. 36:25-29). The people who reject the Messiah will be baptized with fire, the eschatological wrath of God upon evil.

Thus, Messiah is a Saviour from wrath. The wrath of God is real and awful. There must be an ultimate cleansing of His threshing floor. Deliverance from that wrath comes, not by religious heritage or practice, but by repenting of sin and believing on the One who came to be the Saviour of the world.

At the same time, it must be noted that John's message is more than a threat of judgment; it is a promise of salvation. The Messiah will baptize His people with the Holy Spirit. Initially fulfilled at Pentecost, this promise extends to all believers through all time (Acts 2:38-39). The promise includes purity of heart (Acts 15:8-9) and power for service (Acts 1:8). The evidence of this baptism with the Spirit, therefore, is the power to witness for Christ in a needy world, and to sustain a holy life in a dirty world.

The Voice from Heaven

Matthew 3:13-17

> 13 Then cometh Jesus from Galilee to Jordan unto John, to be baptized of him.
> 14 But John forbad him, saying, I have need to be baptized of thee, and comest thou to me?
> 15 And Jesus answering said unto him, Suffer it to be so now: for thus it becometh us to fulfil all righteousness. Then he suffered him.
> 16 And Jesus, when he was baptized, went up straightway out of the water: and, lo, the heavens were opened unto him, and he saw the Spirit of God descending like a dove, and lighting upon him:
> 17 And lo a voice from heaven, saying, This is my beloved Son, in whom I am well pleased.

John's ministry of baptizing reaches a significant and puzzling climax when Jesus presents himself for baptism. Long lines of confessed sinners had been baptized, and *then cometh Jesus!* John demurred. Somehow he discerned in Jesus the Mightier One whose coming he had heralded. Should the lesser baptize the Mightier? The other way around, surely! But Jesus insists, in words whose meaning still provokes debate, and John consents. Whatever doubts the Baptizer had are removed when a voice speaks from heaven, saying, *This is my beloved Son, in whom I am well pleased* (17).

1. *The "why" of God's speech has special significance.* Here One stands with others as a candidate for baptism. All those others have confessed their sins and have evi-

denced their repentance as the condition of baptism. Now One has come whom John discerns as the promised Messiah, the Saviour. Admittedly, those others cannot save themselves or one another. Why should He who comes to save be in that company? The Father's speech, without removing the mystery, vindicates the character of Jesus. With Him, with His whole life, the Father is pleased. The Sinless One stands among the sinners.

Upon Jesus, the Spirit can descend like a dove, energizing and guiding Him for the messianic ministry, because, contrary to appearances, He who stands among sinners is the Father's only Son (as *beloved* implies), who does always the Father's will.

2. *The "what" of God's speech is also highly instructive.* His words allude to Psalm 2, where the messianic King is addressed as the Son of God; and to Isaiah 42, where the Servant of God is introduced whose sufferings atone for sin. Thus the address blends what has been termed the "coronation-formula" of the King and the "ordination-formula" of the Servant. Both of these figures, the Ruler and the Sufferer, are joined now in the one Person, Jesus.

From this unique synthesis Jesus knows precisely what the nature and direction of His messiahship must be. His rule will be redemptive. He will deliver His people from their sins through suffering in their stead. The baptism at the Jordan is a prelude to the baptism at the Cross, where He will be identified with sinners in fathomless depths of suffering love.

3. *The "when" of God's speech is sobering in its implication.* He is *well pleased* with Jesus precisely as Jesus identifies himself with sinners. This gives special urgency to the words of Jesus, *"Let it be so now"* (15, RSV). Jesus will not always take the sinner's place. He came to be baptized, to suffer death in atoning love for our sakes. But scripture declares that He will come again, this time not to bear sin but to finally judge sinners. John the Baptist made it clear that the One who *now* saves the penitent and believing from the coming wrath will then be the very subject of that wrath, visiting the final judgment of God upon

all who reject God's Suffering Servant! *Now,* while God is well pleased to make Him an Offering for sin, our repentance and faith have urgent priority over all else.

Jesus came to baptize with the Spirit, but first He must be baptized in the suffering of the Cross. The gift of life awaits the death of the Son.

MATTHEW 4

The Voice of the Tempter

Matthew 4:1-11

> 1 Then was Jesus led up of the spirit into the wilderness to be tempted of the devil.
> 2 And when he had fasted forty days and forty nights, he was afterward an hungred.
> 3 And when the tempter came to him, he said, If thou be the Son of God, command that these stones be made bread.
> 4 But he answered and said, It is written, Man shall not live by bread alone, but by every word that proceedeth out of the mouth of God.
> 5 Then the devil taketh him up into the holy city, and setteth him on a pinnacle of the temple,
> 6 And saith unto him, If thou be the Son of God, cast thyself down: for it is written, He shall give his angels charge concerning thee: and in their hands they shall bear thee up, lest at any time thou dash thy foot against a stone.
> 7 Jesus said unto him, It is written again, Thou shalt not tempt the Lord thy God.
> 8 Again, the devil taketh him up into an exceeding high mountain, and sheweth him all the kingdoms of the world, and the glory of them;
> 9 And saith unto him, All these things will I give thee, if thou wilt fall down and worship me.
> 10 Then saith Jesus unto him, Get thee hence, Satan: for it is written, Thou shalt worship the Lord thy God, and him only shalt thou serve.
> 11 Then the devil leaveth him, and, behold, angels came and ministered unto him.

Then Jesus was led up by the Spirit . . . to be tempted by the devil (1, RSV). *Then!* Having received the Spirit as His power for service, He must decide the direction His service will take. Having been identified as the Ruler-Sufferer, He must decide to actualize the agony implied. Having heard the voices of forerunner and Father, He must hear the voice of the tempter, striving subtly and desperately to dissuade Him from a scriptural to a national messiahship.

1. *Satan speaks to Jesus as a lexicon-maker.* At the waters of baptism God had said, *This is my . . . Son.* Now in the wilderness of testing Satan twice says, *"If you are the Son of God"* (3, 6, RSV). His strategy is one of definition. Scripture defines sonship as obedience. Satan would re-define sonship as privilege, masking responsibility by emphasizing rights. Should the Son of God be hungry (for bread or men's acceptance) when He has power to turn stones to bread? But Jesus places himself in subjection to God's written words, affirming, *" 'Man shall not live by bread alone, but by every word that proceeds from the mouth of God' "* (4, RSV). Sonship for himself and for all mankind must be defined as obedience to the Father.

God's terms with the devil's meanings are strategies of destruction. In this way grace has been perverted to law, gospel to moralism, and the Church to empire in the history of Christianity. We dare not take vocabulary from God and definition from Satan, for this destroys sonship.

2. *Satan speaks to Jesus as a proof-texter.* He tries to manipulate the Word, to which Jesus has expressed allegiance. Live by God's Word? Very well, then, press the promise of protection made in Psalm 91 into the service of gaining a following as Messiah. Jesus said, Live by *every* word; but Satan sets part against the whole, wresting a scripture from its context and setting scripture against scripture.

The reply of Jesus exposes the trap. *It is written again* (7). Not by isolated proof texts is truth served and integrity maintained, but by submission to the whole tenor of the Scriptures. The strength of heresy has always been its appeal to scripture, just enough scripture to distract the careless mind from the need for more scripture.

3. *Satan speaks to Jesus as an option-giver.* In the third temptation he suggests an alternative to the Cross. *Worship me,* and receive *the kingdoms of the world* as a gift (8-9). In the psalm to which the voice from heaven alluded, God promises the nations to His Son (Ps. 2:8). The third temptation gathers up the force of the first two. Spare yourself. Forget the Suffering-Servant scriptures. Don't

win the kingdoms by the hard way of suffering and death. Take another and easier way to the goal. If Satan cannot change the goal, he seeks to change the route. He always offers an option to the expressed will of God.

Again he is defeated by One who understands sonship as obedience to all the word of God. Israel, called out of Egypt as the son of God, was tested in the wilderness and failed. Jesus, the Son of God, called out of Egypt (2:15), himself the true Israel, was likewise tested but stood. He overcame the tempter, quoting passages of scripture from the very record of old Israel's experience (Deut. 8:3; 6:16; 6:13).

And He conquered temptation as *Man,* i.e., in a representative capacity, as the Exemplar for His followers. He used no divine powers, but only such means as we also have available—knowledge of and obedience to the written Word of God.

The Voice of the Saviour

Matthew 4:12-25

12 Now when Jesus had heard that John was cast into prison, he departed into Galilee;
13 And leaving Nazareth, he came and dwelt in Capernaum, which is upon the sea coast, in the borders of Zabulon and Nephthalim:
14 That it might be fulfilled which was spoken by Esaias the prophet, saying,
15 The land of Zabulon, and the land of Nephthalim, by the way of the sea, beyond Jordan, Galilee of the Gentiles;
16 The people which sat in darkness saw great light; and to them which sat in the region and shadow of death light is sprung up.
17 From that time Jesus began to preach, and to say, Repent: for the kingdom of heaven is at hand.
18 And Jesus, walking by the sea of Galilee, saw two brethren, Simon called Peter, and Andrew his brother, casting a net into the sea: for they were fishers.
19 And he saith unto them, Follow me, and I will make you fishers of men.
20 And they straightway left their nets, and followed him.
21 And going on from thence, he saw other two brethren, James the son of Zebedee, and John his brother, in a ship with Zebedee their father, mending their nets; and he called them.
22 And they immediately left the ship and their father, and followed him.
23 And Jesus went about all Galilee, teaching in their synagogues, and preaching the gospel of the kingdom, and healing all manner of sickness and all manner of disease among the people.
24 And his fame went throughout all Syria: and they brought unto him all sick people that were taken with divers diseases and torments,

and those which were possessed with devils, and those which were lunatick, and those that had the palsy; and he healed them.
25 And there followed him great multitudes of people from Galilee, and from Decapolis, and from Jerusalem, and from Judaea, and from beyond Jordan.

John was cast into prison; so Jesus *departed into Galilee* (12). Herod may arrest the prophet but he cannot restrain the announced Kingdom. So far from intimidating the work of God, events are set in motion that fulfill ancient prophecy. Light bursts forth on Galileans who lived in *the shadow of death.* The voice of the intrepid forerunner is stilled, but the voice of Messiah himself now sounds forth, preaching, healing, and saving with unprecedented authority.

1. *The voice of Jesus is heard as a Preacher. "Jesus began to preach"* (17). The nearing Kingdom must be heralded, if not by John, then by the King himself.

The New Testament understands preaching as heraldry. Preaching is a man voicing forth a "given" message, the Word of God, and not his own or others' opinions. God speaks the word and men are not at liberty either to withhold it or to alter it. Seen in this light, every suggested moratorium on preaching is unbelieving nonsense.

The message of preaching, as done by Jesus, is summarized in the phrase *the gospel of the kingdom* (23). The message is good news, for God is acting to assert His kingly reign over His people. Because that rule over demons, disease, and death has drawn near, men who hope to enter the Kingdom are summoned to *repent.* The living God is ready to judge sin and save sinners in the ministry of the Messiah.

2. *The voice of Jesus is heard as a Recruiter,* also (18-22). Matthew records here the calling of four disciples—Peter, Andrew, James, and John—to become Jesus' Kingdom helpers.

The recruiting discloses the kind of man Jesus is. He is a Ruler, the King who lays claim absolutely upon men's lives, saying, *Follow me.* He is a Leader, who says to *follow,* not simply to go! He does not impose a burden He will not himself carry, or demand a labor He will not himself perform. And He is a Maker, who promises, *I will make you fishers of men.* Following Him, learning from Him, men's minds and lives are graciously reconstructed, enabling them to reach their fellowmen for the Kingdom.

The recruiting discloses, also, the kind of men Jesus calls. They were ordinary men and occupied men. Kingdom work is not easy, and its rewards are not material. Men bound by sloth or greed or pride do not qualify for the task.

The recruiting shows us, too, the kind of ministry Jesus shares. As these four leave nets and boats and homes to follow Jesus, He goes about Galilee, *teaching* . . . *preaching* . . . and *healing.* Before long He will confer upon them authority to continue this same gracious ministry to the bodies, minds, and spirits of men (cf. 10:1 f.).

3. *The voice of Jesus is heard as an Instructor* (23). He teaches in the synagogues, in a manner similar to many rabbis, but with an authority equalled by none. To the teaching ministry of Jesus, Matthew gives large place, structuring his Gospel around five blocks of teaching material. His teaching blends old and new, interpreting and applying truths already given to Israel, and speaking fresh and greater truths that belong to the new covenant.

The epitome of Jesus' ministry in 4:23 explains the throngs who followed Him and introduces the first block of teaching.

First Teaching Section:
The Sermon on the Mount
Matthew 5:1—7:29

MATTHEW 5

The "Blesseds"

Matthew 5:1-16

1 And seeing the multitudes, he went up into a mountain: and when he was set, his disciples came unto him:
2 And he opened his mouth, and taught them, saying,
3 Blessed are the poor in spirit: for theirs is the kingdom of heaven.
4 Blessed are they that mourn: for they shall be comforted.
5 Blessed are the meek: for they shall inherit the earth.
6 Blessed are they which do hunger and thirst after righteousness: for they shall be filled.
7 Blessed are the merciful: for they shall obtain mercy.
8 Blessed are the pure in heart: for they shall see God.
9 Blessed are the peacemakers: for they shall be called the children of God.
10 Blessed are they which are persecuted for righteousness' sake: for theirs is the kingdom of heaven.
11 Blessed are ye, when men shall revile you, and persecute you, and shall say all manner of evil against you falsely, for my sake.
12 Rejoice, and be exceeding glad: for great is your reward in heaven: for so persecuted they the prophets which were before you.
13 Ye are the salt of the earth: but if the salt have lost his savour, wherewith shall it be salted? it is thenceforth good for nothing, but to be cast out, and to be trodden under foot of men.
14 Ye are the light of the world. A city that is set on an hill cannot be hid.
15 Neither do men light a candle, and put it under a bushel, but on a candlestick; and it giveth light unto all that are in the house.
16 Let your light so shine before men, that they may see your good works, and glorify your Father which is in heaven.

The first block of teaching in Matthew is the Sermon on the Mount (cc. 5—7). No piece of ethical literature has been more influential in the course of history. Admittedly, it is hard to interpret, with human assessments ranging all the way from "interim ethics" to "counsels of perfection."

Difficult as it is to understand, the "sermon" is even harder to implement in daily life! No one but Jesus has ever fully lived out its rugged moral demands. Wesley said that in the light of 1 Corinthians 13 every man falls short. The same can be affirmed of the Sermon on the Mount. None are exempt from the responsibility of living by its truth, however. The sermon is, as A. M. Hunter has phrased it, a pattern for life.

Verses 1-16 are a kind of introduction to the rest, as Psalm 1 is to the whole collection of psalms. The introduction deals with two principal matters—what disciples are and what they do.

1. *What disciples are is covered in the Beatitudes.* They are people in poverty, *the poor in spirit.* The phrase describes those who are conscious of deserving nothing and needing everything from God. They accept with gratitude what He bestows, and without bitterness what He withholds. Their trust is not in human resources, but in divine faithfulness.

Such poverty of spirit encloses the remaining "blesseds." They *mourn,* for their humility is exploited by the proud, who add affliction to their days. They are *meek,* accepting the burdens imposed without hatred and looking to God for vindication. They *hunger and thirst after righteousness,* desiring for themselves and others that knowledge and doing of God's will which produces right order in the world. They are *merciful;* having received kindness from God and knowing affliction from men, they are quick to understand, sympathize, forgive, and help the troubled about them. They are *pure in heart,* single-minded in their consecration to God's will, who has granted them life and cleansing. They are *peacemakers;* for having been afflicted themselves, they do not wish to impose hurt. Rather, they seek conditions of peace and friendship with and among others.

The sixth beatitude shines with special luster: *Blessed are the pure in heart: for they shall see God.* The word *are* points to heart purity as a present possibility, as the context indicates. Men are now meek, merciful, peacemakers, and persecuted. They can also be *pure in heart* now. Pure *(katharoi)* implies cleansing, for the heart is unclean by nature (cf. Mark 7:21-22). This divine cleansing of the disciple's inner life issues in single-minded devotion to God's will. As Kierkegaard put it, "Purity of heart is to will one thing." The heart is fixed on God (cf. Jas. 4:8). Such moral purity is a requisite for seeing God. Here, as elsewhere, holiness and hope are joined together (cf. Heb. 12: 14; 1 John 3:3).

Disciples are people with promises. Those who know their poverty and look to God's bounty are not disappointed. They possess *the kingdom of heaven,* living under Messiah's healing and saving reign. They are *comforted,* receiving the strength of God's presence in their sufferings. They *inherit the earth,* receiving the Kingdom for their inheritance as Israel received the land of promise. They are *satisfied,* as God enables them to know and do His will for their lives. They *receive mercy,* both from God and from the beneficiaries of their own acts of mercy. They *see God,* live in His joyful fellowship, partially now and perfectly in the consummation of the Kingdom. They are *sons of God,* recognized by the discerning as those who reflect the Father's reconciling love. The promises hang together in a beautiful cluster and, like the Kingdom itself, have partial fulfillment in this age and total consummation in the age to come.

Disciples are people under persecution. In this world, righteousness is not desired or honored by all. The life-style of the kingdom of heaven is so different from worldly social structures that followers of Jesus cannot escape verbal and physical mistreatment. But life with the King and in the Kingdom overcompensates for the hostility and hurt endured. This is their reward *in heaven,* i.e., from God.

2. *What disciples do is expressed under figures of salt and light.* Salt does not exist for itself, but for the enhancement of soil and food. Light does not exist for itself, but for the illumination of human activity. Even so, the blessedness of disciples is not self-contained. The disciples are in the

world to serve the world, even though they suffer at the hands of the world.

And just as the candle is consumed in order to shine, service will prove costly and sacrificial. The quality of life described in the "sermon" is the "candlepower" of disciples, in the light of which God is glorified as men are helped.

The "Buts"

Matthew 5:17-48

17 Think not that I am come to destroy the law, or the prophets: I am not come to destroy, but to fulfil.
18 For verily I say unto you, Till heaven and earth pass, one jot or one tittle shall in no wise pass from the law, till all be fulfilled.
19 Whosoever therefore shall break one of these least commandments, and shall teach men so, he shall be called the least in the kingdom of heaven: but whosoever shall do and teach them, the same shall be called great in the kingdom of heaven.
20 For I say unto you, That except your righteousness shall exceed the righteousness of the scribes and Pharisees, ye shall in no case enter into the kingdom of heaven.
21 Ye have heard that it was said by them of old time, Thou shalt not kill; and whosoever shall kill shall be in danger of the judgment:
22 But I say unto you, That whosoever is angry with his brother without a cause shall be in danger of the judgment: and whosoever shall say to his brother, Raca, shall be in danger of the council: but whosoever shall say, Thou fool, shall be in danger of hell fire.
23 Therefore if thou bring thy gift to the altar, and there rememberest that thy brother hath ought against thee;
24 Leave there thy gift before the altar, and go thy way; first be reconciled to thy brother, and then come and offer thy gift.
25 Agree with thine adversary quickly, whiles thou art in the way with him; lest at any time the adversary deliver thee to the judge, and the judge deliver thee to the officer, and thou be cast into prison.
26 Verily I say unto thee, Thou shalt by no means come out thence, till thou hast paid the uttermost farthing.
27 Ye have heard that it was said by them of old time, Thou shalt not commit adultery:
28 But I say unto you, That whosoever looketh on a woman to lust after her hath committed adultery with her already in his heart.
29 And if thy right eye offend thee, pluck it out, and cast it from thee: for it is profitable for thee that one of thy members should perish, and not that thy whole body should be cast into hell.
30 And if thy right hand offend thee, cut it off, and cast it from thee: for it is profitable for thee that one of thy members should perish, and not that thy whole body should be cast into hell.
31 It hath been said, Whosoever shall put away his wife, let him give her a writing of divorcement:
32 But I say unto you, That whosoever shall put away his wife, saving for the cause of fornication, causeth her to commit adultery: and whosoever shall marry her that is divorced committeth adultery.
33 Again, ye have heard that it hath been said by them of old time, Thou shalt not forswear thyself, but shalt perform unto the Lord thine oaths:

34 But I say unto you, Swear not at all; neither by heaven; for it is God's throne:

35 Nor by the earth; for it is his footstool: neither by Jerusalem; for it is the city of the great King.

36 Neither shalt thou swear by thy head, because thou canst not make one hair white or black.

37 But let your communication be, Yea, yea; Nay, nay: for whatsoever is more than these cometh of evil.

38 Ye have heard that it hath been said, An eye for an eye, and a tooth for a tooth:

39 But I say unto you, That ye resist not evil: but whosoever shall smite thee on thy right cheek, turn to him the other also.

40 And if any man will sue thee at the law, and take away thy coat, let him have thy cloak also.

41 And whosoever shall compel thee to go a mile, go with him twain.

42 Give to him that asketh thee, and from him that would borrow of thee turn not thou away.

43 Ye have heard that it hath been said, Thou shalt love thy neighbour, and hate thine enemy.

44 But I say unto you, Love your enemies, bless them that curse you, do good to them that hate you, and pray for them which despitefully use you, and persecute you;

45 That ye may be the children of your Father which is in heaven: for he maketh his sun to rise on the evil and on the good, and sendeth rain on the just and on the unjust.

46 For if ye love them which love you, what reward have ye? do not even the publicans the same?

47 And if ye salute your brethren only, what do ye more than others? do not even the publicans so?

48 Be ye therefore perfect, even as your Father which is in heaven is perfect.

The Sermon on the Mount makes two things clear, the devotion of Jesus to law and His opposition to legalism. He did not come *to destroy, but to fulfil* the law (17). His opposition to the legalism of scribes and Pharisees was misread as antinomianism. Jesus avoided both evils. He will not countenance those who break the commandments or who influence others to break them. When He is heard saying, *But I say unto you,* the adversative conjunction is not opposed to the law of God but to the traditions of men by which law was perverted.

The law was given in a context of grace, to a people already saved by God from bondage (Exod. 20:1-2). To make it a system of gaining favor with God in order to be saved distorts its meaning. Jesus addresses the law of this sermon to His *disciples,* those who have already been graciously invited into a Kingdom where God alone is the Saviour and man has no merit, only poverty of spirit. The righteousness which exceeds that of *scribes and Pharisees*

(20), therefore, is not an intensified legalism which out-pharisees the Pharisees. It is the grateful obedience of those who recognize the claims of Jesus upon them as Lord, and who acknowledge Him as the One who puts them right with God by fulfilling His role as the Suffering-Servant Messiah. This is the perspective from which we view the Sermon on the Mount, that Jesus countenances neither legalism nor antinomianism.

1. In this section of the sermon *the authority of Jesus is stressed.* Six times He uses the words, *But I say unto you.* Twice He says, *Verily* (Gk., *amen;* RSV, *truly*) *I say unto you.* Once He says, *I say unto you.* The conjunction is adversative and the first-person pronoun is emphatic. This mode of address was unique in Israel and implies volumes concerning His uniqueness as the Son of God.

The prophets prefaced their messages with the formula, *Thus says the Lord.* They were conscious of possessing no personal inherent authority. They did not dare speak on their own. The rabbis added an *amen* to the word of God; they did not begin their own statements in this manner. The scribes cited "authorities" to buttress their interpretations of law, but using such a formula as Jesus here employs would have been unthinkable to them. Clearly He is conscious of possessing an authority unprecedented among His people. He is not another spokesman for God; He is the speaking God incarnate. His words are to be taken with the same full seriousness of those which prefaced the Decalogue: *And God spoke all these words, saying . . .*

2. In this section of the sermon *the interiority of law is emphatic.* Not actions only, but intentions also come under the judgment of God.

Murder is prohibited, but equally condemned is the anger that would wish another's destruction (21-26). The difficult injunction in verses 23-26 certainly teaches us that being reconciled to God involves also being reconciled to men. The mere absence of anger, however, is not enough. A disposition to forgiveness and fellowship is a necessary element in genuine righteousness.

Adultery is forbidden, but equally condemned is inward lust (27-32). The strong passage about severing a hand or plucking out an eye tells us that an incomplete life is better than an impure life. Whatever becomes a source of temptation to evil must be abandoned and avoided.

This radicalizing of ethics extends also to speech (33-37). Christ's followers are to be so known for truthfulness that no supporting oath is needed to make their words convincing. A yes that means yes, a no that means no is adequate. Such sincerity of speech argues honesty of intention; no duplicity or deception lurks behind the spoken words.

So emptied of ill will and selfish interest should disciples be that they respond to abuse without retaliation (38-42). They do not seek the redress which good laws permit. Nor do they begrudge the impositions which bad laws require. Instead, they give more than litigation demands, adding tunic to cloak; and they do more than forced service demands, carrying a soldier's baggage two miles rather than one. They give and lend to relieve the poor, not to exploit another's straits by finding loopholes which permit circumvention of laws pertaining to usury.

3. In this section of the sermon *the catholicity of love is prescribed*. Kingdom disciples are not to exclude anyone from the command, *Love thy neighbour*. To return love for love is no challenge; tax collectors and Gentiles (terms of opprobrium to most of the Jews in that day) do this. Kingdom disciples are to love as God loves, including in their active goodwill men who are *enemies, unjust,* and *evil*.

And loving means doing for others. God loves, and sends sun and rain and Jesus. If we love, we will *do good, bless,* and *pray* for even those who *hate, curse,* and *persecute* us.

Unquestionably, this is a lofty ethic. The standard is not fixed to accommodate weak human nature. Rather, it is grounded in the character of God. Like God, we are to be complete and sincere in the range of our loving, excluding none because they are unlike us or dislike us.

Catching God's Eye

Matthew 6:1-18

1 Take heed that ye do not your alms before men, to be seen of them: otherwise ye have no reward of your Father which is in heaven.
2 Therefore when thou doest thine alms, do not sound a trumpet before thee, as the hypocrites do in the synagogues and in the streets, that they may have glory of men. Verily I say unto you, They have their reward.
3 But when thou doest alms, let not thy left hand know what thy right hand doeth:
4 That thine alms may be in secret: and thy Father which seeth in secret himself shall reward thee openly.
5 And when thou prayest, thou shalt not be as the hypocrites are: for they love to pray standing in the synagogues and in the corners of the streets, that they may be seen of men. Verily I say unto you, They have their reward.
6 But thou, when thou prayest, enter into thy closet, and when thou hast shut thy door, pray to thy Father which is in secret; and thy Father which seeth in secret shall reward thee openly.
7 But when ye pray, use not vain repetitions, as the heathen do: for they think that they shall be heard for their much speaking.
8 Be not ye therefore like unto them: for your Father knoweth what things ye have need of, before ye ask him.
9 After this manner therefore pray ye: Our Father which art in heaven, Hallowed be thy name.
10 Thy kingdom come. Thy will be done in earth, as it is in heaven.
11 Give us this day our daily bread.
12 And forgive us our debts, as we forgive our debtors.
13 And lead us not into temptation, but deliver us from evil: For thine is the kingdom, and the power, and the glory, for ever. Amen.
14 For if ye forgive men their trespasses, your heavenly Father will also forgive you:
15 But if ye forgive not men their trespasses, neither will your Father forgive your trespasses.
16 Moreover when ye fast, be not, as the hypocrites, of a sad countenance: for they disfigure their faces, that they may appear unto men to fast. Verily I say unto you, They have their reward.
17 But thou, when thou fastest, anoint thine head, and wash thy face;
18 That thou appear not unto men to fast, but unto thy Father which is in secret: and thy Father, which seeth in secret, shall reward thee openly.

Jesus has insisted upon good works that can be seen by men (5:16). Here *good works* performed *to be seen of men* are condemned (1). Motive is the differentiating factor. The *good works* He commends are done to give glory to the Father. The pious practices He condemns are done to have glory from men. The practices themselves are not wrong, but the reason for doing them may be. And motive governs manner; if to glorify God, they are done humbly and discreetly; if to be praised by men, they are paraded and publicized. Whose eye do we seek to catch, God's or men's?

1. *Almsgiving in secret is enjoined* (2-4). Almsgiving in itself is good. It is one way by which the disciple can be *merciful* (5:7), and the destitute can be served. Some almsgiving took place in *synagogues* and *streets,* attended by maximum publicity for the donors. It was done with fanfare, because the givers desired a reputation for righteousness. The intention spoiled the action. The reward they got was less than they expected. They wanted favor with God but received no more than notice from men. And this was all they got. Jesus said, *They have their reward.* *Have* translates the Greek verb *apecho,* used in transactions where receipts were given, and carrying the sense of "paid in full."

He who gives secretly, out of concern for his brother and gratitude to his Father, will be rewarded *openly.* *Openly* is probably a reference to the final judgment (cf. 25:34-40).

2. *Praying in secret is commanded* (5-8). Choosing times and places for prayer which are designed to attract notice and elicit praise from men is reprehended. Again, the notice of men pays in full the one who prays; God remains unimpressed. Sincere prayer shuts the disciple in with God, where poverty of spirit (5:3) controls the approach to the throne of grace. Not word-piles mechanically intoned, but simple, short, sincere praise and petition is heard by God.

Within this context Jesus supplies the model prayer (9-13). The term of address recognizes that God is over us in power and for us in grace. He is *in heaven,* but He is *our Father.* The first concern of prayer is God's glory—the hallowing of His name, the doing of His will. The second concern is man's good—his need for bread, forgiveness, and deliverance from the evil one. The pronouns are plural, for when we close ourselves in our rooms we do not close our brothers from our hearts. And the forgiveness we petition from God we must extend to men. Indeed, this is a model prayer! That it has often become a heaping up of *empty phrases* (RSV) such as Jesus here criticizes is one of the ironies of church history.

3. *Fasting in secret is ordered* (16-18). The words of Jesus indicate that some, eager for reputations as pious men, made sure that others knew when they were fasting by disfiguring their faces to effect a greater solemnity. They resorted to what Floyd Filson called "uglifying cosmetics."

In contrast, the Lord requires His disciples to appear normally, even cheerfully, before men, bearing the sorrow that prompts them to fast in their hearts, not on their faces.

Trusting God's Love

Matthew 6:19-34

19 Lay not up for yourselves treasures upon earth, where moth and rust doth corrupt, and where thieves break through and steal:
20 But lay up for yourselves treasures in heaven, where neither moth nor rust doth corrupt, and where thieves do not break through nor steal:
21 For where your treasure is, there will your heart be also.
22 The light of the body is the eye: if therefore thine eye be single, thy whole body shall be full of light.
23 But if thine eye be evil, thy whole body shall be full of darkness. If therefore the light that is in thee be darkness, how great is that darkness!
24 No man can serve two masters: for either he will hate the one, and love the other; or else he will hold to the one, and despise the other. Ye cannot serve God and mammon.
25 Therefore I say unto you, Take no thought for your life, what ye shall eat, or what ye shall drink; nor yet for your body, what ye shall put on. Is not the life more than meat, and the body than raiment?
26 Behold the fowls of the air: for they sow not, neither do they reap, nor gather into barns; yet your heavenly Father feedeth them. Are ye not much better than they?
27 Which of you by taking thought can add one cubit unto his stature?
28 And why take ye thought for raiment? Consider the lilies of the field, how they grow; they toil not, neither do they spin:
29 And yet I say unto you, That even Solomon in all his glory was not arrayed like one of these.
30 Wherefore, if God so clothe the grass of the field, which to day is, and to morrow is cast into the oven, shall he not much more clothe you, O ye of little faith?
31 Therefore take no thought, saying, What shall we eat? or, What shall we drink? or, Wherewithal shall we be clothed?
32 (For after all these things do the Gentiles seek:) for your heavenly Father knoweth that ye have need of all these things.
33 But seek ye first the kingdom of God, and his righteousness; and all these things shall be added unto you.
34 Take therefore no thought for the morrow: for the morrow shall

take thought for the things of itself. Sufficient unto the day is the evil thereof.

"I tell you, do not worry" (25, NIV)! Did Jesus ever issue a command more difficult to obey? Man needs things. He must have food, clothes, and shelter, or he will die. Worry about how to get and keep things has destroyed more mental, physical, and spiritual health than anyone can calculate. What is the antidote? Trust. Man doesn't live in a neutral zone where things just happen. He will either worry or trust.

1. *Jesus teaches that anxiety destroys life.* The more important material things become, the less secure a person feels in pursuit of them. The destructiveness is threefold.

First, anxiety deceives. *Treasures upon earth* are subject to the moth, rust, and thief. They can be destroyed or stolen, just when a person thinks he has walled out trouble and threat. No measure of accumulated wealth secures, for sooner or later we lose it or we leave it. Banks can fail. Governments can collapse. Property can be confiscated. There is just no security in things.

The man with his heart wedded to things cannot see straight. His eye is diseased and his mind is darkened (22-23). The man with *treasures in heaven*, whose heart is fixed on God, has a clear vision and unclouded future.

Second, anxiety enslaves. Man will have a master, either God or mammon (24). Service to God is true freedom, releasing every faculty of human personality to achieve the purpose for which it was created. But service to mammon, putting things first, brings one into bondage. Materialism is idolatry, and idolatry is slavery, distorting the meaning of life and forcing man into a false role.

Third, anxiety paganizes. Worry over material things is precisely what drives the unconverted *Gentiles* who know not Israel's faithful God (32).

2. On the other hand, *Jesus teaches that trust secures life.* The God who feeds the birds, who cannot provide their own sustenance, who clothes the transient lilies with unrivalled splendor, will surely care for His creature man, who is *better than they.*

Security, then, is a matter of providence. In two phrases Jesus establishes the ground of trust and discloses the secret of security: *"Your heavenly Father knows"* (32, RSV); *"Your heavenly Father feeds"* (26, RSV). God is neither ignorant of our needs nor indifferent to them. To worry about food, drink, or clothing is a species of infidelity, for worry indirectly accuses God of either not knowing or not caring. Worry slanders God.

Security is a matter of priority. *Seek ye first the kingdom of God, and his righteousness; and all these things shall be added unto you* (33). God provides the necessities of those who place His will over all else in life. But the Kingdom can never be a "bonus" for those who seek first to secure their lives by the accumulation of things. The reign of God over us in love is our only real security, and our only true satisfaction!

Jesus adds, with a delightful touch of irony, a final word on the futility of worry. Each today brings enough trouble to cope with, so don't borrow ahead from tomorrow's trouble. To live adequately in the actual situation is challenge enough without struggling with imagined situations.

MATTHEW 7

Don't Judge Your Brother

Matthew 7:1-6

> 1 Judge not, that ye be not judged.
> 2 For with what judgment ye judge, ye shall be judged: and with what measure ye mete, it shall be measured to you again.
> 3 And why beholdest thou the mote that is in thy brother's eye, but considerest not the beam that is in thine own eye?
> 4 Or how wilt thou say to thy brother, Let me pull out the mote out of thine eye; and, behold, a beam is in thine own eye?
> 5 Thou hypocrite, first cast out the beam out of thine own eye; and then shalt thou see clearly to cast out the mote out of thy brother's eye.
> 6 Give not that which is holy unto the dogs, neither cast ye your pearls before swine, lest they trample them under their feet, and turn again and rend you.

Humility in the practice of piety has been enjoined upon the disciples of Jesus. Now harshness in the practice of judging is condemned. The words of Jesus cannot be construed as a blanket prohibition of judging. No man lives with his critical faculties in suspended animation. Life demands choices, and our decisions are based upon judgments, whether good or bad.

1. *There is a kind of judgment which Jesus forbids.* *"Judge not"* can mean only, Judge not harshly, unfairly, censoriously. The words are aimed at the faultfinder who has a good eye on himself and a bad eye on everyone else.

"Judgees" should not be judgers. Those who stand under the judgment of God, and all men do, should not usurp His prerogative as though they were gods, all-seeing and all-knowing. Jesus warns that such judging has a boomerang effect: *"With the judgment you pronounce you will be judged"* (2, RSV). The severe judgment of men upon their brothers is unjust; the just judgment of God upon such men will be severe. Censorious persons are hard on others, easy on themselves. Wesley thought it was an evidence of spiritual growth when he demanded more of himself and less of others.

Blinded men make poor oculists. The faultfinder is like a man who tries to remove a tiny speck from another's eye while a log jammed into his own eye prevents clear vision (3-5). The hyperbole makes the point more emphatic and memorable than pedestrian prose could. Norman Rockwell's paintings include one of a coal deliverer trying to remove a speck of coal dust from his partner's eye, using a handkerchief nearly black with soot. Your portrait? Mine?

2. On the other hand, *there is a kind of judgment which Jesus enjoins* (6). Where condemnation of others is wrong, discrimination with others is right. What is *holy* should not be given to *dogs*, nor *pearls* cast before *swine*. Some people have no more capacity to value spiritual truths than dogs and hogs have to value the sacred and costly. The answer to censoriousness should not be gullibility. The disciple must be sensitive to each situation, knowing when to speak, when to be silent.

John Broadus sees this verse as "a warning against

mistaken zeal in trying to make converts or to correct men's faults." We only worsen the guilt of wicked men if we present the gospel in a situation where beastly rejection is a foregone conclusion. We need wisdom to "select the fit occasion and discover the wise method."

Christ's caution must not be pressed to the point of paralyzing evangelism. As always, Christ is our best Example. His speeches and silences are equally eloquent and instructive. But there were times when He spoke and acted knowing full well that He would be attacked by unbelieving men. What is Calvary if not history's supreme instance of a pearl of great price being trampled by swinish men?

So we must not judge harshly, but we must judge sensibly. We must be generous but not gullible. And we must not allow an undiscerning application of Jesus' words to become an excuse for having no convictions or attempting no evangelism.

Don't Misjudge Your Father
Matthew 7:7-12

> 7 Ask, and it shall be given you; seek, and ye shall find; knock, and it shall be opened unto you:
> 8 For every one that asketh receiveth; and he that seeketh findeth; and to him that knocketh it shall be opened.
> 9 Or what man is there of you, whom if his son ask bread, will he give him a stone?
> 10 Or if he ask a fish, will he give him a serpent?
> 11 If ye then, being evil, know how to give good gifts unto your children, how much more shall your Father which is in heaven give good things to them that ask him?
> 12 Therefore all things whatsoever ye would that men should do to you, do ye even so to them: for this is the law and the prophets.

This section of the "sermon" can stand alone, but it also has relevance for the preceding admonitions concerning judging. If the disciples are to be charitable without being gullible, they need resources of grace and wisdom beyond their natural abilities. Such spiritual resources may be obtained from God, so the words about asking and receiving are well placed in Matthew's collection of Jesus' teachings. Where the foregoing verses caution against judging our brothers, these would help us not to misjudge our Father.

1. *We misjudge Him if we think the Father does not care.* Jesus reminds His hearers that they are radically evil men *(If ye then, being evil)*, and yet they *give good gifts* to their children. *How much more shall your Father . . . give good things to them that ask him?* (11). The righteous God is surely more dependable than evil men!

Earthly fathers do not practice cruel tricks on their children, giving stones instead of bread, serpents instead of fish. The Heavenly Father loves more perfectly. What He does is never cruel; what He gives is never bad.

The character of God is the firmest assurance that prayer avails.

2. *We misjudge Him if we think the Father cannot help* (7-8). It is not unthinkable that human fathers should care but find themselves unable to give. Not so the divine Father. That He is *in heaven,* a verbal symbol for His majesty and might, assures us that His resources are inexhaustible. He can always match power to love.

Therefore, asking will not go unanswered. God will always answer the knock at His door, for He is never embarrassed by having nothing to give. Heaven is not a Mother Hubbard's cupboard. So confident of God does Jesus want His disciples to be, that the asking-seeking-knocking action and the receiving-finding-opening result are repeated for the sake of emphasis. The one is as sure as the other. The power that responds to prayer is as constant as the need that prompts to prayer.

Nor does God have pets among His children: *Every one* who prays is heard and answered.

The admonition to confident prayer is followed by the golden rule (12). Similar statements are found in other sources, both Jewish and Gentile. The others are stated negatively, as in the Apocrypha: "What you hate do not do to anyone" (Tobit 4·15). Jesus preferred to put it positively, Treat others as you want them to treat you. Withholding evil is not enough; practicing good is mandatory upon His followers.

Life by this golden rule *is the law and the prophets,* a summary phrase for the Old Testament. The law inculcated fair treatment for every person. The prophets made the demand for such social justice one of the chief concerns of their preaching. Jesus summarizes and enforces the whole tenor of man-to-man ethics in the Old Testament by His terse, positive golden rule.

It fits well the context beginning at 5:17. Jesus would have the law fulfilled, not destroyed. So far as its precepts governing interpersonal relationships are concerned, golden-rule living fulfills the law.

The Two Ways

Matthew 7:13-23

> 13 Enter ye in at the strait gate: for wide is the gate, and broad is the way, that leadeth to destruction, and many there be which go in thereat:
> 14 Because strait is the gate, and narrow is the way, which leadeth unto life, and few there be that find it.
> 15 Beware of false prophets, which come to you in sheep's clothing, but inwardly they are ravening wolves.
> 16 Ye shall know them by their fruits. Do men gather grapes of thorns, or figs of thistles?
> 17 Even so every good tree bringeth forth good fruit; but a corrupt tree bringeth forth evil fruit.
> 18 A good tree cannot bring forth evil fruit, neither can a corrupt tree bring forth good fruit.
> 19 Every tree that bringeth not forth good fruit is hewn down, and cast into the fire.
> 20 Wherefore by their fruits ye shall know them.
> 21 Not every one that saith unto me, Lord, Lord, shall enter into the kingdom of heaven; but he that doeth the will of my Father which is in heaven.
> 22 Many will say to me in that day, Lord, Lord, have we not prophesied in thy name? and in thy name have cast out devils? and in thy name done many wonderful works?
> 23 And then will I profess unto them, I never knew you: depart from me, ye that work iniquity.

The connection of this section with the previous one is tenuous. However, living by the golden rule strikes any honest person as a difficult task. Those who seriously attempt it soon know they have entered a narrow gate to travel a hard way. By contrast, the way of self-interest and retaliation is easier and more popular.

1. *Two ways are described* (13-14). One is *hard* (RSV), so seldom traveled that it is not easily found. The other is *easy,* very accessible and heavily traveled. But the hard way leads to life, and the easy way to death.

The doctrine of the two ways is rooted in the Old

Testament. In his farewell address Moses set before Israel "a blessing and a curse" (Deut. 11:26). "Blessing" summarized the benefits accruing to obedience, and "curse" summarized judgments befalling disobedience. Both promises and threats were stipulated in the covenant God imposed upon Israel. Rabbinical tradition interpreted this as "the two ways." It is somewhat paralleled in "the way of light" and "the way of darkness" expounded in the Qumran literature (cf. also, Jer. 21:8; Psalm 1).

The hard way that few find is the way of righteousness described throughout the sermon, the life of true discipleship. By contrast, the easy way is all life outside the Kingdom, which in its social, political, and religious aspects is congenial to fallen nature and popular with evil men.

The hard way leads to *life,* the eternal life of the consummated Kingdom. The easy way leads to *destruction,* the loss of God's presence forever (cf. 2 Thess. 1:9).

2. *Two warnings are issued* (15-23). First, *Beware of false prophets.* They appear innocent but they are destructive. If we would *find* the hard way that leads to life, we must not be deceived by misleading guides. We have suggested that the Sermon on the Mount (indeed the whole of Matthew's Gospel) reflects our Lord's repudiation of both legalism and antinomianism. Teaching that produces either is the false guidance warned against here.

Since the false prophets appear as sheep, how can they be recognized as wolves? Changing figures, Jesus says, *by their fruits.* That good trees produce good fruit, that thorns do not yield grapes, is axiomatic. Just so, false teaching produces false living. *Evil fruit* is life disobedient to God's will as taught in Jesus' words.

The second warning is, Beware of false professions. We can miss the way by deceiving ourselves, as surely as we can through being deceived by others, as Plummer points out. We mislead ourselves when we are content with an empty profession, calling Jesus, *Lord, Lord,* but not doing the will of God.

How searching and solemn are these verses! Men may preach, exorcise demons, and perform miracles in the very name which their lives contradict, the name of *Lord.* But their vaunted service records will not spare them from His judgment upon their evil lives. His verdict will be *Depart!* They professed to know Him, He denies knowing them. The horror of that moment of truth is impossible to describe!

In using the title *Lord,* and in representing himself as the final Judge of men, Jesus makes claims for himself that cannot be reconciled with any but the highest Christology. To reduce Him to the status of mere prophet or rabbi is absurd question-begging. The claims lend awful urgency to the closing words of the sermon.

The Two Destinies

Matthew 7:24-29

> 24 Therefore whosoever heareth these sayings of mine, and doeth them, I will liken him unto a wise man, which built his house upon a rock:
> 25 And the rain descended, and the floods came, and the winds blew, and beat upon that house; and it fell not: for it was founded upon a rock.
> 26 And every one that heareth these sayings of mine, and doeth them not, shall be likened unto a foolish man, which built his house upon the sand:
> 27 And the rain descended, and the floods came, and the winds blew, and beat upon that house; and it fell: and great was the fall of it.
> 28 And it came to pass, when Jesus had ended these sayings, the people were astonished at his doctrine:
> 29 For he taught them as one having authority, and not as the scribes.

The contrast between two ways and two trees is followed by a third which closes the Sermon on the Mount, a contrast between two builders, cast in the form of parabolic illustration. The story is told in simple terms with an obvious meaning.

1. *The parable as it concludes the sermon* is our first concern. *"Therefore, everyone who hears these words of mine . . ."* (24, NIV). The demonstrative, *these words,* certainly refer to what He spoke on this occasion, everything in chapters 5—7, if we assume the unity of the sermon. However, the sermon seems intended as a sample and summary of His teaching ministry. *He taught,* in verse 29, translates a participial phrase with the sense of "He habitually taught." *These words of mine* in verses 24 and 25 are equivalent to His habitual teaching. Men are

obliged to hear and do all that Jesus said in all the times and places of His teaching.

Furthermore, 10:14, 40 make it clear that He spoke through His disciples. To receive them and their teaching was to receive Him and His teaching. Their teaching became the New Testament. To say that destiny hinges upon obedience or disobedience to His words is equivalent to saying that destiny hinges upon response to the Bible. To oppose apostles to Jesus as some scholars have done is indefensible.

2. *The parable as it divides the hearers* is our next consideration. The one builder is *wise;* the other is *foolish.*

Division of men into two and only two classes was typical of Jesus, and reflects His knowledge of and consent to the Old Testament literature. Compare the *wicked* and the *righteous* in Psalms and Proverbs. Elsewhere in Matthew's Gospel, Jesus speaks of *wise* and *foolish* virgins, and of *sheep* and *goats* in parables fraught with judgment teaching (25:2, 32). He is unimpressed by our artificial and arbitrary human divisions. All that really matters is whether one will be saved or lost.

And the dividing factor is clear. The issue is that of doing or not doing the words of Jesus. Both builders are hearers of His words; only one is a doer. The Psalmist prayed, *Teach me to do thy will.* Most men know better than they do. Our major problem is not ignorance but rebellion. On the issue of obedience destiny depends. The life obedient to Jesus' words will stand in the judgment. The life disobedient will collapse.

3. *The parable as it universalizes His lordship* is of paramount significance. *Everyone that heareth!* His words have persisted through the centuries among all nations. He claims to be the final Judge, as He is the real Lord, of all. Those who would make Him one way among options, who would place the "scriptures" of other religions alongside His words as having equal validity, tread a ruinous route. Jesus indeed raises "the offense of particularity," but His refusal to share His place with others is a gracious intol-

erance. He knows that He is Lord of all mankind, and their only Saviour.

Matthew closes this block of teaching with a formula repeated, with slight variations, after each of the five discourses (cf. 11:1; 13:53; 19:1; 26:1): *And when Jesus finished these sayings . . .* (28, RSV).

The people were astonished at His teaching, not simply by its originality (for much of it interpreted and applied what others had said), but by its *authority*. He possessed unique authority, and the subsequent narrative section will justify the amazement His authority evoked by the miracles which it produced.

Second Narrative Section: Ministry in Galilee

Matthew 8:1—9:38

MATTHEW 8

Authority over Illness

Matthew 8:1-17

1 When he was come down from the mountain, great multitudes followed him.

2 And, behold, there came a leper and worshipped him, saying, Lord, if thou wilt, thou canst make me clean.

3 And Jesus put forth his hand, and touched him, saying, I will; be thou clean. And immediately his leprosy was cleansed.

4 And Jesus saith unto him, See thou tell no man; but go thy way, shew thyself to the priest, and offer the gift that Moses commanded, for a testimony unto them.

5 And when Jesus was entered into Capernaum, there came unto him a centurion, beseeching him,

6 And saying, Lord, my servant lieth at home sick of the palsy, grievously tormented.

7 And Jesus saith unto him, I will come and heal him.

8 The centurion answered and said, Lord, I am not worthy that thou shouldest come under my roof: but speak the word only, and my servant shall be healed.

9 For I am a man under authority, having soldiers under me: and I say to this man, Go, and he goeth; and to another, Come, and he cometh; and to my servant, Do this, and he doeth it.

10 When Jesus heard it, he marvelled, and said to them that followed, Verily I say unto you, I have not found so great faith, no, not in Israel.

11 And I say unto you, That many shall come from the east and west, and shall sit down with Abraham, and Isaac, and Jacob, in the kingdom of heaven.

12 But the children of the kingdom shall be cast out into outer darkness: there shall be weeping and gnashing of teeth.

13 And Jesus said unto the centurion, Go thy way; and as thou hast believed, so be it done unto thee. And his servant was healed in the selfsame hour.

14 And when Jesus was come into Peter's house, he saw his wife's mother laid, and sick of a fever.

15 And he touched her hand, and the fever left her: and she arose, and ministered unto them.

16 When the even was come, they brought unto him many that were

possessed with devils: and he cast out the spirits with his word, and healed all that were sick:
17   That it might be fulfilled which was spoken by Esaias the prophet, saying, Himself took our infirmities, and bare our sicknesses.

The Sermon on the Mount astonishes the crowds with the authority of Jesus. A lengthy narrative section follows which further illustrates this unique authority by 10 miracles which Jesus performs. They carry on the motif of fulfilled prophecy, and they indicate the incursion of God's future kingdom into this present age.

The first three are healing miracles as *great multitudes followed him,* and lonely sufferers were touched by Him.

1. *Jesus heals a leper* (1-4). *Moved with compassion* (a detail supplied by Mark) Jesus *touched him,* spoke a word of healing, and *immediately* the leprosy was gone.

The dialogue between Jesus and the leper is arresting. The leper said, *"Lord, if you will, you can make me clean"* (2, RSV). He was sure of Jesus' power, less certain of His willingness to help. But Jesus replied, *"I will; be clean"* (3, RSV). His love equals His power, and physical restoration takes place.

His love also honors the law. Jesus sends the leper to the priest to undergo the ritual by which readmission into society was granted. Lepers were ostracized, and social restoration needs to follow physical restoration, for men live fully only when they live in community. The touch of Jesus has already suggested that renewed fellowship, but that touch is not substituted for the law under which the leper lived. The love of Jesus is never antinomian.

2. *Jesus heals a paralytic* (5-13). The victim of disease was the servant of an army officer. In this case Jesus does not approach or touch the sick person. (There is no record of His ever doing so with a Gentile.) Rather, He heals from a distance by the authority of His word.

Again the dialogue is intriguing. It implies a profound principle of authority. The centurion is under authority, and has men under his command. He only is fit to give orders who knows how to obey them. The officer believes that Jesus, sent by God, has authority over disease. *Speak the word,* give the order, *and my servant shall be healed* (8).

Jesus marvels at his faith, as He marvels elsewhere at the unbelief of His own people (Mark 6:6). He sees in the centurion an omen of the *many* Gentiles who will believe on Him, in contrast to the Jews who will reject Him. These Gentiles will enter the Kingdom and find joy, but the *children of the kingdom* will be rejected and find grief.

3. *Jesus heals a fevered woman* (14-17). Entering Peter's house (where Jesus was "at home" in Capernaum), he found Peter's mother-in-law sick abed with a fever. In gentle compassion *he touched her hand, and the fever left her.*

In a sense the touch was the secret of His healing. For the summary passage which follows (16-17) speaks of the healings as fulfillment of prophecy in Isa. 53:4, where the Suffering Servant "takes" and "bears" diseases. Healing involved suffering-identification with the sick, and the touch beautifully symbolizes this identification.

The sequel to healing was service. *She arose, and ministered unto them.* Health is a gift to be invested, not hoarded. Some manuscripts read "him," not "them." No matter. We cannot really love and serve Him unless we also love and serve them.

Authority over Nature

Matthew 8:18-27

18 Now when Jesus saw great multitudes about him, he gave commandment to depart unto the other side.
19 And a certain scribe came, and said unto him, Master, I will follow thee withersoever thou goest.
20 And Jesus saith unto him, The foxes have holes, and the birds of the air have nests; but the Son of man hath not where to lay his head.
21 And another of his disciples said unto him, Lord, suffer me first to go and bury my father.
22 But Jesus said unto him, Follow me; and let the dead bury their dead.
23 And when he was entered into a ship, his disciples followed him.
24 And, behold, there arose a great tempest in the sea, insomuch that the ship was covered with the waves: but he was asleep.
25 And his disciples came to him, and awoke him, saying, Lord, save us: we perish.
26 And he saith unto them, Why are ye fearful, O ye of little faith? Then he arose, and rebuked the winds and the sea; and there was a great calm.

27 But the men marvelled, saying, What manner of man is this, that even the winds and the sea obey him!

Two men impulsively volunteer to accompany Jesus. To the first, He speaks of the privations of discipleship. The *Son of man* is often homeless, His existence more precarious than that of foxes and birds. To the second, He speaks of the priority of discipleship. The spiritually dead can bury the physically dead, but the work of the Kingdom was too urgent to admit of delay. Whatever difficulty we have in translating and interpreting verses 18-22, one thing is clear—the claims of Jesus upon would-be disciples are radical!

Here for the first time in Matthew occurs the title *Son of man,* subject of much spirited debate among New Testament scholars. The Old Testament occurrences point to factors of both humility and power, and in this section both aspects are emphasized. The Son of Man is the lonely, humble, sacrificial Servant. But He is also the Bearer and Exerciser of a power that can still the tempest on Lake Galilee, wrenching from astounded disciples the question, *What manner of man is this* (27)? Three replies are suggested.

1. *This is a tired Man.* As winds shrieked and waves pounded, alarming the disciples, *he was asleep.* So fully human was Jesus that the activities of the day had exhausted Him. He did not possess and utilize supernatural strength that permitted Him to serve and help without being drained.

He was truly human, worn-out from working for God! Our causes for deep weariness are usually self-related. Scripture tells of two men so exhausted they could sleep through a storm at sea. One was Jonah, worn-out by dodging God's work; and the other is Jesus, worn-out by doing God's work. The sleeping Christ is adequate refutation of every docetic heresy.

2. *This is a triumphant Man.* If the sleeping underlines His weakness, the stilling emphasizes His power. Shaken from sleep by terrified disciples, He rebuked the unbelief

of the men and the fury of the sea, restoring both to calmness.

Storms can come and go with surprising suddenness on Lake Galilee, and some would posit the miracle in the minds of the disciples, betrayed by a timely coincidence in nature. The Gospel relates the story to stress the authority of Jesus as Lord of nature.

This power is commensurate with the need. *There arose a great tempest,* and *there was a great calm.* The same Greek adjective describes both the storm and the calm. Jesus was fully adequate to the situation.

3. *This is a "theanthropic" Man.* The humility of the Sufferer and the authority of the Ruler are blended throughout the Gospel to teach us that Jesus is the God-man, at once fully and truly human and divine.

Faith can confess what reason cannot prove. The person of Jesus is a mystery whose depths we cannot fathom. The tiredness we can comprehend; the triumph leaves us, like the disciples, marveling at what baffles analysis. We understand analogically, and there are no analogies by which to capture the unique. Jesus is like us, but unlike us. He is one of a kind.

But the calming of the storm assures us that we are in good hands when we submit to His radical claims. Who follow Him need not cower before tempests. The ship that holds Jesus is sure to reach the shore. The battered Church of Matthew's day, and of ours, treasures the story for the assurance it conveys.

Authority over Demons

Matthew 8:28-34

28 And when he was come to the other side into the country of the Gergesenes, there met him two possessed with devils, coming out of the tombs, exceeding fierce, so that no man might pass by that way.
29 And, behold, they cried out, saying, What have we to do with thee, Jesus, thou Son of God? art thou come hither to torment us before the time?
30 And there was a good way off from them an herd of many swine feeding.
31 So the devils besought him, saying, If thou cast us out, suffer us to go away into the herd of swine.
32 And he said unto them, Go. And when they were come out, they went into the herd of swine: and, behold, the whole herd of swine ran violently down a steep place into the sea, and perished in the waters.

33 And they that kept them fled, and went their ways into the city, and told every thing, and what was befallen to the possessed of the devils.
34 And, behold, the whole city came out to meet Jesus: and when they saw him, they besought him that he would depart out of their coasts.

The variant readings for the geographical location of this miracle make it unwise if not impossible to identify the exact place. No matter. What happened is more important than where it occurred.

Only Matthew's Gospel mentions *two* demoniacs. This has spawned critical problems and prolific guesses. Perhaps the simplest answer is the truest—there were two. If there was one, there could have been two. If there was two, there had to be one. One, two, or a yardful, Jesus is adequate for their deliverance.

1. *The demons are suppliant.* They *pleaded* with Jesus, *Allow us to go into the herd of pigs* (Anchor Bible). There is something immensely reassuring about the demons' recognition of the superior power of Jesus, whom they acknowledge as the *Son of God* (29). Just as Satan had to get a permit to test Job, so here the demons, who will not leave the men until Jesus commands, cannot enter the pigs until He allows!

There is a dualism in the New Testament. The demons recognize in Jesus an "essentially hostile power" (Plummer). Jesus and the demons represent two kingdoms, that of God and that of evil, between whom peaceful coexistence is impossible.

But the dualism is temporal, not eternal; for it is ethical, not metaphysical. The phrase *before the time* (29) suggests the coming ultimate overthrow and destruction of every demonic power that blights the world. The exorcisms of Jesus are prophetic of that doom. Evil in any form exists only by the permission of God. There is mystery here, admittedly, but there is comfort also.

2. *The Christ is sovereign.* The fierce and malevolent demoniacs who denied passage to all other men could not intimidate Jesus. Conscious of His superior authority, He calmly hears out their nervous pleas, and speaks a single

word of command, *Go!* He is majestically in control of the situation.

The demons obey, but the pigs stampede. *The whole herd rushed down the steep bank into the sea, and perished* (32, RSV). This is what always happens when demonic forces drive pigs or people! The direction is down, the speed is fast, and the end is ruin. By contrast, the men are restored by the loving power of Jesus to sanity and to society.

Some have contended that the drowning of the pigs mars the character of Jesus. Such criticism is misplaced. Demons seek a "base of operations." If the choice is between people or pigs, one person is worth vastly more than a thousand pigs. Dead in a lake or dead in a skillet, it's much the same with pigs! Jesus is not capriciously sovereign but lovingly sovereign.

3. *The crowds are stupid.* Terrified herdsmen spread the news and *the whole city came out to meet Jesus.* But instead of making Him welcome and bringing other needy persons for His help, *they begged him to leave* (34, RSV). The same Greek verb is used of the demons and the crowd. The demons begged to depart from Jesus; the crowd begged Jesus to depart from them!

Poor, stupid people! They were as fearful of Jesus as they had been of the demons, and in the same way. They were threatened by a power they could neither understand nor manipulate. Further, a heavy blow had been dealt the hog market, and like others whom Jesus encountered, they thought more of money than of people (cf. 12:9-14; Luke 13:10-17).

To their foolish request He gave a fateful assent. He got into a boat and recrossed the lake to Capernaum. They forfeited a priceless opportunity to share the benefits of the presence and power of Jesus! He never stays where He is not welcome. Sovereign though He is, He does not coerce people to accept Him. The one ray of light in the picture is the two healed men who remained among their short-sighted neighbors. The effect of their witness we do not know.

Putting Men on Their Feet

Matthew 9:1-9

> 1 And he entered into a ship, and passed over, and came into his own city.
> 2 And, behold, they brought to him a man sick of the palsy, lying on a bed: and Jesus seeing their faith said unto the sick of the palsy; Son, be of good cheer; thy sins be forgiven thee.
> 3 And, behold, certain of the scribes said within themselves, This man blasphemeth.
> 4 And Jesus knowing their thoughts said, Wherefore think ye evil in your hearts?
> 5 For whether is easier, to say, Thy sins be forgiven thee; or to say, Arise, and walk?
> 6 But that ye may know that the Son of man hath power on earth to forgive sins, (then saith he to the sick of the palsy,) Arise, take up thy bed, and go unto thine house.
> 7 And he arose, and departed to his house.
> 8 But when the multitudes saw it, they marvelled, and glorified God, which had given such power unto men.
> 9 And as Jesus passed forth from thence, he saw a man, named Matthew, sitting at the receipt of custom: and he saith unto him, Follow me. And he arose, and followed him.

Verse 36 of this chapter says *he saw the multitudes.* Verse 9 says *he saw a man.* He was deeply moved by the needy masses, but He never lost sight of the individual within the crowd. "Jesus rediscovered the individual." Some talk with great concern for masses who never do anything for persons. The opening verses of chapter 9 show Jesus ministering to individuals.

Of two men we read, *he arose*—one a paralytic, the other a publican. Getting to their feet, they demonstrate the power of Jesus to heal both physically and morally.

1. *The healing of the paralytic* is first (2-8). He is brought to Jesus by friends and healed before enemies. The faith of the anonymous friends becomes visible; *Jesus saw their faith* (RSV) and responded with healing love. The unbelief of the *scribes* becomes audible; they murmur among themselves, and Jesus, *knowing their thoughts,* replies in stinging rebuke. This is the first of the "conflict stories" in Matthew, disclosing the growing hostility of Jewish leaders toward Jesus.

In the charged atmosphere of faith and unbelief, Jesus speaks three transforming words to the paralytic.

First he speaks a cheering word: *Son, be of good cheer.* Long-standing illness produces deep depression. Jesus knows the man is psychologically unfitted to hear anything else until he is first heartened.

Next Jesus speaks a forgiving word: *"Your sins are forgiven"* (2, RSV). Where illness is directly caused by sin or produced by guilt, forgiveness is necessary to healing. Such, it seems, was this case.

Pronouncing forgiveness evoked the dissent of the scribes. Only God is man's Pardoner. How dare this man usurp the divine prerogative? Blasphemy! Jesus bluntly charges them with thinking evil in their hearts, for sin had blinded them to who He was, *the Son of man* with *power on earth to forgive sins.*

So He then speaks a healing word: *Arise, take up thy bed, and go* . . . The man carried in on the bed obeys and carries the bed out on him. The miracle in the visible realm validates the authority in the invisible realm. The onlookers marvel that God has given Jesus such power for the benefit of men.

2. *The calling of the publican* is told next (9). Matthew, assuming he wrote this Gospel, humbly and briefly relates his "conversion." Jesus passes by the tax office where Matthew is employed, and issues the call to discipleship by which the 12 apostles were summoned, *Follow me. And he arose, and followed him.*

Matthew was a Jew who collected taxes for Rome. Nothing made a Jew more odious in the eyes of his countrymen than this "collaboration" with the hated foreign power that occupied their land. The Gospel of Matthew does not blink the popular contempt for the "publicani." Tax collectors are bracketed with *sinners* (meaning notorious violators of Mosaic law) and with *harlots* (9:10; 11:19; 21:31-32). Where others detested him, Jesus loved him; and lonely Matthew loses no time in responding to love's invitation.

The calling of Matthew is logically, if not chronologically, correct. The "conflict stories" have begun. Jesus' authority has been challenged by the nation's religious leaders. When they have expressed their final rejection of that authority, Jesus will condemn them because tax collectors and prostitutes entered the kingdom of God, while these who professed allegiance to God's will stubbornly refused to enter (21:28-32). Both reactions are here seen taking place at the very beginning of the conflict. The authority of Jesus is amply validated by the physical and spiritual healing that puts paralytic and publican on their feet. Rejection of that authority is inexcusable.

Putting Critics in their Place

Matthew 9:10-17

> 10 And it came to pass, as Jesus sat at meat in the house, behold, many publicans and sinners came and sat down with him and his disciples.
> 11 And when the Pharisees saw it, they said unto his disciples, Why eateth your Master with publicans and sinners?
> 12 But when Jesus heard that, he said unto them, They that be whole need not a physician, but they that are sick.
> 13 But go ye and learn what that meaneth, I will have mercy, and not sacrifice: for I am not come to call the righteous, but sinners to repentance.
> 14 Then came to him the disciples of John, saying, Why do we and the Pharisees fast oft, but thy disciples fast not?
> 15 And Jesus said unto them, Can the children of the bridechamber mourn, as long as the bridegroom is with them? but the days will come, when the bridegroom shall be taken from them, and then shall they fast.
> 16 No man putteth a piece of new cloth unto an old garment, for that which is put in to fill it up taketh from the garment, and the rent is made worse.
> 17 Neither do men put new wine into old bottles: else the bottles break, and the wine runneth out, and the bottles perish: but they put new wine into new bottles, and both are preserved.

The "conflict stories" continue and the gap widens between Jesus and those who oppose His ministry. In this section opposition comes, not only from waspish Pharisees, but also from certain misguided disciples of John the Baptist. Each group puts questions to Jesus which bear a critical flavor, and He replies with flawless and searching logic.

1. *From the Pharisees comes the question of the legalists* (10-13). It is directed to the disciples but is really intended

for Jesus: *"Why does your teacher eat with tax collectors and sinners?"* (11, RSV).

Jesus was dining in Matthew's house (so Luke informs us, Luke 5:29-32), and a number of tax collectors and "sinners" were present. Perhaps Matthew was celebrating his conversion and attempting a bit of fellowship evangelism with his friends. At any rate, the Pharisees were scandalized by the bad company which Jesus kept. The "sinners" sat loose to Mosaic requirements and Pharisaic traditions alike. And the tax collectors, handling pagan money with pagan inscriptions and iconography, were continually defiled. Their question implies that Jesus was violating the law himself. They were saying, in effect, "A man is known by the company he keeps."

And Jesus replies, in effect, "Wrong! A man is known for the reason he keeps company." He was among sinners for the reason a doctor is with the sick, to help them. His answer does not mean the Pharisees are really righteous and not in need of His help. The words are ironic. Not admitting their sin, they cannot receive His salvation.

He then tells them to *go . . . and learn* the meaning of the very scripture in which they felt expert. In 11:28-29, He invites, *Come . . . and learn.* Here He says, *Go . . . and learn.* Those who will not repent and learn as His disciples are sent away to learn, if they can, from others.

2. *From the disciples of John the Baptist comes the question of the ritualists: "Why do we and the Pharisees fast, but your disciples do not fast?"* (14-17, RSV). If Pharisees were scandalized by His bad company, these were offended by His good times. The one thought He was in the wrong crowd; the other thought He was in the wrong mood.

His first reply was, I am doing what comes supernaturally, calling sinners to repentance. He now replies, My disciples are doing what comes naturally, enjoying the Bridegroom's presence as His friends. It was a time for rejoicing. The Kingdom was being preached; sinners were pressing into it; and its power was giving life and health and peace to those who had been sick. Fasting would be unreal and mere religion artificial in those circumstances.

Frequent fasting on calendar dates was not required

by the law but by tradition. Jesus honors the former but repudiates the latter, a motif Matthew began in the Sermon on the Mount.

Jesus knows these conflicts will intensify, and eventuate in His death. He speaks, therefore, of the taking away of the Bridegroom. Then sorrow will grip His disciples and fasting will be natural.

The following words about old and new wineskins, and old and new cloth, apply to John's disciples. They constitute, not only a contrast between Judaism's forms and the Kingdom's force, but also an indictment of those who were seeking to perpetuate a John the Baptist sect. The great forerunner's mission was accomplished. Now it was time for all his disciples to give allegiance to the One whose coming John had announced. The dawning reign of God was creating a situation of joy in which they should share, rather than cling to a pre-Kingdom system that withheld from them the Messiah's blessings. John would be truly honored as his disciples followed Jesus. The messianic Kingdom was God's new thing, not a prolongation of the forerunner's ministry. It's no longer Jesus or John; it's Jesus or nothing!

The Unintimidated Christ

Matthew 9:18-26

> 18 While he spake these things unto them, behold, there came a certain ruler, and worshipped him, saying, My daughter is even now dead: but come and lay thy hand upon her, and she shall live.
> 19 And Jesus arose, and followed him, and so did his disciples.
> 20 And, behold, a woman, which was diseased with an issue of blood twelve years, came behind him, and touched the hem of his garment:
> 21 For she said within herself, If I may but touch his garment, I shall be whole.
> 22 But Jesus turned him about, and when he saw her, he said, Daughter, be of good comfort; thy faith hath made thee whole. And the woman was made whole from that hour.
> 23 And when Jesus came into the ruler's house, and saw the minstrels and the people making a noise,
> 24 He said unto them, Give place: for the maid is not dead, but sleepeth. And they laughed him to scorn.
> 25 But when the people were put forth, he went in, and took her by the hand, and the maid arose.
> 26 And the fame hereof went abroad into all that land.

Jesus continues to exercise an authority so obviously from God that His critics are inexcusable. A *ruler,* whom

Mark names and identifies as a synagogue official, implores Jesus to raise up his daughter from death. And *Jesus arose, and followed him*. These are beautiful words! In verse 9 we read *he arose, and followed him,* the response of Matthew to the summons of Jesus as Lord. Now He who commands others places himself at the disposal of a grieving father; commanded by human need, He obeys in love! But He is in command; no challenge to His power can daunt Him.

1. *Jesus was unintimidated by disease* (20-22). En route to the ruler's home, He is touched by the pitiful victim of a hemorrhage doctors have been powerless to cure (cf. Mark 5:26; Luke 8:43), and His power proves adequate for her healing.

She touched Him in faith. What she said to herself becomes public utterance later: *If I may but touch his garment, I shall be whole.* Coming up behind Him in that confidence, she touched with trembling fingers the tassels of His cloak. The contact of faith released the flow of power.

Her desire for secrecy was dictated by the nature of the disease. It made her ceremonially unclean and thus defiled whomever she touched. But Jesus had no fear of this ritual impurity, and made the secret event an open matter.

He adopted her in love! He called her *daughter* (we have no record of His using the word for any other woman), and assured her that faith had healed her.

2. *Jesus was unintimidated by death* (23-26). Reaching the ruler's house, he found the flute players and wailers already gathered and the customary mourning begun. He put them out, took the girl by the hand, and she arose. *Jesus arose* (19) in response to human plight. *The maid arose* in response to divine power.

To the noisy crowd Jesus had said, *"The girl is not dead, but sleeping"* (24, RSV). He shows throughout the Gospels a reluctance to use the word "death" (cf. John 11: 11-14). He preferred the figure of sleep, furnished from the Old Testament (Dan. 12:2), with its built-in implications of awakening and continued activity (cf. 1 Thess. 4:13-16; 1 Cor. 15:51).

He refuses to acknowledge the power of death. In the Gospels, Jesus interrupts every funeral He encounters by raising the dead to life again (Matt. 9:25; Luke 7:14-15; John 11:43-44). He is the Incarnation of divine holiness, and His unrelenting hostility to sin necessarily extends to death, since death is the final outworking of sin (Rom. 5: 12; Jas. 1:15).

3. *Jesus was unintimidated by disbelief* (24). *They laughed him to scorn. But* . . . their scornful skepticism could not prevent the triumphant exertion of His power. They who mocked were the losers, for they were denied the privilege of witnessing His triumph. He put them out, and only the parents and three of His disciples were favored to observe the raising of the girl from death (Mark 5:37, 40). Unbelieving men will not receive the benefit of Jesus' ministry, but even crowds of scoffers cannot prevent His gracious work for those who trust in Him.

The contrast between the Gadarenes and Jairus is significant. The Gadarenes begged Jesus to leave, and He left. Jairus begged Him to come, and He came. He will not intrude His help upon those who despise their opportunity. But He will not withhold that help from those who ask and believe.

The Incomparable Christ

Matthew 9:27-34

> 27 And when Jesus departed thence, two blind men followed him, crying, and saying, Thou son of David, have mercy on us.
> 28 And when he was come into the house, the blind men came to him: and Jesus saith unto them, Believe ye that I am able to do this? They said unto him, Yea, Lord.
> 29 Then touched he their eyes, saying, According to your faith be it unto you.
> 30 And their eyes were opened; and Jesus straitly charged them, saying, See that no man know it.
> 31 But they, when they were departed, spread abroad his fame in all that country.
> 32 As they went out, behold, they brought to him a dumb man possessed with a devil.
> 33 And when the devil was cast out, the dumb spake: and the multitudes marvelled, saying, It was never so seen in Israel.
> 34 But the Pharisees said, He casteth out devils through the prince of the devils.

Following the raising of Jairus' daughter, *the fame* of Jesus *went abroad into all that land.* The excited reports would occasion more healings and cause greater hostility. Both happen in this section.

1. *The healing of the blind: a challenge to faith.* Two blind men follow Jesus, calling Him by the messianic title *Son of David,* and crying for mercy. Jesus does not respond until He enters a house, not wishing to inflame the mistaken messianic hopes of the crowds. There He puts the challenge to faith: *According to your faith be it unto you.*

Their eyes were opened according to mercy. The blind men have no claim upon Him. They do not pretend to deserve His help. Rather, they make themselves pensioners on His bounty of compassion, crying, *Have mercy on us.*

Their eyes were opened according to power. Jesus puts the question, *"Do you believe that I am able to do this?"* And they respond with an appropriate title, *"Yes, Lord"* (RSV). His lordship extended to the realm of men's physical condition. What they had heard about Him (v. 26) convinced them of the adequacy of His power as a Healer.

Their eyes were opened according to faith. Repeatedly in the Gospels, the healing miracles take place in response to faith, and in the absence of faith people do not benefit from the mercy and power of Jesus (cf. 13:58).

Jesus enjoined secrecy upon them, again to prevent a messianic clamor that would precipitate a premature clash with governing officials. The joy of the now-sighted men outstrips their disposition to obey and they *spread abroad his fame* still further. They acknowledged His lordship in the matter of healing power, then disregard that lordship when it contradicts strong natural impulses.

2. *The healing of the dumb: a challenge to history.* A mute was brought to Jesus, whose inability to speak was attributed to demon possession. The demon is exorcised and *the dumb spake.* As a consequence the crowds marvelled, exclaiming to one another, *"Never was anything like this seen in Israel"* (34, RSV).

There has never been another like Jesus. The mercy

and power He exercised impressed the multitudes as unique. Before their eyes some ancient scriptures were having literal fulfillment. Had not Isaiah written, *Then the eyes of the blind shall be opened, and the ears of the deaf unstopped; then shall the lame man leap like a hart, and the tongue of the dumb sing for joy* (Isa. 35:5-6, RSV)? And this would occur when *the glory of the Lord* was revealed as He came to *save* Israel. How easily, then, could the exalted titles of *Son of David* and *Lord* be given to this compassionate Healer!

And through the continuing history of the Church, those who have denied the uniqueness of Jesus—ranking Him among prophets, teachers, and reformers but denying Him as Lord—have not benefited from His power.

With a jealous eye upon His burgeoning popularity, the enemies of Jesus had another explanation for His feats of deliverance: *"He casts out demons by the prince of demons"* (34, RSV). Their motives were as insincere as their logic was faulty. Unwilling to acknowledge Him as Messiah, unable to deny the evidences of His power, they seek to vindicate themselves and discredit Him by charges of complicity with demons.

He is the incomparable One in this respect, also. No other ever aroused greater continuing hostility than Jesus. The believing disciples, the marveling crowds, the slandering critics form a motif in Matthew. Jesus is the Divider of men, a Challenge to faith and to history.

Help Wanted

Matthew 9:35-38

> 35 And Jesus went about all the cities and villages, teaching in their synagogues, and preaching the gospel of the kingdom, and healing every sickness and every disease among the people.
> 36 But when he saw the multitudes, he was moved with compassion on them, because they fainted, and were scattered abroad, as sheep having no shepherd.
> 37 Then saith he unto his disciples, The harvest truly is plenteous, but the labourers are few;
> 38 Pray ye therefore the Lord of the harvest, that he will send forth labourers into his harvest.

This brief section is transitional. The ministry of Jesus has attracted enormous crowds with vast needs. The dimensions of the task indicate the need for help, and thus the passage serves to introduce the third block of teaching, namely, the instructions that preface the mission of the 12 disciples.

1. The passage shows *how Jesus helps people.* Verse 35 is another of Matthew's summary descriptions of Jesus' ministry in Galilee (cf. 4:23) as one of teaching, preaching, and healing.

The *teaching* took place largely *in their synagogues.* This would suggest exposition and application of Old Testament scriptures, as was the practice in synagogue worship. The thrust of our Lord's teaching would be those scriptures that point to Messiah's ministry and the imminent kingdom of heaven. Luke 4:16-21 is descriptive of such a message and method. It would be good for churches everywhere to recover such a ministry of Bible exposition!

The *preaching* is concerned with *the gospel of the kingdom.* Probably the accent fell on the liberating effect of God's reign. It was customary for rulers, on accession to their thrones, to proclaim special freedoms in the form of exemption from taxes or legal penalties. Jesus proclaims freedom from sin, from its guilt and power.

The *healing* would outwardly signify the inward effects of the teaching and preaching. Emancipation from *every sickness and every disease* would illustrate in the physical realm the liberation from sin and guilt in the spiritual realm (cf. 9:6).

2. The passage shows also *how Jesus views crowds. "When he saw the multitudes, he was moved with compassion"* (36). The Greek word for *compassion,* except in parables, is used only of Jesus in the Gospels. In seven instances the word describes His motivation for acting to help others.

He saw the crowds as helpless, like shepherdless sheep scattered to the mercy of thorns and wolves. *Scattered* translates the Greek *eskulmenoi,* a strong term that means literally thrown to the earth, like a man felled by a blow or collapsed in drunkenness. Emphasis is on the helplessness implied.

He saw the crowds as a harvest, another image that may reflect another source. The harvest needs to be gathered before a storm can strike and the value be lost. So there is an "eschatological urgency" about His talk that prompts the admonition to the disciples in verses 37-38.

3. The passage shows *how Jesus needs others.* So many to reach by the teaching, preaching, healing ministry! So little time in which to gather the imperiled harvest! What urgency marks His words: *"The harvest is plentiful, but the laborers are few; pray therefore the Lord of the harvest to send out laborers into his harvest"* (37-38, RSV).

Laborers are urgently needed, now as then. But why must the *Lord of the harvest* be importuned? If it is *his harvest,* is He not much more concerned than outside help could ever be? Indeed, the concern of the Lord of the harvest lies back of Jesus' appeal, as reference to His *compassion* shows. But only those who care enough to pray, to share His concern, will respond when the Lord issues His "help wanted" bulletin.

There is a risk in prayer! In the following chapter the very disciples who were admonished to pray are called and sent into the harvest.

Some cling to a doctrine of absolute divine sovereignty that will not permit them to speak of the Lord "needing" anyone. Jesus felt and spoke differently, saying even of a donkey, *The Lord has need of it* (Mark 11:3, RSV). God's work is done through people in this world. Without exalting man or belittling God, we insist that Jesus needs help to gather His harvest.

Second Teaching Section:
The Charge to the Twelve
Matthew 10:1—11:1

MATTHEW 10

The Mission of the Twelve

Matthew 10:1-15

1 And when he had called unto him his twelve disciples, he gave them power against unclean spirits, to cast them out, and to heal all manner of sickness and all manner of disease.
2 Now the names of the twelve apostles are these; The first, Simon, who is called Peter, and Andrew his brother; James the son of Zebedee, and John his brother;
3 Philip, and Bartholomew; Thomas, and Matthew the publican; James the son of Alphaeus, and Lebbaeus, whose surname was Thaddaeus;
4 Simon the Canaanite, and Judas Iscariot, who also betrayed him.
5 These twelve Jesus sent forth, and commmanded them, saying, Go not into the way of the Gentiles, and into any city of the Samaritans enter ye not:
6 But go rather to the lost sheep of the house of Israel.
7 And as ye go, preach, saying, The kingdom of heaven is at hand.
8 Heal the sick, cleanse the lepers, raise the dead, cast out devils: freely ye have received, freely give.
9 Provide neither gold, nor silver, nor brass in your purses,
10 Nor scrip for your journey, neither two coats, neither shoes, nor yet staves: for the workman is worthy of his meat.
11 And into whatsoever city or town ye shall enter, enquire who in it is worthy; and there abide till ye go thence.
12 And when ye come into an house, salute it.
13 And if the house be worthy, let your peace come upon it: but if it be not worthy, let your peace return to you.
14 And whosoever shall not receive you, nor hear your words, when ye depart out of that house or city, shake off the dust of your feet,
15 Verily I say unto you, It shall be more tolerable for the land of Sodom and Gomorrha in the day of judgment, than for that city.

In chapter 10, the third block of teaching, the Lord of the harvest calls and sends the 12 disciples into His harvest. Here they are called *apostles* for the first and only time in the Gospels. Whether the term goes back to Jesus or reflects the post-Easter usage of the Church is inconsequential. *Apostle* means one sent on a mission, and is appropriate to this setting. Since the Twelve are not sent on another mission until after the Resurrection, further use of the term in Matthew is unnecessary.

1. *The men are named.* The list of names not only identifies those who shared this original mission, but reminds us that the call of Christ must be heard and answered by individuals, in the particularity of each one's personal life. The prayer for *labourers* ultimates, not in some anonymous and amorphous group, but in Peter, Andrew, James, John, etc.

The names are those of men chosen but not choice. The weakness and failure of them all is documented in scripture (cf. 26:56). The work of the Kingdom would never get done if it awaited perfect men. Further, the names are of men well known and virtually unknown. Apart from their appearance in the "disciple lists" we never hear again of some of them. Christ's mission is continued not alone by those whose work is highly publicized, but also by those who labor in obscurity.

Matthew arranges the names in pairs. Probably they were sent out two by two (cf. Luke 10:1), to give encouragement and reinforcement to one another. That Peter is designated the *first* (cf. 16:18) and that Judas is named last is certainly no accident, for this is not the chronological order of their call to follow Jesus. The order has theological implications.

2. *The mission is outlined.* Three items are of special significance.

a. The authority Jesus imparts. He *gave them authority* (1, RSV) to exorcise demons, heal the sick, raise the dead, and proclaim the imminence of the Kingdom. His own authority, underlying His teaching and illustrated in His healings (cc. 5—9), is now transmitted to His disciples for this mission. Such authority for the achievement of Kingdom objectives is a gift, and not the consequence of personality, talent, or wit. Persons of unusual ability and resources can utterly fail as disciples and apostles;

while ordinary people, filled with the Spirit, may achieve extraordinary victories in Kingdom service. Demons are not subject to dollars or diplomas, but to the name of Jesus.

b. The restriction Jesus imposes. He confines their mission to *the lost sheep of the house of Israel,* specifically excluding Gentile territory (6). The mission is not so broad as the Lord's compassion, but its limits are dictated by the horizons of His own earthly task (cf. 15:24), and the exigencies of the time at their disposal. Beyond the Crucifixion-Resurrection a global mission will be laid upon His disciples. It is always true that a follower of Jesus may embrace in his heart more than he can reach with his hands, and the necessary restriction upon his mission is the prerogative of Jesus as Lord of the harvest.

c. The destinies Jesus implies. The disciples are to accept support from those whom they serve, and bless those who receive them in peace. But from those who refuse a welcome and a hearing they are to *depart.* Their departure will symbolize abandonment to judgment of those who reject the gospel of the Kingdom with its offer of salvation. *Sodom and Gomorrha,* called by Filson "proverbial examples of extreme wickedness," will be less severely judged. Plainly the destinies of men, individually and corporately, hinge upon their acceptance or rejection of the word Christ sends through disciples of His choosing. To accept them is to accept Him; to reject them is to reject Him.

Sheep in a Wolf Pack

Matthew 10:16-33

16 Behold, I send you forth as sheep in the midst of wolves: be ye therefore wise as serpents, and harmless as doves.
17 But beware of men: for they will deliver you up to the councils, and they will scourge you in their synagogues;
18 And ye shall be brought before governors and kings for my sake, for a testimony against them and the Gentiles.
19 But when they deliver you up, take no thought how or what ye shall speak: for it shall be given you in that same hour what ye shall speak.
20 For it is not ye that speak, but the Spirit of your Father which speaketh in you.
21 And the brother shall deliver up the brother to death, and the father the child: and the children shall rise up against their parents, and cause them to be put to death.

22 And ye shall be hated of all men for my name's sake: but he that endureth to the end shall be saved.

23 But when they persecute you in this city, flee ye into another: for verily I say unto you, Ye shall not have gone over the cities of Israel, till the Son of man be come.

24 The disciple is not above his master, nor the servant above his lord.

25 It is enough for the disciple that he be as his master, and the servant as his lord, If they have called the master of the house Beelzebub, how much more shall they call them of his household?

26 Fear them not therefore: for there is nothing covered, that shall not be revealed; and hid, that shall not be known.

27 What I tell you in darkness, that speak ye in light: and what ye hear in the ear, that preach ye upon the housetops.

28 And fear not them which kill the body, but are not able to kill the soul: but rather fear him which is able to destroy both soul and body in hell.

29 Are not two sparrows sold for a farthing? and one of them shall not fall on the ground without your Father.

30 But the very hairs of your head are all numbered.

31 Fear ye not therefore, ye are of more value than many sparrows.

32 Whosoever therefore shall confess me before men, him will I confess also before my Father which is in heaven.

33 But whosoever shall deny me before men, him will I also deny before my Father which is in heaven.

Parts of this section certainly look beyond the swift and limited mission on which the Twelve were sent during Jesus' life on earth. Instructions are included which are relevant only to that wider "all nations" mission to which they are assigned by the risen Lord (28:16-20). This does not require us to regard the passage as Early Church addenda to the sayings of Jesus. Granted the social, political, and religious situation in Palestine, even without special clairvoyance Jesus could foresee that proclamation of His kingdom would produce conflict among the Jews and provoke reaction among the Gentiles. Arrest, trial, prison, and torture would inevitably befall some of His apostles. Accordingly, He prepares them for it by a frank statement of the cost of discipleship. They will be *as sheep in the midst of wolves.*

1. *Christ's witnesses can expect hostility from men.* The kingdom of heaven is not only different from the kingdoms of this world; it is in opposition to them, insofar as they operate by principles of force, greed, and hatred. Christ's emissaries can only expect misunderstanding, distrust, and abuse. How radical the forms of this hostility may

become are indicated in the strong verbs employed—dragged, flogged, killed, hated.

This hostility may come from family members. One may be *handed over* (Anchor Bible) to persecuting authorities by one's own brother, or parent, or child, who in misguided zeal or fear consents to one's death. What Jesus predicted, history has recorded.

The hostility will come from society leaders, whose vested interests are threatened by Christ's claims. *Councils, synagogues, governors,* and *kings* are mentioned. Civil and religious authorities will conspire against Christ's witnesses as they did against Christ.

The hostility is for Jesus' sake, breaking out against the disciples because they bear His name. The servant will be treated as was the Master, who was maligned with the title Beelzebul, the chief of demons.

2. *Christ's witnesses can expect help from God.* They are sheep among wolves, but not sheep without a Shepherd.

God's help, however, is not for escape but for endurance. Limited periods of escape may come as they *flee* from one place *into another.* But even flight is not in order to purchase immunity from persecution, but in order to perpetuate the mission and witness! All will be hated, and some will be killed, but *he who endures to the end will be saved* (22, RSV), i.e., received into the eternal kingdom of God.

Help from God will take the form of wisdom and words. The persecution itself will provide opportunity for *testimony before* (RSV) officials, and the Spirit will give needed words to accused disciples.

For this reason His witnesses are not to fear. What has been received in private instruction must be proclaimed in public testimony. The God who cares for sparrows and numbers the insignificant hairs on one's head will care for His own. They are not to fear men, who can kill the body but wreak no injury beyond death. Rather, they are to fear God, who as righteous Judge has power to consign the whole person to everlasting punishment.

The destinies of men are at stake in the situations of threat and persecution. If people confess Jesus before men, even at the cost of their lives, He will acknowledge them as His own before the Father. If, to save themselves from persecution, they deny Him before men, He will repudiate them before the Father. How easily the bravest may be tempted to deny Him is shown in the case of Peter (26:69-75), who also demonstrates that a momentary lapse need not be final.

Christ is worth having at the cost of life. Life is not worth having at the cost of hell.

The Great Divider

Matthew 10:34—11:1

> 34 Think not that I am come to send peace on earth: I came not to send peace, but a sword.
> 35 For I am come to set a man at variance against his father, and the daughter against her mother, and the daughter in law against her mother in law.
> 36 And a man's foes shall be they of his own household.
> 37 He that loveth father or mother more than me is not worthy of me: and he that loveth son or daughter more than me is not worthy of me.
> 38 And he that taketh not his cross, and followeth after me, is not worthy of me.
> 39 He that findeth his life shall lose it: and he that loseth his life for my sake shall find it.
> 40 He that receiveth you receiveth me, and he that receiveth me receiveth him that sent me.
> 41 He that receiveth a prophet in the name of a prophet shall receive a prophet's reward; and he that receiveth a righteous man in the name of a righteous man shall receive a righteous man's reward.
> 42 And whosoever shall give to drink unto one of these little ones a cup of cold water only in the name of a disciple, verily I say unto you, he shall in no wise lose his reward.
> 1 And it came to pass, when Jesus had made an end of commanding his twelve disciples, he departed thence to teach and to preach in their cities.

The saying of Jesus about a *sword* has perplexed translators and exegetes no end. That the messianic purpose was to divide is difficult for many to accept. That the messianic ministry had this effect, all must admit. We can only go from this point, admitting, however, that Jesus' intention was neither to impose an enforced peace nor to wage war, but to divide the just from the unjust by a different kind of messiahship.

1. The passage speaks of *the deepest division that Christ causes: "A man's foes shall be they of his own household"* (36). No cleavage is so painful as that which divides (the

Greek is *dichazō*) parents from children, that sunders the serenity and joy of a family. But this inevitably happens when some within the home opt to follow Jesus while others refuse to do so. Jesus himself experienced misunderstanding and rejection at home, though He was not persecuted physically by unbelieving members of His family circle. Some have been, and no cross weighs more heavily than does this one.

Without equivocation Jesus calls upon His followers to establish a priority of relationships that puts Him first, all others second. To love anyone more than Him is to prove unworthy of Him, disqualified to advance His mission in a hostile world.

2. The passage speaks of *the highest sacrifice that Christ demands* (38-39). He makes a hard saying even harder by insisting that one is unsuited to follow Him in this Kingdom enterprise who will not give up life itself for His sake. The cross must be accepted, not as symbol of irritations endured, but of life surrendered. The cross was a form of gallows, an instrument of violent and shameful death. Jesus expected His own life to end on a cross. He demands of all who follow Him a like commitment to the Kingdom, whether it is actualized in every individual's experience or not.

The cost of discipleship is death to self-will always, physical death often. But precisely in physical life purchased by compromise lies spiritual death, while surrender to the point of martyrdom for Christ's sake means eternal life.

3. The passage speaks, also, of *the surest rewards that Christ promises.* The faithful servant of Christ's kingdom *shall in no wise lose his reward* (42). To receive His missioners is to receive Him. To support them is to support Him. And He will never allow such loyalty and assistance to go unrewarded. Indeed, those who *receive* and *give* shall have the same reward dispensed to those who are the prophets, righteous men, and little ones actively engaged in publishing the gospel of the Kingdom.

It is possible to translate the *prophet* and the *righ-*

teous man as titles for Jesus himself. Whether scholars can ever agree on the rendering of this difficult passage, the truth stands, that the humblest service rendered sincerely to Jesus and His harvest-workers will be crowned with gracious and unfailing reward.

MATTHEW 11

This section of Matthew is closed with His typical editorial formula, marking the transition back to narrative discourse: *When Jesus had finished instructing his twelve disciples, he went on from there to teach and preach in their cities* (11:1, RSV). The ministry is resumed which He has called them to share.

Third Narrative Section:
Conflict and Rejection
Matthew 11:2—12:50

Rebuke and Tribute for John

Matthew 11:2-19

2 Now when John had heard in the prison the works of Christ, he sent two of his disciples,

3 And said unto him, Art thou he that should come, or do we look for another?

4 Jesus answered and said unto them, Go and shew John again those things which ye do hear and see:

5 The blind receive their sight, and the lame walk, the lepers are cleansed, and the deaf hear, the dead are raised up, and the poor have the gospel preached to them.

6 And blessed is he, whosoever shall not be offended in me.

7 And as they departed, Jesus began to say unto the multitudes concerning John, What went ye out into the wilderness to see? A reed shaken with the wind?

8 But what went ye out for to see? A man clothed in soft raiment? behold, they that wear soft clothing are in kings' houses.

9 But what went ye out for to see? A prophet? yea, I say unto you, and more than a prophet.

10 For this is he, of whom it is written, Behold, I send my messenger before thy face, which shall prepare thy way before thee.

11 Verily I say unto you, Among them that are born of women there hath not risen a greater than John the Baptist: notwithstanding he that is least in the kingdom of heaven is greater than he.

12 And from the days of John the Baptist until now the kingdom of heaven suffereth violence, and the violent take it by force.

13 For all the prophets and the law prophesied until John.

14 And if ye will receive it, this is Elias, which was for to come.

15 He that hath ears to hear, let him hear.

16 But whereunto shall I liken this generation? It is like unto children sitting in the markets, and calling unto their fellows,

17 And saying, We have piped unto you, and ye have not danced; we have mourned unto you, and ye have not lamented.

18 For John came neither eating nor drinking, and they say, He hath a devil.

19 The Son of man came eating and drinking, and they say, Behold a man gluttonous, and a winebibber, a friend of publicans and sinners. But wisdom is justified of her children.

Two matters arrest our attention in this section of the narrative: the evident misunderstanding of John, and the high tribute paid to him by Jesus.

1. *Jesus sends a gentle rebuke to John.* Rebuke is certainly implied in the words, *And blessed is he who takes no offense at me* (6, RSV). Languishing in Herod's prison the courageous forerunner, because of doubt or impatience, seems to have misunderstood the messianic work of Jesus. He sends certain of his loyal followers to ask, *"Are you the one who was to come, or should we expect someone else?"* (3, NIV). John had heard of *the works of Christ,* such works as Matthew has been describing as illustrations of Jesus' unique authority. Possibly John wondered, Since He is doing messianic works, why is He not more plainly and publicly identifying himself by messianic titles? Why this ambiguity that keeps men guessing? It's time to say, I am, or I am not, the Messiah.

For answer Jesus sends another report such as John already had received: Miracles of healing are taking place and the gospel is inviting the poor to enter the Kingdom. This is a clear reference to Isa. 35:5 and 61:1-3, two acknowledged messianic scriptures. Jesus adds a beatitude which chides the impatience and calls for John to exercise faith. Jesus is indeed the Coming One whom John had heralded. Now let John trust Him to do His work in His own time and way.

Jesus is so faithful to a man's needs! He will rebuke even a loyal friend when such wounding can promise healing as its consequence.

2. *Jesus then delivers a glowing tribute to John.* The crowd must know that His rebuke was not a disparagement of John's person or work.

John was no self-indulgent, time-serving tool of the civil powers. Had he been such a man, he would now be housed in the palace, not in the prison. No, he was a true prophet, worthy to stand in that noble succession of truth-speaking men who bore God's word to a rebellious Israel.

Indeed, he was *more than a prophet,* for he had the added privilege and responsibility of announcing the imminent kingdom of God and the arrival of Messiah. And yet, he was less than the humblest neophyte in the Kingdom, for John belonged to the old order with its inferior blessings, not to the dawning reign of God with its greater freedoms. The comparisons marked by *greater* and *least* are not comparisons of moral worth but of covenant privileges.

Plummer suggests that the high praise of Jesus for John may almost be called "the funeral oration of the Baptist," for he was soon to be martyred. Perhaps in the anticipation of that coming execution, and of His own, Jesus goes on to speak of violent men launching violent attacks upon the dawning Kingdom. Despite the hostility and aggression of such men, however, those with *ears to hear* would know that John was the forerunner of Messiah, the Elijah who was to come as Malachi had prophesied. Thus they would also know that Jesus was indeed the Messiah, whose advent the faithful prophet had announced.

The tribute to His friend passes into an indictment of His enemies. When men reject God's Word, they can always rationalize their unbelief by their dislike for the personalities of those who preach. Like pouting children who refuse to play wedding or funeral, they charged Jesus with being too merry, John with being too morose. Nevertheless, *wisdom is justified by her deeds* (RSV). In the course of history the ministry of both John and Jesus will be vindicated by their results. The Kingdom will come.

Cities That Failed

Matthew 11:20-24

> 20 Then began he to upbraid the cities wherein most of his mighty works were done, because they repented not:
> 21 Woe unto thee, Chorazin! woe unto thee, Bethsaida! for if the mighty works, which were done in you, had been done in Tyre and Sidon, they would have repented long ago in sackcloth and ashes.
> 22 But I say unto you, It shall be more tolerable for Tyre and Sidon at the day of judgment, than for you.
> 23 And thou, Capernaum, which art exalted unto heaven, shalt be brought down to hell: for if the mighty works, which have been done in thee, had been done in Sodom, it would have remained until this day.
> 24 But I say unto you, That it shall be more tolerable for the land of Sodom, in the day of judgment, than for thee.

Man is as truly social as he is individual. Sin and guilt, accordingly, have a corporate as well as a personal dimension. Here Jesus solemnly denounces three cities for failure to repent. The King had entered these cities, but these cities had not entered the Kingdom. Their refusal is inexcusable, for His mighty works were sufficient evidence that in His ministry God was summoning them to decision.

1. These cities had *a day of opportunity*. They could have repented and did not. Their opportunity was created by His miracles. Healings and exorcisms had demonstrated a power at work on their behalf mightier than the demonic forces that blinded and bound them. They had their chance to ally themselves with the liberating power of God's inbreaking kingdom. Instead, they let Jesus come and go, content to form curious crowds who watched a few individuals benefit from His touch.

His accusation is simply, *They repented not*. They are not charged with violence against Him, nor does He suggest that their sins and crimes were worse than the ancient cities of Tyre, Sidon, or Sodom. They had rejected Him in cool indifference. Pride was a factor in their failure to repent; this is implied in His challenging question to Capernaum, *"Will you be exalted to heaven?"* (RSV). (Textual evidence for reading His words as a question seems conclusive.)

2. These cities would have *a day of judgment*. His words, *I say unto you*, hold an implicit and impressive claim to divine authority. He is confident of their fate, for He will be their Judge.

Temporal judgments point to final judgment. Jesus said that Sodom *would have remained until this day* had they repented. Yet He includes them in *the day of judgment* yet future. The overthrow and disappearance of Sodom was a judgment in time that presaged *the* judgment at the end of time.

Light graduates guilt. The punishment of Chorazin, Bethsaida, and Capernaum will be greater than the punishment of Tyre, Sidon, and Sodom because they had more favorable opportunity. No such mighty works had been wrought in those ancient wicked cities, but *most* of Jesus' miracles had occurred in the Galilean cities which He upbraids. Capernaum is especially reprehensible, for there Jesus was *at home* (cf. 9:1; Mark 2:1, RSV). Capernaum was headquarters for His Galilean ministry. The city refused Him in pride, lifting itself to the heavens in civic boasting. It would be cast down to *the depths* (NIV), by the inexorable judgment of God. (The Greek for *depths* is *hades*, not *gehenna;* the underworld, not the place of fiery punishment. The term marks a contrast; it does not detail a fate.)

Jesus sounds like the prophets who brought oracles of woe, and taunt songs of coming disaster, upon impenitent cities in Old Testament days (cf. Isa. 14:13-15; Jer. 25:22; Ezek. 26:3-7). But no prophet ever spoke with the direct personal authority that sounds in these words. The following passage shows why.

Revelation and Invitation

Matthew 11:25-30

> 25 At that time Jesus answered and said, I thank thee, O Father, Lord of heaven and earth, because thou hast hid these things from the wise and prudent, and hast revealed them unto babes.
> 26 Even so, Father: for so it seemed good in thy sight.
> 27 All things are delivered unto me of my Father: and no man knoweth the Son, but the Father; neither knoweth any man the Father, save the Son, and he to whomsoever the Son will reveal him.
> 28 Come unto me, all ye that labour and are heavy laden, and I will give you rest.
> 29 Take my yoke upon you, and learn of me; for I am meek and lowly in heart: and ye shall find rest unto your souls.
> 30 For my yoke is easy, and my burden is light.

Answered, in verse 25, is a Matthean device for introducing this important passage. Jesus is not replying to a question but to a situation. He has been rejected, but gives thanks because God's purposes have not failed. Though proud leaders have scorned Him, He has revealed the Father to some humble commoners. And He extends an invitation for others to join the circle of His disciples. The passage turns on the twin poles of revelation and invitation.

1. *Revelation is the subject of Jesus' thanksgiving.* He praises the Father for both concealing and revealing *these things.* This phrase refers to His *mighty works* done in the Galilean cities just denounced. They were hidden from

men who fancied themselves *wise and understanding,* such as the scribes and Pharisees, who failed to discern in Jesus' miracles the sign of God's irrupting kingdom. They were revealed to *babes,* the humble and trusting disciples who were entering the Kingdom.

Jesus views this revelation as sovereignly made; it is the work of Him who is *Lord of heaven and earth.*

The revelation is also graciously made; the hiding and showing were God's *gracious will* (RSV).

Jesus is not condemning intelligence or sanctifying ignorance. It is the pride, not the intellect, of the wise that prompts them to reject Jesus. It is the simpleheartedness and not the simplemindedness of the *babes* that permits them to accept Him.

Jesus alone can make the saving disclosure to men. Only the Father knows the Son; only the Son knows the Father. Jesus is conscious of being uniquely the Son of God and wills to share His knowledge of the Father with His disciples (cf. John 14:8-9; 2 Cor. 4:6; Heb. 1:1-3).

2. *Invitation should be the subject of our thanksgiving!* The gracious words of verses 28-30 are found only in Matthew, and they constitute a call to share the revelation. *Come unto me* stands in sharpest contrast to the words He will speak to false teachers at the judgment, *Depart from me* (7:23).

The invitation is to learning: *Take my yoke upon you, and learn of* (i.e., from) *me.* Some scholars are convinced that taking the yoke was a verbal symbol for becoming a disciple. *Yoke* implies a task, for discipleship is both learning and doing God's will (cf. 7:24-27).

And yet, the invitation is to liberty: *Ye shall find rest.* Jesus promises freedom from the oppressive yoke imposed by the false teachers, who made the law a grievous burden (cf. 23:4). Legalism leaves one *heavy laden,* for it piles rule after rule upon a conscience whose guilt it cannot remove. Jesus, who is *gentle and humble in heart* (NIV), imposes a *yoke,* but it is *easy;* and a *burden,* yet it is *light.* His heart will not allow Him to make things harder for an already lost, confused, and oppressed humanity.

The invitation strikes a universal note. It is extended to *all who labor and are heavy laden* (RSV). It extends to us.

MATTHEW 12

Lord of the Sabbath

Matthew 12:1-8

> 1 At that time Jesus went on the sabbath day through the corn; and his disciples were an hungred, and began to pluck the ears of corn, and to eat.
> 2 But when the Pharisees saw it, they said unto him, Behold, thy disciples do that which is not lawful to do upon the sabbath day.
> 3 But he said unto them, Have ye not read what David did, when he was an hungred, and they that were with him;
> 4 How he entered into the house of God, and did eat the shewbread, which was not lawful for him to eat, neither for them which were with him, but only for the priests?
> 5 Or have ye not read in the law, how that on the sabbath days the priests in the temple profane the sabbath, and are blameless?
> 6 But I say unto you, That in this place is one greater than the temple.
> 7 But if ye had known what this meaneth, I will have mercy, and not sacrifice, ye would not have condemned the guiltless.
> 8 For the Son of man is Lord even of the sabbath day.

The "conflict stories" are resumed and the hostility toward Jesus becomes deeper. Blinded by their legalism, which subordinated human need to religious tradition, the Pharisees regard Jesus and His disciples as lawbreakers. Here the specific law in question was the prohibition of work on the Sabbath day. The passage reads like a trial.

1. *The accused were the disciples.* Their act of plucking grain was considered harvesting by the accusers. And harvesting was one of 39 forms of activity classified as work in the tradition of the Pharisees.

The charge was made directly against the disciples, but indirectly against Jesus as their Teacher. Those who have taken His yoke (11:29), it is implied, have been wrongly instructed. It requires scant imagination to know where voice stress was placed when the charges were made: *"Look, your disciples are doing what is not lawful to do on the sabbath"* (2, RSV). *Your* disciples!

2. *The Defender was Jesus.* No accused ever had a wiser or better Advocate to represent them.

He cites the accusers to the precedent of David. When he and his followers were hungry, they ate *the bread of the Presence* from *the house of God* (RSV), which the law reserved for the priests. Hunger justified the action, and it was hunger which motivated the disciples.

Jesus drew a second example from *the law.* On the Sabbath the priests who serve the Temple offer sacrifices, working on the day of rest, but are guiltless. *Something greater than the temple* refers to the Kingdom service which the disciples share with Jesus (6). The ministry of Jesus is far more important than the ministry of the priests, for He is *the Son of man,* the One sent from God to redeem mankind from sin.

His next words accuse the accusers. They are ignorant of the very scriptures which they purport to teach. They do not know the meaning of the prophet's words, *I will have mercy, and not sacrifice* (Hos. 6:6).

3. *The verdict was acquittal.* The disciples are *guiltless.*

Having rendered a verdict, Jesus asserts His authority. *The Son of man is lord . . . of the sabbath* (8). The Pharisees had made their accusation on the basis of their own interpretation of the Sabbath legislation. But Jesus is the Lord, whose day the Sabbath is. Decisions concerning its observance are His province, not theirs.

What comfort, when wrongfully accused, to have Jesus as an Advocate to defend and a Judge to acquit! And greater comfort still, when justly condemned, to have Him as a Saviour who forgives!

Withered Hands, Withered Hearts

Matthew 12:9-21

> 9 And when he was departed thence, he went into their synagogue:
> 10 And, behold, there was a man which had his hand withered. And they asked him, saying, Is it lawful to heal on the sabbath days? that they might accuse him.
> 11 And he said unto them, What man shall there be among you, that shall have one sheep, and if it fall into a pit on the sabbath day, will he not lay hold on it, and lift it out?

12 How much then is a man better than a sheep? Wherefore it is lawful to do well on the sabbath days.
13 Then saith he to the man, Stretch forth thine hand. And he stretched it forth; and it was restored whole, like as the other.
14 Then the Pharisees went out, and held a council against him, how they might destroy him.
15 But when Jesus knew it, he withdrew himself from thence: and great multitudes followed him, and he healed them all;
16 And charged them that they should not make him known:
17 That it might be fulfilled which was spoken by Esaias the prophet, saying,
18 Behold my servant, whom I have chosen; my beloved, in whom my soul is well pleased: I will put my spirit upon him, and he shall shew judgment to the Gentiles.
19 He shall not strive, nor cry; neither shall any man hear his voice in the streets.
20 A bruised reed shall he not break, and smoking flax shall he not quench, till he send forth judgment unto victory.
21 And in his name shall the Gentiles trust.

Jesus entered *their* synagogue, i.e., the one attended by the Pharisees with whom He had just disputed. He was in the habit of attending on the Sabbath, and would not permit hypocrites to keep Him away. There a healing miracle occurred, and a plot to kill the Healer was hatched.

1. The incident shows *Jesus' love for the incapable.* A man is present whose hand is *withered.* The Pharisees raise the question of the legality of healing on the Sabbath. Healing was work, and the Sabbath was for rest. They would rescue a stray sheep from *a pit* on the Sabbath, but they object to the healing of a man. Their value system was structured by love for money; His, by love for men: *A man [is] better than a sheep!* By the measure of his capacity for reason, speech, worship, and immortality a man outvalues an animal. As *Lord . . . of the sabbath* (8), Jesus rules that *"it is lawful to do good"* on that day (RSV), and He implements the ruling by healing the man.

2. The incident shows *Jesus' power for the impossible.* He commands the victim to *stretch forth* his hand, as earlier He had directed a paralytic to rise and walk. In faith the man attempts the impossible, and His hand *was restored whole.*

Jesus was always commanding the impossible. Rise and walk! Love your enemies! Sin no more! But as George Truett observed, "His commands are inverted promises"; what He demands, He enables.

3. The incident shows *Jesus' judgment upon the implacable*. The Pharisees did not rejoice at the healing; rather, they *held a council,* and the agenda was, How can we kill this Healer who tramples our tradition? When Jesus learned of their plot, *he withdrew.* An awesome judgment, and so quietly executed! He simply leaves the place; they forfeit His presence. Everything looks the same as it did before He came, but all is subtly and terribly changed.

Many follow Him, and He graciously heals the sick among them. He *charged* them not to publicize Him. He does not want His opportunity for service to their needs destroyed by untimely clashes with the authorities.

This prompts one of Matthew's Old Testament quotations, prefaced by the "fulfillment-formula" (17). Jesus is the gentle Servant of Yahweh of whom Isaiah spoke, refusing to wrangle in the streets, but persisting in His mission against all opposition encountered. The quotation draws a contrast between the gentle Healer of men and the heartless critics of His works in these "conflict stories."

Three things stand out in the description of the Servant (18-21). (1) His power. *I will put my spirit upon him.* His ministry of love is accomplished in the creative power of the living God. (2) His purpose. *"He brings justice to victory"* (RSV). The prophetic concept of justice emphasized "judgment on evil and salvation for the poor" (Filson). (3) His patience. Enduring all opposition encountered, the Servant refuses to be discouraged from His mission until it is completed. *He shall proclaim justice . . . till he brings justice to victory* (RSV).

God is saying to our injustice-ridden world today, *Behold my servant!*

The Kingdom of God Has Come

Matthew 12:22-37

22 Then was brought unto him one possessed with a devil, blind, and dumb: and he healed him, insomuch that the blind and dumb both spake and saw.
23 And all the people were amazed, and said, Is not this the son of David?
24 But when the Pharisees heard it, they said, This fellow doth not cast out devils, but by Beelzebub the prince of the devils.
25 And Jesus knew their thoughts, and said unto them, Every king-

dom divided against itself is brought to desolation; and every city or house divided against itself shall not stand:

26 And if Satan cast out Satan, he is divided against himself; how shall then his kingdom stand?

27 And if I by Beelzebub cast out devils, by whom do your children cast them out? therefore they shall be your judges.

28 But if I cast out devils by the Spirit of God, then the kingdom of God is come unto you.

29 Or else how can one enter into a strong man's house, and spoil his goods, except he first bind the strong man? and then he will spoil his house.

30 He that is not with me is against me; and he that gathereth not with me scattereth abroad.

31 Wherefore I say unto you, All manner of sin and blasphemy shall be forgiven unto men: but the blasphemy against the Holy Ghost shall not be forgiven unto men.

32 And whosoever speaketh a word against the Son of man, it shall be forgiven him: but whosoever speaketh against the Holy Ghost, it shall not be forgiven him, neither in this world, neither in the world to come.

33 Either make the tree good, and his fruit good; or else make the tree corrupt, and his fruit corrupt: for the tree is known by his fruit.

34 O generation of vipers, how can ye, being evil, speak good things? for out of the abundance of the heart the mouth speaketh.

35 A good man out of the good treasure of the heart bringeth forth good things: and an evil man out of the evil treasure bringeth forth evil things.

36 But I say unto you, That every idle word that men shall speak, they shall give account thereof in the day of judgment.

37 For by thy words thou shalt be justified, and by thy words thou shalt be condemned.

The healing of a blind and mute demoniac prompts the amazed onlookers to ask, *Is not this the son of David?* The Pharisees move quickly to chill the messianic fervor that is rising, and their hostility provokes a severe warning from Jesus. This pericope is a typical "conflict story" preserved by the disciples. It explains the opposition Jesus met in His career and that which they were meeting in theirs. A clash of kingdoms, not of ideologies, was taking place.

1. Verses 22-27 record *an inexcusable slander.* The Pharisees dare to accuse Jesus of conspiracy with demons. The power they cannot deny they choose to defame, insisting angrily that its source is *Beelzebul, the prince of demons* (RSV).

Their slander was condemned by the quality of Jesus' deeds. *Satan* means "adversary." Every member of the hierarchy of evil is committed to the anti-welfare of people. But every action of Jesus to which these critics object has promoted human welfare. Gifts of sight and speech and health restore what God has created. Such good works cannot have an evil source.

Their slander was also condemned by the force of His logic. *Every kingdom divided against itself is brought to desolation* (25). Satan doesn't cast out Satan. He is too wise to divide his empire of evil. The works of Jesus do not represent civil-war victories. Rather, the demonic kingdom is being invaded and conquered from without.

2. Verses 28-30 witness to *an irresistible power. "The kingdom of God has come upon you"* (28, RSV). The mighty is under siege by the Almighty. A stronger than Satan is plundering his house, recovering stolen property!

The kingdom of God is a binding power. As thieves would bind a strong man in order to loot his home, so the inbreaking reign of God has restrained Satan in order to release his captives. The binding of Satan looks back to the temptation of Jesus, and to every successive victory of the Lord whenever their kingdoms have clashed.

The kingdom of God is a freeing power. It liberates from demonic forces and crippling illnesses as Jesus exorcises and heals. It liberates from the guilt and power of sin as Jesus forgives and renews. In undoing the worst that Satan has done, Jesus leaves no doubt that God's reign cannot be successfully resisted.

In this collision of kingdoms there can be no neutrality: *He that is not with me is against me* (30). Again Jesus divides men into two classes (cf. 7:24-29). Since the kingdom of God, the power of the age to come, is operative in the ministry of Jesus, *the Pharisees* and *the people* have just two choices: Either they join with Jesus or decamp to the enemy. This no-neutrality factor leads to a serious warning.

3. Verses 31-37 caution against *an unforgivable sin: "The blasphemy against the [Holy] Spirit will not be forgiven"* (RSV). *Every sin,* with this one exception, is pardonable. But the blasphemy of attributing to Satan the work done by the Spirit is unpardonable, both *in this age* and *in the age to come* (RSV). He who speaks this awful warning is

the very One who claimed and demonstrated *authority* . . . *to forgive* (cf. 9:6, RSV).

Three things are postulated concerning this unforgivable sin. (1) It arises out of an evil heart: *Out of the abundance of the heart the mouth speaketh.* (2) It is expressed in blasphemous speech. When the heart is hostile, the mouth is hurtful. Hatred so intense as that which Jesus met cannot be passive, but speaks and acts violently. (3) It is condemned in ultimate judgment. This narrative section in Matthew (cc. 11—12) is replete with references to the final judgment. The phrase *the day of judgment* occurs three times, and *the judgment* twice. Early and late in Matthew's Gospel, Jesus identifies himself as the final Judge of men (7:21-23; 25:31-46). He knows that speech will be judged as well as action (v. 37), and He tells in advance what the verdict upon blasphemy against the Spirit will be.

The Sign of Jonah

Matthew 12:38-45

> 38 Then certain of the scribes and of the Pharisees answered, saying, Master, we would see a sign from thee.
> 39 But he answered and said unto them, An evil and adulterous generation seeketh after a sign; and there shall no sign be given to it, but the sign of the prophet Jonas:
> 40 For as Jonas was three days and three nights in the whale's belly; so shall the Son of man be three days and three nights in the heart of the earth.
> 41 The men of Nineveh shall rise in judgment with this generation, and shall condemn it: because they repented at the preaching of Jonas; and, behold, a greater than Jonas is here.
> 42 The queen of the south shall rise up in the judgment with this generation, and shall condemn it: for she came from the uttermost parts of the earth to hear the wisdom of Solomon; and, behold, a greater than Solomon is here.
> 43 When the unclean spirit is gone out of a man, he walketh through dry places, seeking rest, and findeth none.
> 44 Then he saith, I will return into my house from whence I came out; and when he is come, he findeth it empty, swept, and garnished.
> 45 Then goeth he, and taketh with himself seven other spirits more wicked than himself, and they enter in and dwell there: and the last state of that man is worse than the first. Even so shall it be also unto this wicked generation.

The very request of these scribes and Pharisees for *a sign* was depressingly insincere. They had contradicted Jesus' words and slandered His deeds, while the people marveled at the unique authority which marked those words and deeds. Now, having attributed His ministry to the devil, they come asking for a compelling sign, as though they really were open to persuasion. They are like a man demanding to hear who stands with fingers jammed into his ears, or demanding to see when he has put on a blindfold.

Jesus calls them *evil and adulterous.* In Old Testament times Israel was labeled adulterous by the prophets when Yahweh was forsaken for idols (Isa. 57:3; Hos. 3:1). The figure was apt in view of the sexual orgies that accompanied much of the Canaanite religion. Now the idols are not heathen gods but human traditions by which the law has been distorted into an oppressive burden.

The only sign they will receive is *the sign of the prophet Jonah* (39, RSV). His deliverance from the sea monster serves to prefigure the resurrection of Jesus. What else could be a sign? Further exorcisms and healings would be "more of the same" which they had already rejected. This one sign will not be an addition to His works, but a reversal of their work. They had resolved to kill Him (14); and when their rejection of His ministry would reach this climax, God would raise Him from the dead.

1. *The one sign given was sufficient.* The Resurrection would validate His claims to be the Son of Man, claims explicit in His words and implicit in His miracles. If He were a demoniac or a maniac, an impostor as they asserted, God would not raise Him from the dead. A holy God will not lend credence to the claims of a deluded fanatic or deliberate charlatan.

The nature of His ministry made impenitence and unbelief inexcusable. Rejecting the Resurrection will make it unpardonable. Jesus anticipates this further rejection in the sayings about judgment. *The queen of the south* (the Sabaeans occupied southern Arabia) went to great lengths to hear the wisdom of Solomon. These Pharisees were going to great lengths to discredit the teachings of *a greater than Solomon. The men of Nineveh* repented at Jonah's preaching, but these rejected the proclamation of *a greater than Jonas. In the judgment* those who made better responses to lesser privileges will condemn these who thrust away the gospel of Jesus Christ.

2. *An insufficient response is contrasted to the sufficient sign.* The parable of *the unclean spirit* who leaves the house temporarily, but returns with seven worse companions, illustrates the futility of "reformation without regeneration." Some exegetes apply these words to those who were physically healed by exorcism of demons but did not become followers of Jesus spiritually. Others apply them to the crowds who thronged to John's baptism but did not enter the kingdom of heaven at the preaching of Jesus. Still others refer the parable to the Jewish nation generally, who having been delivered from bondage and captivity in the past, fell victim to a legalistic, ritualistic system that could not save, but served to trigger their suicidal hostility to the Saviour.

The important thing is to have enough courage to apply Jesus' words to ourselves. Do we face up to the truth that when He is rejected a man or a nation is doomed, though the ultimate worse state may be masked for a while by the *empty, swept, and garnished* condition produced by inadequate reformations? Men do not exist in spiritual vacuums. Someone will occupy the *empty* house. In Luther's rough phrasing, "Man is a saddle-horse. Either God or the devil will ride him."

The Family of Jesus
Matthew 12:46-50

46 While he yet talked to the people, behold, his mother and his brethren stood without, desiring to speak with him.
47 Then one said unto him, Behold, thy mother and thy brethren stand without, desiring to speak with thee.
48 But he answered and said unto him that told him, Who is my mother? and who are my brethren?
49 And he stretched forth his hand toward his disciples, and said, Behold my mother and my brethren!
50 For whosoever shall do the will of my Father which is in heaven, the same is my brother, and sister, and mother.

While Jesus was replying to the calumnies of His enemies, He was informed that His mother and brothers had arrived and desired to speak with Him. Besides the blasphemous opposition of His enemies, He had to bear the burden of His family's misunderstanding and unbelief. The passage places in contrast two families, the physical and the spiritual.

1. *The physical family.* At this time only His mother and brothers are mentioned. Joseph had died. In 13:56, sisters are mentioned. Whether these brothers and sisters were siblings or cousins has been debated for centuries. Whatever, they were close to His heart. He who loved all people could not fail of deep affection toward the members of His own household. Who can doubt that their rejection was His heaviest grief?

Of this family two things are noteworthy in this passage from Matthew. (1) They were *outside.* He was in a house teaching and they *stood without.* But they were outside in another, more significant way. (2) They were opposed (cf. 30). The depth of their misunderstanding is indicated in Mark 3:21, 31; they thought Jesus was mentally ill (cf. John 7:5-7).

2. *The spiritual family.* Jesus does not rush out to the physical family. As the Messiah, He has another family, His community of disciples. They are sharing the opposition and criticism He receives, and He is moved with appreciation (cf. 9:14; 10:42; 12:2). Stretching His hand toward them, He names them as His true family. The spiritual ties are stronger than the physical ties. The children of His Heavenly Father are nearer to Him than those of His earthly mother. Blood is not always thicker than water.

Of this spiritual family, also, two things are disclosed: (1) It is constituted by obedience. *"Whoever does the will of my heavenly Father is my brother, my sister, my mother"* (50, NEB). (2) It is open to all: *whosoever.* We cannot choose our ancestors, but we can choose to belong to the family of Jesus. And this privilege is open to all who hear the gospel.

Joshua said, *As for me and my house, we will serve the Lord* (Josh. 24:15). Jesus had to say, Even without My house, I will serve the Father. Such was the heartache and loneliness He accepted for our sakes. Do we sometimes stand alone, our foes being those of our own households? The author of Hebrews bids us, *Consider him who endured from sinners such hostility against himself, so that you may not grow weary or fainthearted* (Heb. 12:3, RSV). If your physical family opposes you, His spiritual family will share love and strength and encouragement with you.

Third Teaching Section:
The Parables of the Kingdom
Matthew 13:1-52

MATTHEW 13

Kingdom-Mystery Stories (1)

Matthew 13:1-23

1 The same day went Jesus out of the house, and sat by the sea side.

2 And great multitudes were gathered together unto him, so that he went into a ship, and sat; and the whole multitude stood on the shore.

3 And he spake many things unto them in parables, saying, Behold, a sower went forth to sow;

4 And when he sowed, some seeds fell by the way side, and the fowls came and devoured them up:

5 Some fell upon stony places, where they had not much earth: and forthwith they sprung up, because they had no deepness of earth:

6 And when the sun was up, they were scorched; and because they had no root, they withered away.

7 And some fell among thorns; and the thorns sprung up, and choked them:

8 But other fell into good ground, and brought forth fruit, some an hundredfold, some sixtyfold, some thirtyfold.

9 Who hath ears to hear, let him hear.

10 And the disciples came, and said unto him, Why speakest thou unto them in parables?

11 He answered and said unto them, Because it is given unto you to know the mysteries of the kingdom of heaven, but to them it is not given.

12 For whosoever hath, to him shall be given, and he shall have more abundance: but whosoever hath not, from him shall be taken away even that he hath.

13 Therefore speak I to them in parables: because they seeing see not; and hearing they hear not, neither do they understand.

14 And in them is fulfilled the prophecy of Esaias, which saith, By hearing ye shall hear, and shall not understand; and seeing ye shall see, and shall not perceive:

15 For this people's heart is waxed gross, and their ears are dull of hearing, and their eyes they have closed; lest at any time they should see with their eyes, and hear with their ears, and should understand with their heart, and should be converted, and I should heal them.

16 But blessed are your eyes, for they see: and your ears, for they hear.

17 For verily I say unto you, That many prophets and righteous men have desired to see those things which ye see, and have not seen them; and to hear those things which ye hear, and have not heard them.

18 Hear ye therefore the parable of the sower.

19 When any one heareth the word of the kingdom, and understandeth it not, then cometh the wicked one, and catcheth away that which was sown in his heart. This is he which received seed by the way side.

20 But he that received the seed into stony places, the same is he that heareth the word, and anon with joy receiveth it;

21 Yet hath he not root in himself, but dureth for a while: for when tribulation or persecution ariseth because of the word, by and by he is offended.

22 He also that received seed among the thorns is he that heareth the word; and the care of this world, and the deceitfulness of riches, choke the word, and he becometh unfruitful.

23 But he that received seed into the good ground is he that heareth the word, and understandeth it; which also beareth fruit, and bringeth forth, some an hundredfold, some sixty, some thirty.

Chapter 13 is comprised of the third block of teaching material in Matthew. It contains seven parables of the kingdom of heaven, most of them peculiar to the first Gospel.

Matthew uses the term *parable* for the first time in this chapter, marking a contrast between Jesus' previous mode of teaching and the method now adopted. Jesus did not originate the parable form, but He made larger and more effective use of it than any other teacher before or since.

These homely stories conveying religious truth may contain allegorical elements, as His explanation of two of them shows (18-23, 36-43). But they are not, strictly speaking, allegories, and the attempt to make every detail mean something encourages fanciful interpretation. Many details are simply local color which every good story requires.

The purpose of the parabolic method is disclosed by one of Matthew's "formula quotations" (10-17). There has been a persistent rejection of the preaching and teaching of Jesus to this point. That the parables will fall upon deaf ears, that their light will strike blind eyes, is a judgment upon those who reject the proclamation of the Kingdom. On the other hand, the disciples, by responding in faith to the proclamation, can receive *the mysteries of the kingdom of heaven*. The parables, like the miracles, benefit only those who will recognize in Jesus' ministry the in-breaking kingdom of God. Others will become hostile and rejecting. Thus the parables call for decision, as did the prior proclamation, and divide the audience into those who truly *hear* and those who merely listen.

The subject matter of the parables is termed the *mysteries* of the kingdom of heaven. Mystery refers to the plans of God, existing as His prior, eternal decisions, which are disclosed to chosen men by special revelation. That the kingdom of God would come at the end of the present age, striking apocalyptically and supernaturally into history, and transforming human society by the destruction of evil, was no mystery. Rather, it was a commonly held Jewish belief. The mystery lay in the fact that this eschatological Kingdom has been brought into the present age without completely transforming it. There has been fulfillment but not consummation. The Kingdom is future, but also present. And it is present precisely in the work of Jesus, which receives a mixed reception, and creates a community of faith to whom the Kingdom is given. To those who have responded in faith-obedience to Jesus' ministry, a capacity to know the mysteries is given.

The first of these kingdom-mystery stories is the parable of the sower.

The sower is Jesus, who has been flinging broadcast the seed, *the word of the kingdom,* which is the subject matter of the preceding chapters in Matthew. At the time Matthew wrote, of course, the sowing was being done by the witnessing Church. In every case the sower's intention was the same, and the seed's potential was the same, but the soil's response varied. Just so, the kingdom of heaven has but partial success in the present as human responses to the word of Jesus vary.

Precisely this situation obtained at the time Jesus spoke the parable. Most of the ministry had produced no harvest. Yet among the many who rejected were the few, the disciples, who believed. In their lives the fruit of the Kingdom was being produced in varied amounts.

The kingdom of God was expected as an irresistible force before which there could stand no immovable object.

When it came it would shatter evil, destroy the wicked, and create a perfect human society. The parable teaches that the Kingdom has come, but in an unexpected way. The Kingdom is proclaimed in a word that can be resisted, because the forces opposed to the Kingdom (the evil one, the cares of this age, etc.) continue to operate.

To see in the ministry of Jesus, to which only a minority had responded in faith, the kingly reign of God begun among men was the challenge of the parable. And still is!

Kingdom-Mystery Stories (2)

Matthew 13:24-43

> 24 Another parable put he forth unto them, saying, The kingdom of heaven is likened unto a man which sowed good seed in his field:
> 25 But while men slept, his enemy came and sowed tares among the wheat, and went his way.
> 26 But when the blade was sprung up, and brought forth fruit, then appeared the tares also.
> 27 So the servants of the householder came and said unto him, Sir, didst not thou sow good seed in thy field? from whence then hath it tares?
> 28 He said unto them, An enemy hath done this. The servants said unto him, Wilt thou then that we go and gather them up?
> 29 But he said, Nay; lest while ye gather up the tares, ye root up also the wheat with them.
> 30 Let both grow together until the harvest: and in the time of harvest I will say to the reapers, Gather ye together first the tares, and bind them in bundles to burn them: but gather the wheat into my barn.
> 31 Another parable put he forth unto them, saying, The kingdom of heaven is like to a grain of mustard seed, which a man took, and sowed in his field:
> 32 Which indeed is the least of all seeds: but when it is grown, it is the greatest among herbs, and becometh a tree, so that the birds of the air come and lodge in the branches thereof.
> 33 Another parable spake he unto them; The kingdom of heaven is like unto leaven, which a woman took, and hid in three measures of meal, till the whole was leavened.
> 34 All these things spake Jesus unto the multitude in parables; and without a parable spake he not unto them:
> 35 That it might be fulfilled which was spoken by the prophet, saying, I will open my mouth in parables; I will utter things which have been kept secret from the foundation of the world.
> 36 Then Jesus sent the multitude away, and went into the house: and his disciples came unto him, saying, Declare unto us the parable of the tares of the field.
> 37 He answered and said unto them, He that soweth the good seed is the Son of man;
> 38 The field is the world; the good seed are the children of the kingdom; but the tares are the children of the wicked one;
> 39 The enemy that sowed them is the devil; the harvest is the end of the world; and the reapers are the angels.

40 As therefore the tares are gathered and burned in the fire; so shall it be in the end of this world.
41 The Son of man shall send forth his angels, and they shall gather out of his kingdom all things that offend, and them which do iniquity;
42 And shall cast them into a furnace of fire: there shall be wailing and gnashing of teeth.
43 Then shall the righteous shine forth as the sun in the kingdom of their Father. Who hath ears to hear, let him hear.

The parable of the sower and its explanation is followed by three other parables: the weeds, the mustard seed, and the leavened meal. Then the setting changes. Jesus dismisses the crowds and enters a house with His disciples. There He responds to their request for an explanation of the parable of the weeds. In that private setting He continues to set forth three additional stories.

1. *The parable of the weeds* (24-30, 36-43). The sower of *good seed is the Son of man.* The sower of weeds is *the devil.* The whole ministry of Jesus is presented as a conflict between irreconcilable hostile powers, the kingdom of God and the kingdom of Satan (cf. 8:29; 12:22-29). Notice that the field is *his field,* not the enemy's. This world, even in its fallen and sinful situation, is God's world. Satan is the usurper, not the owner!

The field is *the world.* At this point the story reaches beyond the personal ministry of Jesus, which was confined to the Jews, to the global mission of His Church (cf. 15:24; 28:19). This implies, however, that the Church enters into and extends His ministry. He remains the Sower. He is the Subject, and not simply the subject matter of the Church's proclamation and teaching of the gospel.

The sowings produce a mixed field, both wheat and weeds. This was contrary to popular Jewish expectation. The coming of the Kingdom would mean the destruction of the wicked, leaving only the sons of the Kingdom to inherit the earth. At the end of the age, Jesus teaches, this will indeed happen. The harvest is the end of the age, and then the angels of the Son of Man will cleanse from the field every offensive thing, every iniquitous person. The righteous shall shine forth splendidly in the Kingdom which is then delivered over to the Father. Prior to harvest, however, is sowing and growing. The Kingdom is even now present, and men are being called to enter it by the Word proclaimed. That Word invites and challenges men to see in the person of Jesus the present hidden and secret, but assured, operation of the Kingdom. The end will depend upon the response made to Jesus in this overlapping of the old and new ages with its continued mixed society.

Meanwhile, Jesus' servants are forbidden to play God, forbidden to function as judges who divide the wheat from the weeds before the harvest. One of the surest ways to do this, and a constant temptation, is to identify the Church and the Kingdom. The Church becomes an enemy-punishing empire in this case.

2. *The parable of the mustard seed.* The mustard seed, not literally but proverbially, is *the least of all seeds.* It grows rapidly to heights of 10 feet, attracting birds to its branches. The terms *least* and *greatest* are the thrust of the parable. In its ultimate consummation the kingdom of heaven will be a great tree. Meanwhile, it is present in a small and inconspicuous form, the ministry of Jesus and the little group of followers that share the mysteries of the Kingdom. From outward appearance that tiny messianic movement, scorned and rejected by the "best" people, had neither power nor worth to assure its continued existence. But it was the seed without which there would not be the tree; and its success was assured, not by human canons, but by God.

3. *The parable of the leavened meal* (33). Again the enormous contrast is the point of the story. Compared to the lump of dough, the leaven was tiny and appeared inconsequential. But its hidden operation would leaven the entire bushel of meal. Even so, the kingdom of God, present in the ministry that had resulted in a number of healings, exorcisms, and conversions, would one day dominate the entire world, brooking no competition from the kingdom of evil. The consummation awaits in the future, but fulfillment has begun in Jesus Christ. Those who understand will identify themselves with Him at any cost, and that cost becomes emphatic in the next parables.

Kingdom-Mystery Stories (3)

Matthew 13:44-52

44 Again, the kingdom of heaven is like unto treasure hid in a field; the which when a man hath found, he hideth, and for joy thereof goeth and selleth all that he hath, and buyeth that field.
45 Again, the kingdom of heaven is like unto a merchant man, seeking goodly pearls:
46 Who, when he had found one pearl of great price, went and sold all that he had, and bought it.
47 Again, the kingdom of heaven is like unto a net, that was cast into the sea, and gathered of every kind:
48 Which, when it was full, they drew to shore, and sat down, and gathered the good into vessels, but cast the bad away.
49 So shall it be at the end of the world: the angels shall come forth, and sever the wicked from among the just,
50 And shall cast them into the furnace of fire: there shall be wailing and gnashing of teeth.
51 Jesus saith unto them, Have ye understood all these things? They say unto him, Yea, Lord.
52 Then said he unto them, Therefore every scribe which is instructed unto the kingdom of heaven is like unto a man that is an householder, which bringeth forth out of his treasure things new and old.

The remaining Kingdom parables in chapter 13 were delivered to the disciples away from the crowds. Those who have ears to hear and not merely to listen must realize that the kingdom of God is worth everything—and more. And they must know that the community created by the Kingdom is a mixed lot, of which the eschatological judgment will preserve only the righteous. These are the supreme values of the last three parables.

1. *The worth of the Kingdom* (44-46). The story of the hidden *treasure* and of the *pearl of great price* reinforce a truth which Jesus had earlier set forth in different words: The kingdom of heaven is worth the sacrifice of life itself to obtain it (cf. 5:10-12; 10:21-22, 28, 39). In each story the person involved sells all that he has, and purchases thereby something of far greater worth.

In neither case is Jesus saying that men can buy or earn God's saving favor. The Kingdom is received as a gift. But the gift can be received only from One who is despised, rejected, and will be crucified. Fellowship with Him in a world like this can make the cost of discipleship extremely heavy.

The glory of the age to come would make the worth

of the Kingdom self-evident. The real issue lies in the present hidden form of the Kingdom. Fellowship with Jesus and the motley assortment of people gathered about Him did not fit the notion of the kingdom of heaven in the minds of most of His contemporaries. But this life, this saving fellowship, was actually the kingdom of God present and operative in the midst of men. It was the Kingdom in this scorned and *incognito* form that men were challenged to see as life's highest value.

A perfect illustration of one who sought the Kingdom but would not pay the price of discipleship is given later in the Gospel (19:16-22).

2. *The judgment of the Kingdom* (47-50). The parable of the net describes the present "catch" and the final form of the Kingdom. As a dragnet encloses *good* and *bad* fish, so the proclamation of the Kingdom creates a community whose composition is mixed. There are true and false disciples. At the close of the age there will be a severance of the just from the wicked.

The case of Judas illustrates the mixed character of the Kingdom in its mystery form, even in Jesus' own day. The parable calls us to recognize that the imperfect society does not mean that the kingdom of God is not being fulfilled, but only that it is not yet being fully consummated. The Kingdom creates a sinless order only at the close of the age.

3. *The scribes of the Kingdom* (51-52). The disciples of the Kingdom are to be scribes, men responsible for receiving and transmitting the word of the Kingdom.

The training of the scribes is precisely what was taking place. Jesus was instructing the disciples *for the kingdom of heaven* (RSV) by revealing to them the mysteries of the Kingdom.

The treasure of the scribe is *new* and *old*. The Sermon on the Mount is a good example. There Jesus interpreted and deepened and applied the old law in a way that fulfilled it as part of the new action of God. These parables are excellent illustrations of the scribes' treasure, also. The ancient Kingdom expectation is affirmed and upheld; and the new factor, the in-breaking of the future Kingdom in the ministry of Jesus, the "realized" eschatology that does not cancel the yet-to-be-realized eschatology, is added. Thus, from the resources of their heritage in Israel and of their participation in Christ's teaching, the Christian scribes can fulfill their responsibility to their households. How splendidly Matthew himself fulfilled this role his Gospel everywhere demonstrates.

Fourth Narrative Section:
Further Ministry in Galilee
Matthew 13:53—17:27

No Welcome Mat for Jesus

Matthew 13:53-58

> 53 And it came to pass, that when Jesus had finished these parables, he departed thence.
> 54 And when he was come into his own country, he taught them in their synagogue, insomuch that they were astonished, and said, Whence hath this man this wisdom, and these mighty works?
> 55 Is not this the carpenter's son? is not his mother called Mary? and his brethren, James, and Joses, and Simon, and Judas?
> 56 And his sisters, are they not all with us? Whence then hath this man all these things?
> 57 And they were offended in him. But Jesus said unto them, A prophet is not without honour, save in his own country, and in his own house.
> 58 And he did not many mighty works there because of their unbelief.

Verse 53 contains the formula sentence by which Matthew makes a transition from the block of teaching to renewed narrative. As the record of ministry continues, the familiar theme of rejection is resumed. Three common elements of the theme are clearly seen in this section.

1. *Element one is the astonished crowd* (54). Jesus enters the synagogue at Nazareth for worship (cf. Luke 4:16-30). A main part of the synagogue service was the reading of scripture followed by an exposition of its contents if anyone competent to do so was present. On this occasion Jesus performed the expositor's role.

Matthew describes the effect of Jesus' teaching, not its contents; *they were astonished.* The wisdom of His words and the power in His deeds amazed them, for they could not account for Him in terms of His heredity or environment. *"Where did this man get this wisdom?"* (54, RSV). They knew Him as *the carpenter's son,* but failed to recognize Him as God's Son.

2. *Element two is the dishonored Prophet* (57). The crowd was amazed, but more to the point, *they were offended.* They were victims of a stupid pride that would not allow them to admit that one reared in their midst could be other or more than one of them.

Jesus responded to their offense with a proverbial saying: *A prophet is not without honour, save in his own country, and in his own house.* He is rejected by His townspeople as nothing more than a woodworker making arrogant and pretentious claims. *His own house* points to the saddest rejection of all. His own family cannot bring themselves to believe that God is at work in this young Man, reared in the same home as themselves, as God has never worked through another.

Jesus designates himself *a prophet.* He was that and very much more. But He indicts them for unbelief on the very lowest level at which they should have recognized Him. Prophets had come before from humble origins, as did Amos, to cite a single example. Whatever excuse these may have had for their not seeing Him as more than a prophet, they had none for seeing Him as less. Those who will believe and follow Him at this point can be led to higher levels of understanding and faith (cf. John 9:11, 17, 38: "man," "prophet," "Lord").

3. *Element three is the forfeited opportunity. "He did not many mighty works there because of their unbelief"* (58). The teachings, healings, and conversions which could have transformed Nazareth never took place. Ultimately, those who reject Him are hurt more than He!

There are no temporal or spatial limits to Jesus' love and power. What He has done sometime, somewhere, He can do anytime, anywhere. The barrier lies not in Him but in those who will not believe.

Verses 57-58 remind us that (1) faith honors the man of God, and (2) God honors the faith of man. The account is more than ancient history. There are Nazareths everywhere. But even where *many* works of might are forfeited by unbelief, a few will transpire to benefit those who trust Jesus.

MATTHEW 14

The Death of John the Baptist
Matthew 14:1-12

1 At that time Herod the tetrarch heard of the fame of Jesus,

2 And said unto his servants, This is John the Baptist; he is risen from the dead; and therefore mighty works do shew forth themselves in him.

3 For Herod had laid hold on John, and bound him, and put him in prison for Herodias' sake, his brother Philip's wife.

4 For John said unto him, It is not lawful for thee to have her.

5 And when he would have put him to death, he feared the multitude, because they counted him as a prophet.

6 But when Herod's birthday was kept, the daughter of Herodias danced before them, and pleased Herod.

7 Whereupon he promised with an oath to give her whatsoever she would ask.

8 And she, being before instructed of her mother, said, Give me here John Baptist's head in a charger.

9 And the king was sorry: nevertheless for the oath's sake, and them which sat with him at meat, he commanded it to be given her.

10 And he sent, and beheaded John in the prison.

11 And his head was brought in a charger, and given to the damsel: and she brought it to her mother.

12 And his disciples came, and took up the body, and buried it, and went and told Jesus.

The martyrdom of John is recounted to explain the superstitious alarms of Herod Antipas. Hearing reports of Jesus' miracles, the guilt-ridden king thinks that John the Baptist is back from the dead with supernatural powers. (During his ministry John performed no miracles.) The grisly drama of death revolves around the prophet, the king, and the queen, with hapless Salome the weak tool of the strong mother.

1. *The story reveals the integrity of the prophet.* To begin with, John rebuked sin in the palace. Herod had "stolen" another's wife, and John had the courage to declare, *It is not lawful for thee to have her.* It is easy for persons in high office to hold themselves above the moral laws that bind common citizens. It is hard for preachers to denounce such "higher-ups" without equivocation. John proved worthy of Elijah's mantle in bringing the judging word of God to bear upon the adulterous alliance between Herod and Herodias.

And John remained true in the dungeon. Prison is hard for anyone; for one schooled in the desert, the dank confinement would be exceptionally intolerable. While John's patience may have faltered (cf. 11:2-3), not for a moment did he entertain the notion of purchasing freedom by compromising his message.

2. *The account accents the stupidity of the king.* He made a stupid promise. Wits addled by drink, lust inflamed by Salome's sensuous dance, *he promised with an oath* (7) to honor any request she made.

He had a warped ethic. Her request shocked Herod, and *the king was sorry* (9) he had made the foolish offer. Unwilling to retract his oath, he ordered John's execution. What confused morality! He would be a murderer rather than be thought a liar!

And so he issued an insane order: *he sent and had John beheaded* (10, RSV). He soaked his conscience in blood, and would henceforth tremble every time reports of a God-attested ministry reached his ears.

Herod's problem was one of misplaced fear. *He feared the people* (5, RSV), and he feared his guests, but he had no fear of God.

3. *The narrative exposes the cruelty of the queen.* Herodias has but one rival for cruelty in the Scriptures—the infamous Jezebel.

Rather than mend her life, she degraded her daughter. The princess provides for drunken men the entertainment usually furnished by slave girls. And then Herodias drags her own daughter down to the level of coconspirator in a wanton murder. A mother's heart is desperately wicked who destroys her own child by the poison of her hatred for God's messenger.

Rather than mend her life she avenged her pride, and bequeathed her name to history as a symbol of contempt and cruelty. There are few scenes in history as gruesome as that of Salome bearing to her gloating mother the head of John the Baptist on a platter (11, RSV).

John's disciples did what they could to honor the martyr. They gave the body a decent burial. Then they *went and told Jesus.* There is not a wiser or better course for any to follow in the shock and sorrow that evil causes. Tell Jesus!

The Bread-Maker

Matthew 14:13-21

13 When Jesus heard of it, he departed thence by ship into a desert place apart: and when the people had heard thereof, they followed him on foot out of the cities.

14 And Jesus went forth, and saw a great multitude, and was moved with compassion toward them, and he healed their sick.

15 And when it was evening, his disciples came to him, saying, This is a desert place, and the time is now past; send the multitude away, that they may go into the villages, and buy themselves victuals.

16 But Jesus said unto them, They need not depart; give ye them to eat.

17 And they say unto him, We have here but five loaves, and two fishes.

18 He said, Bring them hither to me.

19 And he commanded the multitude to sit down on the grass, and took the five loaves, and the two fishes, and looking up to heaven, he blessed, and brake, and gave the loaves to his disciples, and the disciples to the multitude.

20 And they did all eat, and were filled: and they took up of the fragments that remained twelve baskets full.

21 And they that had eaten were about five thousand men, beside women and children.

Grief shuns a crowd. On the news of John's death Jesus withdrew to a desert place. But crowds seek a man who offers help, and they rushed on foot to be present where Jesus came by boat. Upon seeing the throngs, Jesus was *moved with compassion.* (Compassion is the only emotion of Jesus which Matthew mentions, and he refers to it several times. This suffering sympathy was what impressed the Gospel writer most.) The healing ministry is resumed until evening, and provides the background for the miracle of loaves and fish. Two factors stand out, the authority of Jesus and His adequacy.

1. *The authority of Jesus* is expressed in two significant ways. He puts it in opposition to human suffering, and He exercises it over human resources.

a. Jesus opposed human suffering. This passage clearly shows His desire to relieve the basic hurts of human life. The healing miracles tell us that Jesus wills health for the sick. This phase of His ministry has been the mandate and inspiration for the erection of hospitals and clinics, and for the careers of doctors and nurses, throughout subsequent history. All healing is by His power though it may not be in His name. He wills health. The feeding miracle shows us that Jesus wills bread for the hungry. He refused to make bread miraculously to nourish His own hunger (4: 2-4), but He will exercise His powers as the Son of God to feed the crowd. The disciples said, *Send the multitude away* (15). Many still say that, unwilling to support legislation and programs designed to feed the hungry.

b. The authority opposed to human suffering is exercised over human resources. An inventory of the food supply is made: *five loaves, and two fishes.* Jesus commandeers the food, saying, *Bring them hither to me.* Discipleship means holding all that we possess subject to His requisition. Then *he commanded the multitude to sit down.* Not only the food but the eaters are placed under His lordship. The total scene is one of Christ in command. Too often we want Him to feed us but not to rule us. We want Him as a Bread-Maker but not as a Command-Giver. We want Him as Saviour but not as Lord, but He will not concede to our selfish desires. We *bring* and *sit* or we don't eat.

2. *The adequacy of Jesus* is emphasized in two ways.

a. First, by the amount of food. He blessed, broke, and gave the bread and fish to His disciples, who served the crowd. *And they did all eat, and were filled.* Each had enough to fully satisfy his need. Besides that, the leftovers exceeded the original supply—*twelve baskets full.*

b. Second, His adequacy is exhibited in the number of diners. *Five thousand men,* plus some *women and children,* shared this lakeside dinner. The crowds are not usually counted in the Gospels. They are simply designated as great (14). The census taken here is obviously intended to enhance the stress on the adequacy of Jesus to meet human needs in difficult situations.

Jesus cares deeply for people. Because He is for them, He is against the sickness and hunger that blight human existence. His followers should be swift to place at His disposal every available resource to help the ill and the starving. Men are not just souls to save. They are bodies to be fed and healed, also. The concern of Jesus for the whole man should structure the agenda of His Church.

The Sea-Walker

Matthew 14:22-36

> 22 And straightway Jesus constrained his disciples to get into a ship, and to go before him unto the other side, while he sent the multitudes away.
> 23 And when he had sent the multitudes away, he went up into a mountain apart to pray: and when the evening was come, he was there alone.
> 24 But the ship was now in the midst of the sea, tossed with waves: for the wind was contrary.
> 25 And in the fourth watch of the night Jesus went unto them, walking on the sea.
> 26 And when the disciples saw him walking on the sea, they were troubled, saying, It is a spirit; and they cried out for fear.
> 27 But straightway Jesus spake unto them, saying, Be of good cheer; it is I; be not afraid.
> 28 And Peter answered him and said, Lord, if it be thou, bid me come unto thee on the water.
> 29 And he said, Come. And when Peter was come down out of the ship, he walked on the water, to go to Jesus.
> 30 But when he saw the wind boisterous, he was afraid; and beginning to sink, he cried, saying, Lord, save me.
> 31 And immediately Jesus stretched forth his hand, and caught him, and said unto him, O thou of little faith, wherefore didst thou doubt?
> 32 And when they were come into the ship, the wind ceased.
> 33 Then they that were in the ship came and worshipped him, saying, Of a truth thou art the Son of God.
> 34 And when they were gone over, they came into the land of Gennesaret.
> 35 And when the men of that place had knowledge of him, they sent out into all that country round about, and brought unto him all that were diseased;
> 36 And besought him that they might only touch the hem of his garment: and as many as touched were made perfectly whole.

Jesus *constrained* His disciples to head for home in the boat, and then *dismissed the crowds* (RSV). Matthew's strong term indicates an unwillingness to leave in the disciples, and a firm insistence by Jesus. John's Gospel supplies a reason. The miracle of feeding aroused messianic fervor, and the crowd sought to make Jesus King. He did not want the disciples infected by the wrongheaded enthusiasm whipped up on the occasion. The rest of the story points to a far more significant ministry of Jesus to His disciples.

1. *Jesus prays for them—and us.* He *went up into the hills by himself to pray* (23, RSV). He could dismiss men from His presence, but not from His heart. He is concerned to guide them aright and be King on the Father's terms, so

He seeks the quiet place of correction after the heated scene of mistake. Perhaps, in the zealous acclamation of the crowd, He felt a renewal of the third temptation (4:1-12). He needed the reinforcing presence of the Father to still His own and His followers' agitation.

He prays for His disciples. Then in the hills, now in the heavens. According to Heb. 7:25, Jesus has a continuing ministry of intercession.

2. *Jesus comes to them—and us.* The disciples were struggling against pounding waves churned into frenzy by a *contrary* wind. Shortly before dawn *he came to them, walking on the sea* (25, RSV).

Few of the miracle stories have occasioned greater offense than this one. Ingenious efforts to explain it away, sadly lacking in credibility, may be found in a number of commentaries. These rationalizing attempts are aptly described in the Anchor Bible volume on Matthew as "rather pathetic."

Of course, the fact of major importance is not how He came but that He came. The Church in Matthew's day must have seemed to him like a tiny group of people in a rough situation, buffeted by persecution. The story of how Jesus came in a dark hour to rescue His storm-threatened disciples would have comforting effect. The homiletic use, however, does not impugn the facticity of the event.

Thousands of Christians in our day can witness to the faithfulness of Jesus to come to His people when all is dark and desperate.

3. *Jesus saves them—and us.* He assured the terrified disciples that He was not a ghost: *Be of good cheer; it is I; be not afraid* (27). Impulsive and unconvinced Peter exclaimed, *"If it is you, bid me come to you on the water"* (28, RSV). Jesus responded, *Come* (29). Peter's rash attempt failed, and beginning to sink, he cried, *Lord, save me* (30). Then occurs the choicest statement in the whole account: *Immediately Jesus stretched forth his hand, and caught him* (31). Jesus saves men from the fatal consequences of their foolish actions.

Peter is rebuked for unbelief. The rebuke looks back,

not to his sinking, but to his words, *"If it is you."* There was good reason for Jesus to come to them on the sea, but none for Peter to go to Him. The presence and power of the Lord are evidenced by what He does for men, not by what they do. Peter's attempt at sea-walking, if successful, could have served no good purpose.

When Jesus stepped into the boat, *the wind ceased.* The disciples reacted with a gesture of worship, exclaiming, *"Truly, you are the Son of God"* (33, RSV). All that this title means theologically they could not know then, nor do we know now. What it means, practically, can be simply stated: Jesus prays for us, comes to us, and saves us.

MATTHEW 15

Revelation Versus Tradition

Matthew 15:1-9

> 1 Then came to Jesus scribes and Pharisees, which were of Jerusalem, saying,
> 2 Why do thy disciples transgress the tradition of the elders? for they wash not their hands when they eat bread.
> 3 But he answered and said unto them, Why do ye also transgress the commandment of God by your tradition?
> 4 For God commanded, saying, Honour thy father and mother: and, He that curseth father or mother, let him die the death.
> 5 But ye say, Whosoever shall say to his father or his mother, It is a gift, by whatsoever thou mightest be profited by me;
> 6 And honour not his father or his mother, he shall be free. Thus have ye made the commandment of God of none effect by your tradition.
> 7 Ye hypocrites, well did Esaias prophesy of you, saying,
> 8 This people draweth nigh unto me with their mouth, and honoureth me with their lips; but their heart is far from me.
> 9 But in vain they do worship me, teaching for doctrines the commandments of men.

The conflict between Jesus and certain of the scribes and Pharisees came at the point of tradition, not law. Jesus honored the law, but did not respect the body of oral and written tradition which the rabbinate had elevated to the status of law.

The issues of that conflict are sharply etched in this section of Matthew. The picayune nature of the Pharisees' objections to Jesus is made starkly clear by the background of merciful healings in the region of Gennesaret with which chapter 14 closes. To pick at a Man who could perform such beneficial miracles has all the ludicrous aspects of a Chihuahua yapping at a bull elephant.

1. *Tradition is exposed as spurious revelation.* The words of Jesus in verses 3 and 9 show that *commandments of men* have been given par value with the *commandment of God.* The tradition which purported to interpret the word of God is now equated with the word of God. To reject one is to reject the other.

Moreover, the interpretive commentary was *the tradition of the elders.* Thinking was frozen in past terms. The opinions of earlier generations were inordinately revered, as though the fathers had spoken so finally that future generations had only to bow in assent to their ideas. This is not an ancient problem merely. The Church has always confronted the same issue. The theological and ethical understandings of early leaders are given such canonical status that to question them is regarded as heretical.

2. *Tradition is further exposed as hypocritical evasion.* The traditions were structured, in some cases, to provide loopholes in the law. Jesus cites a single example. The command to honor one's parents was circumvented by a tradition which permitted a man to dedicate to the Temple the money or property by which his parents could be supported. Having thus earmarked the funds for God's work, the man could continue to use it for personal advantage while his parents suffered (4-6). Jesus denounces this legalized evasion of God's command as hypocrisy.

The antithesis between the written law and the oral tradition could not be more sharply drawn: *God commanded. . . . But ye say.* The disciples are charged with flouting traditions which had their origin in men. The Pharisees are charged with flouting commandments which had their origin in God. Jesus accepts the latter, but rejects the former.

3. *Tradition is exposed, also, as empty worship.* Jesus accuses these scribes and Pharisees of lip submission to

God and heart rebellion against God. He applies to them the words of Isaiah, an indictment of pious speech contradicted by rebellious lives (8-9). The inward revolt made all the outward apparatus of worship a sham.

When precepts of men are substituted for the commands of God there is great concern for the ritual cleansing of the hands, but little for the actual purifying of the heart. Externalism and legalism flourish, while inward piety and sincerity wane. There is something pathetic about men with corrupt hearts lodging complaints against men with "defiled" hands. And something tragic about men who study tradition in order to faithfully observe it, and study revelation in order to subtly circumvent it. In effect, man tries to judge the Word of God instead of being judged by it, to master the divine Word instead of being mastered by it. The tradition was man's effort to be autonomous while posturing as God's servant.

Real Defilement Versus Ritual Defilment

Matthew 15:10-20

> 10 And he called the multitude, and said unto them, Hear, and understand:
> 11 Not that which goeth into the mouth defileth a man; but that which cometh out of the mouth, this defileth a man.
> 12 Then came his disciples, and said unto him, Knowest thou that the Pharisees were offended, after they heard this saying?
> 13 But he answered and said, Every plant, which my heavenly Father hath not planted, shall be rooted up.
> 14 Let them alone: they be blind leaders of the blind. And if the blind lead the blind, both shall fall into the ditch.
> 15 Then answered Peter and said unto him, Declare unto us this parable.
> 16 And Jesus said, Are ye also yet without understanding?
> 17 Do not ye yet understand, that whatsoever entereth in at the mouth goeth into the belly, and is cast out into the draught?
> 18 But those things which proceed out of the mouth come forth from the heart; and they defile the man.
> 19 For out of the heart proceed evil thoughts, murders, adulteries, fornications, thefts, false witness, blasphemies:
> 20 These are the things which defile a man: but to eat with unwashen hands defileth not a man.

Jesus makes the private dispute a public occasion. He calls the crowd, in order to give His truth the same extension as the scribes' falsehood. Perhaps, also, He wished to give His accused disciples the broadest vindication possible. In this attempt to rescue the crowd from pharisaical influence, several factors are noteworthy.

1. *Jesus corrects a false notion* (10-11). The command, *Hear, and understand,* points to the gravity of His instruction. All religious history reveals how poorly men hear, and how frequently they must relearn this lesson. Real defilement is not outward but inward. Ritual washing cannot remove actual corruption. To the Pharisees, neglect of the ceremonial lustration transferred defilement from hands to food. But Jesus insists that food passing into the mouth does not defile; rather, evil proceeding from unclean hearts into unclean speech is defiling. He does two things at once with these words: (1) He defines defilement in the only significant way; (2) He indicts the hearts of these outwardly pious Pharisees as corrupt.

2. *Jesus affirms an ultimate victory* (12-14). The disciples raised an uneasy question: *"Do you know that the Pharisees were offended?"* (12, RSV). They did not share our Lord's sublime courage under fire. The anger and contempt of the community power-structure intimidated them. Jesus' admonition recorded earlier, *Fear not them which kill the body, but are not able to kill the soul* (10:28), did not become possible for them until Pentecost.

To their uneasy question Jesus returns a comforting answer. *Every plant, which my heavenly Father hath not planted, shall be rooted up.* Every system and teaching that opposes the Word of God is doomed to destruction. No lie will outlive truth. No tradition will outlast revelation. No ritual has the staying power of reality. No man can withstand God.

His reply is capped by a terrifying judgment: *Let them alone.* There is something chilling about this phrase! Can we become so blinded by allegiance to human traditions that neither the appeals nor the rebukes of divine love can reach us? The tragedy of such an impervious condition is its influence over others. *The blind lead the blind* and together stumble into destruction.

3. *Jesus explains His radical saying* (15-20). Peter, self-appointed spokesman for the disciples, requests an ex-

planation of the parable (10-11). Jesus rebukes their lack of understanding, but He goes on to explain the saying. His rebuke is better than His silence! Better to be rebuked than to be left alone.

His explanation radically locates sin. *Out of the heart* come the sinful thoughts, words, and acts that defile human life. Mark's list of sins is longer, containing 13 specified evils. Matthew's contains 7 which are structured in the order of the Decalogue. This serves to emphasize Jesus' awareness and support of the law, while He repudiates conflicting tradition.

The words of Jesus have profound implications for understanding man and salvation. Man's predicament is heart-deep. Evil is not to be dismissed as cultural deficiency. Sin is not equated with ignorance. Education can civilize but it cannot save. Man is radically sinful, and only the cleansing and reorientation of his inner life can save him from the pit. For that, neither human tradition nor divine commandment avails. The recreating power of the Spirit, released from the atoning sacrifice of Jesus, is the only power adequate to change man's heart. Rebirth, not ritual, is his hope.

A Jew for the Gentiles

Matthew 15:21-28

> 21 Then Jesus went thence, and departed into the coasts of Tyre and Sidon.
> 22 And, behold, a woman of Canaan came out of the same coasts, and cried unto him, saying, Have mercy on me, O Lord, thou son of David; my daughter is grievously vexed with a devil.
> 23 But he answered her not a word. And his disciples came and besought him, saying, Send her away; for she crieth after us.
> 24 But he answered and said, I am not sent but unto the lost sheep of the house of Israel.
> 25 Then came she and worshipped him, saying, Lord, help me.
> 26 But he answered and said, It is not meet to take the children's bread, and to cast it to dogs.
> 27 And she said, Truth, Lord: yet the dogs eat of the crumbs which fall from their masters' table.
> 28 Then Jesus answered and said unto her, O woman, great is thy faith: be it unto thee even as thou wilt. And her daughter was made whole from that very hour.

Jesus could not avoid controversy, but He did not relish it. He was not a wrangler. He withdraws from His critics, suiting action to His words, *Let them alone.* Unable to find a place to relax in Jewish territory, He crosses into a Gentile area. But a man with bread cannot hide for long from the hungry, and soon a desperate mother seeks His help. This healing story, in its parts, is exceptionally difficult to understand. As a whole it displays the catholicity of Jesus' love and the invincibility of His power.

1. *The total silence of Jesus defies understanding.* Out for a walk with the disciples, He is followed by a heartbroken Gentile woman imploring His mercy for the healing of a demonized daughter. *But he answered her not a word.*

In view of her plight and His past, this is strange. Matthew notes on several occasions that Jesus was moved to respond by seeing the plight of helpless people under heavy burdens. We would have expected this stricken mother's cry to provoke immediate response. Certainly the disciples expected Him to respond. Their words, *Send her away,* in view of His reply in v. 24, can only mean, Grant her request and let her go on her way. Instead, Jesus does not answer the woman at all.

2. *The total silence is broken by troubling speech.* His mission is to *the house of Israel.* This presents no real difficulty for exegetes and commentators. But what problems they have had trying to grasp and interpret His words to the woman! The common attitude of His fellow Jews, caught up in the *children—dogs* antithesis, sounds so harsh and out-of-character on His lips. Every attempt to soften His words becomes strained and reads like special pleading.

He certainly intended for His disciples a mission beyond the necessary confines of His own, as the closing paragraph in Matthew makes clear (28:16-20). This is already hinted at in 10:18. Furthermore, He has previously responded to a Gentile's plea for help in Galilee (8:5-13). Surely His purpose can include another Gentile in her own territory.

Frankly, His speech is as baffling to me as His silence. I can only assume that something came through to her in His look and tone that doesn't come through to us in print. At any rate, she persisted.

3. *The silence and speech gives way to His triumphant salvation.* With rare humility born of great faith, and with ready wit born of serious plight, she acknowledges the children's rights and accepts the dog's place. But surely the Messiah's bounty allows crumbs for the dogs, without depriving the children!

Jesus exclaimed in approval, *"O woman, great is your faith! Be it done for you as you desire"* (28, RSV). Her daughter was immediately healed. As Luther put it, "she snares Christ in His own words." From all we know of Him in the Gospels, and in our lives, we may be confident that He was a willing Captive!

A lesson of sympathy emerges in this story. The mother pled for her girl, but her words were, *Lord, help me.* She made the girl's need her own. When we can so identify with sufferers, the Saviour will identify with us!

A lesson in persistence emerges also. She did not take silence as refusal. As long as Jesus did not say no, she hoped for yes. When she could not understand His words, she continued to trust His love. By such importunate faith does victory come.

As Jesus grants the wish of this mother, she becomes a symbol of the redemptive benefits which will flow from His love to all people outside of Israel. He is a Jew for the Gentiles.

Great Crowds—Great Compassion

Matthew 15:29-39

> 29 And Jesus departed from thence, and came nigh unto the sea of Galilee; and went up into a mountain, and sat down there.
> 30 And great multitudes came unto him, having with them those that were lame, blind, dumb, maimed, and many others, and cast them down at Jesus' feet; and he healed them:
> 31 Insomuch that the multitude wondered, when they saw the dumb to speak, the maimed to be whole, the lame to walk, and the blind to see: and they glorified the God of Israel.
> 32 Then Jesus called his disciples unto him, and said, I have compassion on the multitude, because they continue with me now three days, and have nothing to eat: and I will not send them away fasting, lest they faint in the way.
> 33 And his disciples say unto him, Whence should we have so much bread in the wilderness, as to fill so great a multitude?
> 34 And Jesus saith unto them, How many loaves have ye? And they said, Seven, and a few little fishes.
> 35 And he commanded the multitude to sit down on the ground.

36 And he took the seven loaves and the fishes, and gave thanks, and brake them, and gave to his disciples, and the disciples to the multitude.
37 And they did all eat, and were filled: and they took up of the broken meat that was left seven baskets full.
38 And they that did eat were four thousand men, beside women and children.
39 And he sent away the multitude, and took ship, and came into the coasts of Magdala.

The healing of the Canaanite girl is followed by one of Matthew's brief summaries of Jesus' ministry of healing and its effects upon the crowds. The summary is followed by the account of another miraculous feeding, this time of 4,000 men plus some women and children. Similarities in the account have prompted some to view this one as duplication. The differences, however, are sufficiently numerous and striking to justify those who treat the two feedings as separate incidents.

1. *A great crowd is described.* Matthew uses the plural, *crowds* (RSV), as he does habitually in his Gospel, when Mark uses the singular. Neither are mere copyists, but editors and theologians in their own right.

There was a great crowd of sufferers, *lame, blind, dumb, maimed, and many others.* No phenomenon of human existence is more persistent and universal than sickness and suffering. The sufferers are often drawn together in large groups for convenience of treatment and for mutual encouragement. It was thus wherever Jesus went.

With the sufferers were a great crowd of sympathizers, and the well were *bringing* (RSV) the sick and hurt to Jesus, putting them at His feet in a plea for help and a gesture of faith. Blessed are the sick who have friends willing to bring them to Jesus. Blessed are the well who see this service as their duty and joy.

2. *A great conquest is recorded.* There was a conquest of illness, and it underscores His power and their praise. *He healed them . . . and they glorified the God of Israel* (30-31).

Many others points to a large variety of ailments. Those specifically named reflect Isa. 35:5, which was interpreted messianically, and forms part of Matthew's witness to Jesus as the Messiah.

The phrase *God of Israel* indicates a number of Gentiles present. No fences of race or class can be erected about His mercy.

There was also a conquest of hunger. Limited resources were placed in hands of unlimited power. The God of Israel, as of old, supplies *bread in the wilderness.* Note the contrast in Jesus' question and the disciples' answer: *How many? . . . A few.* From the perspective of their resources, *few.* From the standpoint of His power, *many.* He was positive, they were negative in the situation.

As in the previous feeding, the Lord provides much from little. He blesses, breaks, and gives to the disciples, and the disciples give in turn to the crowd. We are not amiss in noting that *the bread of life* reaches the world through the ministry of the apostles and their successors, the heralds of the gospel in every age.

3. *A great compassion is extolled.* Jesus said, *I have compassion on the multitude.* In their eagerness to see Him, hear Him, and receive His healing, the crowd has remained for three days, sleeping out of doors, and exhausting what food they brought. They have miles to go before reaching their homes, and He is not willing to send them away hungry. He is touched in His heart by those who come to be touched by His hands.

"I am unwilling to send them away hungry" (32, RSV). Is this not a challenging statement to all responsible for teaching and preaching His Word today?

MATTHEW 16

The Leaven of False Doctrine

Matthew 16:1-13

> 1 The Pharisees also with the Sadducees came, and tempting desired him that he would shew them a sign from heaven.
> 2 He answered and said unto them, When it is evening, ye say, It will be fair weather: for the sky is red.
> 3 And in the morning, It will be foul weather to day: for the sky is red and lowring, O ye hypocrites, ye can discern the face of the sky; but can ye not discern the signs of the times?
> 4 A wicked and adulterous generation seeketh after a sign; and there

shall no sign be given unto it, but the sign of the prophet Jonas. And he left them, and departed.

5 And when his disciples were come to the other side, they had forgotten to take bread.

6 Then Jesus said unto them, Take heed and beware of the leaven of the Pharisees and of the Sadducees.

7 And they reasoned among themselves, saying, It is because we have taken no bread.

8 Which when Jesus perceived, he said unto them, O ye of little faith, why reason ye among yourselves, because ye have brought no bread?

9 Do ye not yet understand, neither remember the five loaves of the five thousand, and how many baskets ye took up?

10 Neither the seven loaves of the four thousand, and how many baskets ye took up?

11 How is it that ye do not understand that I spake it not to you concerning bread, that ye should beware of the leaven of the Pharisees and of the Sadducees?

12 Then understood they how that he bade them not beware of the leaven of bread, but of the doctrine of the Pharisees and of the Sadducees.

Pharisees and Sadducees had little in common, but mutual hostility to Jesus bound them in a temporary alliance to test Jesus. Their insincere demand meets with stern refusal. Soon after, the disciples misunderstand a warning from Jesus and receive a sharp reproof. The common factor in the two accounts is rebuke.

1. *Jesus rebukes His unwise enemies* (1-4). These hostile critics came asking for what they already had—*a sign from heaven.* By all He was and did Jesus supplied abundant evidence that God was uniquely and mightily at work, ushering in the kingdom of heaven. The rejection of His work and words would not be reversed by any celestial sign, such as fire called down from heaven, or a miracle of manna renewed. The truth is, where the Word of God is not believed, no spectacular sign can be convincing (Luke 16:31).

These religious leaders could discern signs of weather, but they could not read the *signs of the times.* As J. H. Jowett put it, they were "weather-wise but not history-wise." The *signs of the times* were the mighty works of Jesus which fulfilled prophecies of the new age. Where love creating justice and bringing forgiveness cannot inspire faith, no miracle can compel it.

Asking for what they had, the critics got what they did not want—*the sign of Jonah* (RSV). The Resurrection is the sign *par excellence* of God's approval upon Jesus' ministry, and upon His claims as Messiah and Lord. This sign too will be rejected, and years later Paul can still write, *Jews demand signs* (1 Cor. 1:22, RSV).

2. *Jesus rebukes His unwise friends* (5-12). He warns against the influence and teaching of the sign-seeking Pharisees and Sadducees, employing the figure of leaven. The disciples misunderstand, feeling that He is displeased at their oversight in not bringing along food for the trip. Reminding them of the previous miracles of loaves and fishes, He chides their scant faith. His words, *Do ye not yet understand, neither remember . . . ,* suggests two important truths: (1) Perception is conditioned by faith; and (2) Faith is strengthened by memory.

Leaven is a fitting symbol for false teaching. A little influences a lot, and it works subtly but surely. The only safety against it is to remember what Jesus has said.

The disciples understood after being rebuked. The cost of their lesson was painful, but well worth it. There is here, as in 15:14-16, a contrast between the judgment of Jesus upon His enemies and the rebuke of Jesus for His friends. Of the sign-demanding Pharisees it is written, *He left them* (4). Better by far to learn His truth at the cost of a thousand rebukes than to be abandoned by Him to ignorance and unbelief.

The Rock and the Church

Matthew 16:13-20

13 When Jesus came into the coasts of Caesarea Philippi, he asked his disciples, saying, Whom do men say that I the Son of man am?
14 And they said, Some say that thou art John the Baptist: some, Elias; and others, Jeremias, or one of the prophets.
15 He saith unto them, But whom say ye that I am?
16 And Simon Peter answered and said, Thou art the Christ, the Son of the living God.
17 And Jesus answered and said unto him, Blessed art thou, Simon Barjona: for flesh and blood hath not revealed it unto thee, but my Father which is in heaven.
18 And I say also unto thee, That thou art Peter, and upon this rock I will build my church; and the gates of hell shall not prevail against it.
19 And I will give unto thee the keys of the kingdom of heaven: and whatsoever thou shalt bind on earth shall be bound in heaven: and whatsoever thou shalt loose on earth shall be loosed in heaven.
20 Then charged he his disciples that they should tell no man that he was Jesus the Christ.

Few passages in the New Testament rival this one for significance or controversy. The modest scope of this book precludes a history of its interpretation, and that history precludes a consensus of exegetical opinion. We are content here to deal with some general matters, while the debate of skilled exegetes continues.

1. *The questions of Jesus.* The first concerns popular opinion: *"Who do men say that the Son of man is?"* (13, RSV). He has used the title of himself; the third-person phrasing would not confuse them. The answers are one: a prophet, though the precise identification varies. Whatever else was true about Him, men recognized Jesus as a fearless, forthright Bearer of God's judging and saving word to Israel.

Not content with popular estimates—which, while not erroneous, are deficient—He challenges the inner circle: *"But who do you say that I am?"* (15, RSV). When the concept of Jesus held in the Church today rises no higher than the opinion of the world, the Church sounds its own death knell. Jesus is not willing to settle for a title and role that calls into question His absolute claims on human life. No prophet spoke as Jesus spoke, claiming direct personal authority, and calling for radical allegiance to himself as Lord. From the uninformed, the title "prophet" is tribute; from His own followers, it is polite blasphemy.

2. *The confession of Peter.* Peter spoke for the group; his confession was representative: "You are the Christ, the Son of the living God." (16, RSV). It soon becomes apparent that Peter is unaware of the full implications of messiahship for Jesus. Nonetheless, he is convinced that the Deliverer awaited by Israel, the Messianic-King whom God named as His Son, was this very Rabbi whose call to discipleship had fetched Peter from his fishing nets.

The confession was not a product of human insight, but of divine revelation, as the beatitude of Jesus affirms. When, where, by what stages that revelation was made is not told us. Peter himself probably could not analyze or describe the inner process of illumination. Only the Son can reveal the Father, and only the Father can reveal the Son. That the revelation is given in parts and stages does not argue defective transmission by God. Rather, it attests imperfect reception by man.

3. *The prediction of the Church.* The word *church* here has offended many scholars, for it occurs in just two Gospel passages, both of them found in Matthew. However, the complaint that Jesus could not have used this word is baseless. He has been confessed as the Messiah, and in Jewish thinking a messianic community was a necessary corollary. As the Greek word *ekklesia* was used in the Septuagint for the congregation of Israel, it was the proper word to replace the Aramaic which Jesus employed. As Messiah, He is saying that a new Israel, a new congregation not congruent with national Israel, will be established.

The foundation of the messianic community will be Peter, the rock, who is recipient of the revelation and maker of the confession (cf. Eph. 2:20). The significant leadership role of Peter is a matter of sober history.

Some expositors see Jesus himself, in His essential deity, as the *rock*. G. Campbell Morgan is an example. *Rock* is used figuratively in the Old Testament some 40 times, always a reference to Deity. Although the Roman Catholic church has exploited the idea to their own ends, the plain sense of the whole statement of Jesus would seem to accord best with the view that the rock on which Jesus builds His Church is Peter.

The formidability of the Church is affirmed in the promise that *the powers of death* (18, RSV) shall not overcome it. The first dramatic proof of this assured triumph was the resurrection of Jesus. Death was flung back defeated! And under the power and guidance of its risen Lord the infant community made inexorable progress against the opposition of fire and sword (cf. Rom. 8:35-30).

The function of the Church is set forth under the figure of *the keys of the kingdom of heaven,* and the power of binding and loosing. By proclamation of the gospel the Kingdom is opened to believing men. Peter's ministry to the household of Cornelius in Acts 10 is a classical illustration. Binding and loosing refer to ethical decisions concerning what is permitted or prohibited to the messianic community. The verb tenses employed in Greek indicate that the Spirit-guided Church will carry out the prior decisions of God, not that God will ratify the prior rulings of men.

The incident closes with a charge not to publicize the messiahship of Jesus just confessed. Too much misunderstanding exists, both in the populace generally and in His disciples as well, for such announcements to do any good. They would only serve to prematurely shorten His ministry by evoking the repressive powers of the government, for Jesus would be looked upon as a political revolutionary.

The Cost of Discipleship

Matthew 16:21-28

> 21 From that time forth began Jesus to shew unto his disciples, how that he must go unto Jerusalem, and suffer many things of the elders and chief priests and scribes, and be killed, and be raised again the third day.
> 22 Then Peter took him, and began to rebuke him, saying, Be it far from thee, Lord: this shall not be unto thee.
> 23 But he turned, and said unto Peter, Get thee behind me, Satan: thou art an offence unto me: for thou savourest not the things that be of God, but those that be of men.
> 24 Then said Jesus unto his disciples, If any man will come after me, let him deny himself, and take up his cross, and follow me.
> 25 For whosoever will save his life shall lose it: and whosoever will lose his life for my sake shall find it.
> 26 For what is a man profited, if he shall gain the whole world, and lose his own soul? or what shall a man give in exchange for his soul?
> 27 For the Son of man shall come in the glory of his Father with his angels; and then he shall reward every man according to his works.
> 28 Verily I say unto you, There be some standing here, which shall not taste of death, till they see the Son of man coming in his kingdom.

The phrase *from that time forth* marks a transition in the ministry of Jesus. In each of the Synoptic Gospels the confession of His messiahship by Peter is a pivotal point. Up to this point His ministry is largely to the crowds. Now He sets His face towards the Cross and concentrates upon the training of the Twelve. Matthew introduces both main sections of Jesus' ministry with the same phrase (cf. 4:17).

1. *The cost of messiahship is now declared.* Jesus makes the first unambiguous prediction of His death. Having been confessed as Messiah, He tells the disciples that

He will suffer, be killed, and be raised again. His death will be brought about by the religious hierarchy of His own nation, *the elders and chief priests and scribes.*

The concept of a suffering Messiah was beyond their comprehension. Peter, the confessor, now becomes rebuker: *"God forbid, Lord! This shall never happen to you"* (22, RSV). What prompts the sharp protest? Doubtless, his love for Jesus. Love can unwisely spare suffering. Perhaps, as well, his concern for himself. If the Master is slain, will the disciples be spared?

Jesus hears the words as a renewal of the third temptation (cf. 4:8-10), the devil's suggestion of a way to the kingdoms without enduring Calvary. His strong reprimand to Peter hints at the strength of the temptation. The idea of sparing himself must not be toyed with, but instantly flung away. The disciple's protest is an offense, a stumbling block, representing man's thinking in opposition to God's. *Get behind me, Satan!* (RSV). Messiah cannot dodge the Cross. The ruling King must be the suffering Servant.

2. *The cost of discipleship is then emphasized.* Not only the Messiah, but all His followers, must tread the way of suffering. *If any man will come after me, let him deny himself, and take up his cross, and follow me* (24). Jesus does not coerce discipleship. A man must will to follow Him. But He does condition discipleship. The suffering Lord cannot be served by self-sparing disciples. To give one's life, not to save one's life, is the law of discipleship. Giving life concentrates upon others, but saving life concentrates upon oneself. Jesus repudiates a self-serving attitude as unworthy of His kingdom.

The way of death is the way to life. If physical life is one's highest good, he will deny the Lord in order to spare himself from suffering and death. In doing so he will forfeit eternal life. But if he follows Jesus, even at the cost of suffering and death, he will gain eternal life. The force of Jesus' words are obvious when the issue is that clear-cut, a choice between recanting one's faith or losing one's life. The words are equally applicable, however, to a situation more common, the choice between investing one's life in service to others or hoarding one's life in selfish ease.

The cost of forsaking Christ is greater than the cost of following Christ. One may gain the world only to forfeit heaven. Any price paid for temporal advantage that ultimates in loss of eternal life is a bad bargain! Any price paid for remaining loyal to Jesus is sound investment, for He leads His disciples through suffering to glory.

The coming judgment casts its long shadow over our present decisions! The *Son of man shall come in the glory of his Father,* and every man's works will then be rewarded.

MATTHEW 17

The Glory on the Mountain

Matthew 17:1-13

> 1 And after six days Jesus taketh Peter, James, and John his brother, and bringeth them up into an high mountain apart,
> 2 And was transfigured before them: and his face did shine as the sun, and his raiment was white as the light.
> 3 And, behold, there appeared unto them Moses and Elias talking with him.
> 4 Then answered Peter, and said unto Jesus, Lord, it is good for us to be here: if thou wilt, let us make here three tabernacles; one for thee, and one for Moses, and one for Elias.
> 5 While he yet spake, behold, a bright cloud overshadowed them: and behold a voice out of the cloud, which said, This is my beloved Son, in whom I am well pleased; hear ye him.
> 6 And when the disciples heard it, they fell on their face, and were sore afraid.
> 7 And Jesus came and touched them, and said, Arise, and be not afraid.
> 8 And when they had lifted up their eyes, they saw no man, save Jesus only.
> 9 And as they came down from the mountain, Jesus charged them, saying, Tell the vision to no man, until the Son of man be risen again from the dead.
> 10 And his disciples asked him, saying, Why then say the scribes that Elias must first come?
> 11 And Jesus answered and said unto them, Elias truly shall first come, and restore all things.
> 12 But I say unto you, That Elias is come already, and they knew him not, but have done unto him whatsoever they listed. Likewise shall also the Son of man suffer of them.
> 13 Then the disciples understood that he spake unto them of John the Baptist.

Years after this event Peter would write, *We ... were eyewitnesses of his majesty ... when he received honor and glory from God the Father ... on the holy mountain* (2 Pet. 1:16-18, RSV). The apostle's words are our best clue to the enigmatic saying which closes chapter 16. Some prefer to link 16:28 to the Cross, others to the Resurrection, and others to the Second Advent. What the three disciples were privileged to experience as eyewitnesses, we can be ear-witnesses to as we listen to the Scriptures.

1. *The vision of Christ's splendor* (1-8). He *was transfigured before them.* While they watched in speechless wonder, an unearthly radiance caused His face to shine and His robes to glisten. The inner glory of His immaculate holiness burst through the veil of His flesh.

Into the vision stepped visitors, Moses and Elijah, representing the Law and the Prophets, gathering up as symbols the entire Old Testament history whose promise was coming to fulfillment in Jesus Christ. They were *talking with him,* and Luke informs us that the topic of conversation was the coming *exodus* that Jesus would accomplish at Jerusalem (Luke 9:31, literal translation). They talked of His death on the Cross, by which a people in bondage to sin and guilt would be liberated.

Peter's words are well understood with emphasis on *here.* He was becoming adept at cross-dodging. *It is good ... to be here,* not down there where a cross awaits!

Into the vision comes a voice, interrupting and silencing Peter. A luminous cloud, recalling the Shekinah that symbolized God's presence in the wilderness and in the Temple, overshadowed them. From the cloud a voice spoke, saying, *"This is my beloved Son, with whom I am well pleased; listen to him"* (5, RSV). The disciples fell on their faces in fear.

The Father's words recall the baptism of Jesus. There He had committed himself to be the Messiah in suffering love, not in smashing force. Now, as His ministry moves toward the Cross, and His disciples misunderstand and protest, the Father again expresses His good pleasure. The words from the cloud reinforce Jesus and rebuke Peter.

Listen to him, said the Father. And the first words which Jesus speaks to them are filled with patience and comfort: *Arise, and be not afraid.* The visitors are gone; the voice is still. They see *Jesus only,* but that really is enough.

2. *The prediction of Christ's sufferings* (9-13). Descending from the mountain, Jesus enjoins silence upon them: *Tell the vision to no man, until the Son of man be risen again from the dead.* Reports of such a vision could serve only to further excite a mistaken populace, and further agitate the nervous rulers who were quick to read political meanings into the concept of messiahship.

The disciples raised a question which reflected popular Jewish thought. *"Why do the scribes say that first Elijah must come?"* (10, RSV). The prophecy of Malachi surely pointed to a more public and longer-lasting ministry than Elijah's appearance on the mount of transfiguration! Jesus replied that Elijah had come, symbolically, in the person and ministry of John the Baptist.

Then followed another prediction of Christ's sufferings. Just as John the Baptist was arrested and executed, *so also the Son of man will suffer at their hands* (12, RSV).

The Father said, *Listen to him.* Then Jesus is heard speaking as (1) the Giver of comfort, (2) the Answerer of questions, and (3) the Proclaimer of the Cross. We need very much to hear Him in precisely these same ways today!

The Misery in the Valley

Matthew 17:14-23

14 And when they were come to the multitude, there came to him a certain man, kneeling down to him, and saying,
15 Lord, have mercy on my son: for he is lunatick, and sore vexed: for ofttimes he falleth into the fire, and oft into the water.
16 And I brought him to thy disciples, and they could not cure him.
17 Then Jesus answered and said, O faithless and perverse generation, how long shall I be with you? how long shall I suffer you? bring him hither to me.
18 And Jesus rebuked the devil; and he departed out of him: and the child was cured from that very hour.
19 Then came the disciples to Jesus apart, and said, Why could not we cast him out?
20 And Jesus said unto them, Because of your unbelief: for verily I say unto you, If ye have faith as a grain of mustard seed, ye shall say unto this mountain, Remove hence to yonder place; and it shall remove; and nothing shall be impossible unto you.

21　Howbeit this kind goeth not out but by prayer and fasting.
22　And while they abode in Galilee, Jesus said unto them, The Son of man shall be betrayed into the hands of men:
23　And they shall kill him, and the third day he shall be raised again. And they were exceeding sorry.

They came to the crowd (14, RSV), from the glory on the mountain to the misery in the valley—to all the ignorance, disease, and sin that any crowd represents. And this is why neither Jesus nor His Church can stay on holy mountains in comfortable isolation. There are crowds of lost, hurting, desperate people to be served. Retreat is only for renewing strength with which to attack again the problems and pain of afflicted humanity.

There in the valley was a heartsick father with a demonized son. Uncontrollable seizures flung the helpless boy often into water or into fire, imperiling his very life. Hunting for Jesus, the father had found the disciples, but they could not deliver the piteous victim of demons and disease. Now Jesus takes command, and soon the lad is normal. Three factors call for our attention in this story.

1. *The failure of the disciples. I brought him to thy disciples, and they could not cure him* (16). The crestfallen disciples proved no match for demons while a crowd witnessed the spectacle of their defeat. They could not heal him, though they wanted to heal him, and though they had healed before! They had been sent on a mission as preachers, healers, and exorcists by Jesus, who conferred upon them authority over evil forces. Then they were successful; now they are failures. That hurts!

2. *The success of the Master. Bring him . . . to me,* Jesus commanded. Anyone who wants His help for a loved one must honor such a command. Where we cannot bring them in our arms, we must bring them in our prayers and by our evangelism.

Jesus knows how little time He has remaining with them and how little men have learned of God from Him. This awareness prompts the outburst which precedes His command. Does it not speak to the perverse unbelief that retards our own discipleship?

The command to the father is followed by another to

the demon. The demon is *rebuked* and the boy is healed. The note of immediacy, *from that very hour,* heightens the witness to the authority of Jesus. Where the disciples failed, the Lord succeeded.

3. *The reason for the difference.* Away from the crowd, and still stung by defeat, the disciples ask, *Why could not we cast him out?* The reply is as swift and incisive as the stroke of a scalpel: *Because of your unbelief.*

The words that follow are designed to encourage faith. Obstacles of mountain size can be removed by faith of mustard-seed size. For it is not the size of one's faith, but the size of its object, that matters. How big is your God?

The reply of Christ makes evasion of personal responsibility impossible. *Your* is emphatic. They could not blame their failure on the absence of the Lord, nor on the presence of the crowd. *Because of your unbelief.* We have an almost instinctive reaction to failure: blame someone else! But we never achieve anything worthwhile in Kingdom service until we accept responsibility personally, quit shifting blame, and start planting mustard seeds.

Many textual critics regard verse 21 as an editorial addition to Matthew, inserted later in an attempt to excuse the disciples from blame. How this could exonerate them is unclear, unless they were excused also from praying!

Verses 22-23 contain another announcement of the coming death and resurrection of Jesus. Placed here, the saying reminds us of the cost at which Jesus brings His healing to our afflicted world.

Tax-exempt Taxpayers

Matthew 17:24-27

24 And when they were come to Capernaum, they that received tribute money came to Peter, and said, Doth not your master pay tribute?
25 He saith, Yes. And when he was come into the house, Jesus prevented him, saying, What thinkest thou, Simon? of whom do the kings of the earth take custom or tribute? of their own children, or of strangers?
26 Peter saith unto him, Of strangers. Jesus saith unto him, Then are the children free.
27 Notwithstanding, lest we should offend them, go thou to the sea, and cast an hook, and take up the fish that first cometh up; and when

thou hast opened his mouth, thou shalt find a piece of money: that
take, and give unto them for me and thee.

Capernaum, owing to its location and population, was
a center for tax collection. Here the annual half-shekel
payment demanded of Jewish males for the support of the
Temple was scrupulously enforced. Coming to Peter, in
whose home Jesus often stayed, the tax collectors ask,
"Does not your teacher pay the tax?" (RSV). Jealous for
the reputation of his Master, Peter gives a hasty affirmative reply. The ensuing conversation between Jesus and
Peter has been a thorny problem for exegetes, but there
clearly emerges some contrast between legal freedom and
moral obligation.

1. *Legal freedom is affirmed. Kings of the earth* exact
tribute from their subjects in order to finance the operation
of their palaces. They do not impose taxes upon their sons.
The upkeep of the Temple, the Father's house, does not
obligate Jesus, the Father's Son, to pay revenue.

Some would interpret differently. Christ is the King;
His disciples are the sons; and their new relationship to
Him frees them from the old obligation to the Temple. The
parabolic question would thus point to the growing split
between the Church and the Temple. That Kingdom had
come which, for all who entered it, would supersede the
cultus of the Temple. Support was due the dawning Kingdom, not the fading dispensation.

However understood, the words of Jesus posit a legal
freedom in the case. The sons are free.

2. *Moral obligation is recognized.* Love limits freedom.
Love ungrudgingly surrenders rights in order to discharge
responsibilities. Rather than *offend,* i.e., cause to stumble,
Jesus gladly submits to the impost.

Offense would occur because His sonship to God was
unrecognized, or His kingship over men unknown. Then,
too, the continuing sacrifices at the Temple would set forth
in symbol what His sacrifice on the Cross would accomplish in fact. And His followers would continue their
association with the Temple for a while, since it afforded
excellent opportunity for evangelism.

These were compelling reasons for wise love to abridge its technical freedom and enhance its moral obligation. Causing needless offense that restricts the chance to reach and help others can claim no precedent in Jesus. His apostles adopted His attitude in their own ministries (cf. Acts 3:1 f.; 1 Cor. 9:19 f.).

In this incident we not only see love limiting freedom, but love sharing necessity. In the fish that he will catch, Peter will find money for his own tax as well as for Jesus' tax. *For me and thee* are words unspeakably precious to those who have found in Jesus a Helper in financial straits.

In chapter 17, Jesus is disclosed as (1) the Lord of glory (1-8), (2) the Saviour of the body (14-18), and (3) the Companion in necessity (24-27). He is, indeed a triumphant, adequate, unfailing Christ.

Fourth Teaching Section:
Discipline in the Church
Matthew 18:1-35

MATTHEW 18

The Big Are the Little

Matthew 18:1-14

1 At the same time came the disciples unto Jesus, saying, Who is the greatest in the kingdom of heaven?

2 And Jesus called a little child unto him, and set him in the midst of them,

3 And said, Verily I say unto you, Except ye be converted, and become as little children, ye shall not enter into the kingdom of heaven.

4 Whosoever therefore shall humble himself as this little child, the same is greatest in the kingdom of heaven.

5 And whoso shall receive one such little child in my name receiveth me.

6 But whoso shall offend one of these little ones which believe in me, It were better for him that a millstone were hanged about his neck, and that he were drowned in the depth of the sea.

7 Woe unto the world because of offences! for it must needs be that offences come; but woe to that man by whom the offence cometh!

8 Wherefore if thy hand or thy foot offend thee, cut them off, and cast them from thee: it is better for thee to enter into life halt or maimed, rather than having two hands or two feet to be cast into everlasting fire.

9 And if thine eye offend thee, pluck it out, and cast it from thee: it is better for thee to enter into life with one eye, rather than having two eyes to be cast into hell fire.

10 Take heed that ye despise not one of these little ones; for I say unto you, That in heaven their angels do always behold the face of my Father which is in heaven.

11 For the Son of man is come to save that which was lost.

12 How think ye? if a man have an hundred sheep, and one of them be gone astray, doth he not leave the ninety and nine, and goeth into the mountains, and seeketh that which is gone astray?

13 And if so be that he find it, verily I say unto you, he rejoiceth more of that sheep, than of the ninety and nine which went not astray.

14 Even so it is not the will of your Father which is in heaven, that one of these little ones should perish.

Chapter 18 contains the fourth block of teaching material that supplies the obvious structure of Matthew's

Gospel. Jesus has been confessed as the Messiah, and has announced His intention to establish a messianic community. Instruction must be given for the ordering of life in that Church, in keeping with the values of Jesus. Part of the necessary instruction is gathered and organized by Matthew into this fourth main discourse.

In the first 14 verses we meet three groups significant for three activities.

1. *The contenders form the first group.* The disciples approached Jesus with an ambitious question: *Who is the greatest in the kingdom of heaven?* We may be sure, from other passages, that each one was ready to nominate himself (cf. 20:20-28). The disciples spent a lot of time arguing the question among themselves. The special prominence given to Peter (16:16-18) and the special privileges accorded Peter, James, and John (17:1-8) must have added fuel to the fires of contention.

To the ambitious question Jesus gives a surprising answer. He calls a child and places him in their midst. They must become childlike to enter the Kingdom, humble and teachable. The Kingdom is not possessed through merit; it is received as a gift. Those who fancy themselves worthy and aspire to eminence are disqualified by their very qualifications. The kingdom of heaven reverses the world's values. The big are the little.

2. *The offenders form the second group.* Jesus issues a warning against those who offend the *little ones* (6) who believe in Him. These little ones are the humble and childlike followers of whatever age. For the selfish, jealous, ambitious, and sophisticated to treat with contempt these lowly followers, and to cause them to stumble into sin, is to evoke the displeasure of God. Better to be drowned in the sea than to face that righteous wrath!

Offenses will come. They are a fact of life. Occasions for sin are inevitable, but that does not make them excusable. They can lead to the *everlasting fire.* Therefore, decisive and drastic action should be taken to remove the occasion for sin. That action is set forth under the startling imagery of amputating a limb or removing an eye, as in

5:29-30. The application is not literal, for a one-eyed man can lust and a one-handed man can kill.

The "millstone" saying urges the truth that there is a fate worse than death. The "mutilation" saying argues that there is a life better than health.

3. *The defenders form the third group.* The little ones are not without defenders, however helpless they may seem to their despisers.

The guardian angels are their defenders. They are friends at court, with constant access to the Father. They watch His face like troops before a commander, ready to carry out the orders to protect or avenge the offended little ones.

The Shepherd-God is their Defender. The little ones are precious to Him. As a shepherd rejoices over the recovery of a single strayed sheep, so the Father seeks and saves the strayed person with joy, not willing that even *one of these little ones should perish.*

The genius of Christianity is the seeking God. Other religions make God the difficult Goal of man's quest. The Bible teaches that God is the Quester and man, undeserving and sinful man, is His goal.

Gaining a Brother

Matthew 18:15-20

> 15 Moreover if thy brother shall trespass against thee, go and tell him his fault between thee and him alone: if he shall hear thee, thou hast gained thy brother.
> 16 But if he will not hear thee, then take with thee one or two more, that in the mouth of two or three witnesses every word may be established.
> 17 And if he shall neglect to hear them, tell it unto the church: but if he neglect to hear the church, let him be unto thee as an heathen man and a publican.
> 18 Verily I say unto you, Whatsover ye shall bind on earth shall be bound in heaven: and whatsoever ye shall loose on earth shall be loosed in heaven
> 19 Again I say unto you, That if two of you shall agree on earth as touching any thing that they shall ask, it shall be done for them of my Father which is in heaven.
> 20 For where two or three are gathered together in my name, there am I in the midst of them.

This section contains the second "church" passage. The messianic community as a local group of believers is discussed. Within the life of the church offenses will come, brother will sin against brother. Such offenses cannot be ignored, but disciplinary measures should not be arbitrary or harsh. The life of the church in a situation where sin has intruded is the theme of this section. The church is seen in three aspects.

1. *The church questing for a brother.* The *if* in v. 15 is hypothetical. Sooner or later, in every congregation, someone sins against another.

Four steps are outlined for dealing with the situation. (1) The sinned-against discusses the matter with the brother who wronged him, avoiding publicity and containing the trouble to prevent its spread. (2) This measure failing, the injured party takes two or three others on another visit to attempt reconciliation. They are neither accusers nor defenders, and certainly not judges, but a team of conciliators. (3) If this step fails, the incident is brought before the whole congregation. (4) Should the offender still remain intransigent, then, by action of the church, not by the individual or lesser group, he is to be regarded as an outsider. The decision made on earth has been made in heaven. (Here the binding and loosing seem to refer, not to ethical decisions, as in 16:19, but to judicial rulings based upon them.)

The four steps have one motive, to gain the brother. The issue is never retaliation or vengeance. Even the terms of reproach, *as a Gentile and a tax collector* (17, RSV), forbid total dissociation, for Jesus welcomed such persons in order to save them. At no point are efforts to win back a person to be discontinued, not even when he must be dealt with as an outsider rather than an insider.

2. *The church praying to the Father.* An agreement in faith, where just two disciples are involved, is enough to assure an answer to their prayer. The God who upholds the judicial action of the whole group honors the believing petition of two brothers in prayer.

The scope of the promise is breathtaking: *any thing that they shall ask!* Stronger incentive and assurance could not be given to small-group prayer.

In context, two significant concerns for those who agree together in prayer are the offended little ones (12-14) and the offending brothers (15-18). Each needs to be recovered from straying, and each is the object of the Father's will to save. More prayer and less gossip might reach many who have wandered.

3. *The church meeting with the Saviour.* Jesus pledges to be present wherever *two or three are gathered together* in His name.

The phrase *in my name* implies submission to His lordship. At His authority they meet together, for the fellowship of the church at worship or in work is not based upon human impulses or decisions. It is His Church (cf. 16:18), not a social structure demanded by or nourished upon human mutualities of color, class, or creed.

Meeting together in His name, to participate in His life, supplies the inspiration for the other activities, namely, questing for a brother and praying to the Father. For in the fellowship of His presence our love, respect, and appreciation for one another are nourished and strengthened. When we realize how much each one means to Him, we cannot endure the thought of losing a brother, and we value the experience of praying with a brother. Christ is with us as the Shepherd of those in the fold and of those who have strayed. His presence, therefore, incites us to the activities of prayer and reconciliation.

Forgiveness Unlimited

Matthew 18:21-35

> 21 Then came Peter to him, and said, Lord, how oft shall my brother sin against me, and I forgive him? till seven times?
> 22 Jesus saith unto him, I say not unto thee, Until seven times: but, Until seventy times seven.
> 23 Therefore is the kingdom of heaven likened unto a certain king, which would take account of his servants.
> 24 And when he had begun to reckon, one was brought unto him, which owed him ten thousand talents.
> 25 But forasmuch as he had not to pay, his lord commanded him to be sold, and his wife, and children, and all that he had, and payment to be made.
> 26 The servant therefore fell down, and worshipped him, saying, Lord, have patience with me, and I will pay thee all.
> 27 Then the Lord of that servant was moved with compassion, and loosed him, and forgave him the debt.

28 But the same servant went out, and found one of his fellowservants, which owed him an hundred pence: and he laid hands on him, and took him by the throat, saying, Pay me that thou owest.
29 And his fellowservant fell down at his feet, and besought him, saying, Have patience with me, and I will pay thee all.
30 And he would not: but went and cast him into prison, till he should pay the debt.
31 So when his fellowservants saw what was done, they were very sorry, and came and told unto their lord all that was done.
32 Then his lord, after that he had called him, said unto him, O thou wicked servant, I forgave thee all that debt, because thou desiredst me:
33 Shouldest not thou also have had compassion on thy fellowservant, even as I had pity on thee?
34 And his lord was wroth, and delivered him to the tormentors, till he should pay all that was due unto him.
35 So likewise shall my heavenly Father do also unto you, if ye from your hearts forgive not every one his brother their trespasses.

The Early Church was not ideal. Enough friction between members arose to prompt the Gospel writers to include in several places the insistence of Jesus upon forgiveness. Here it is Peter who broaches the subject, after hearing Jesus' words about gaining a brother (vv. 15-20). Was Peter having a problem with another of the Twelve? Very likely. The conversation with Jesus proceeds to contrast his human measure of forgiveness with a divine model for forgiveness.

1. *A human measure of forgiveness* (21-22). Forgiveness is constantly needed. Brothers do sin against brothers; that is a fact of life in the Church. We know that we should not, but we do. The worst reaction to such a situation is to pretend that it has not happened. Sin is not remedied, nor is fellowship preserved, by ignoring reality.

A measure of forgiveness is suggested: *Until seven times?* That sounds like a generous figure. People often limit forgiveness to a single instance, adding to the words of pardon the ominous threat, "But if it ever happens again . . ." The Babylonian Talmud limited forgiveness to three times. No doubt Peter felt that his suggestion was magnanimous.

But his measure of forgiveness is corrected: *Until seventy times seven.* The reply of Jesus, in effect, removes all limits. Forgiving love does not keep score. A brother who sins, repents, and desires forgiveness must receive forgiveness no matter how often he has offended. A forgiving disposition should characterize the followers of Jesus. After all, the Church was created as a company of pardoned sinners.

2. *A divine model for forgiveness* (23-35). The ensuing parable sets forth a pattern for pardon under Messiah's reign.

A huge debt is freely forgiven. The king responds to the plea of a servant-debtor by canceling his debt of several million dollars. The king's motive is supplied in a phrase which is used several times of Jesus in this Gospel —moved with compassion.

How such an immense debt could occur is not important. The language is pictorial. Jesus is illustrating the guilt of our sins against God. No sum can exaggerate that indebtedness!

After the huge debt was forgiven, a small forgiveness was refused. The ungrateful man imprisoned a fellow servant over a trifling debt of several dollars. A million to one is a good ratio for expressing the measure of my sins against God compared with anyone's sins against me!

When the small forgiveness was refused, a just anger was kindled. The merciless servant, by order of the wrathful king, was delivered to the jailers (lit., "torturers") *till he should pay all his debt* (34, RSV), which sounds an awful lot like a life sentence.

And then a stern warning was issued: *So also my heavenly Father will do to every one of you, if you do not forgive your brother from your heart* (35, RSV).

The figure of a prison is very appropriate in the story, because forgiveness is a liberation, and without it man remains a prisoner of guilt. To refuse forgiveness to those who offend us is to will that the offender live under an unrelieved burden of guilt, and remain a wretched and tortured prisoner.

Is the angry king a proper figure for God? Would God forgive and then retract forgiveness? We had better believe it! Jesus had earlier described sonship to God in terms of loving as God loves (5:43-48). Here sonship means forgiving as God forgives. Sonship is not defined biologically, allowing us to prate about always being a son no matter how we live. Sonship is defined ethically, as moral resemblance to the Father, who loves and forgives freely and continually. Unless we live like that, we will not have fellowship with Him and cannot honestly bear His name. An unforgiving spirit will separate a man from God, in this or any other world. If we do not show mercy, we shall have justice (cf. 7:1-2).

Fifth Narrative Section:
The Public Ministry Concluded
Matthew 19:1—24:2

MATTHEW 19

Marriage and Divorce

Matthew 19:1-15

1 And it came to pass, that when Jesus had finished these sayings, he departed from Galilee, and came into the coasts of Judaea beyond Jordan;

2 And great multitudes followed him; and he healed them there.

3 The Pharisees also came unto him, tempting him, and saying unto him, Is it lawful for a man to put away his wife for every cause?

4 And he answered and said unto them, Have ye not read, that he which made them at the beginning made them male and female,

5 And said, For this cause shall a man leave father and mother, and shall cleave to his wife: and they twain shall be one flesh?

6 Wherefore they are no more twain, but one flesh. What therefore God hath joined together, let not man put asunder.

7 They say unto him, Why did Moses then command to give a writing of divorcement, and to put her away?

8 He saith unto them, Moses because of the hardness of your hearts suffered you to put away your wives: but from the beginning it was not so.

9 And I say unto you, Whosoever shall put away his wife, except it be for fornication, and shall marry another, committeth adultery: and whoso marrieth her which is put away doth commit adultery.

10 His disciples say unto him, If the case of the man be so with his wife, it is not good to marry.

11 But he said unto them, All men cannot receive this saying, save they to whom it is given.

12 For there are some eunuchs, which are so born from their mother's womb: and there are some eunuchs, which were made eunuchs of men: and there be eunuchs, which have made themselves eunuchs for the kingdom of heaven's sake. He that is able to receive it, let him receive it.

13 Then were there brought unto him little children, that he should put his hands on them, and pray: and the disciples rebuked them.

14 But Jesus said, Suffer little children, and forbid them not, to come unto me: for of such is the kingdom of heaven.

15 And he laid his hands on them, and departed thence.

The opening verse contains the formula by which Matthew concludes the major discourses, *when Jesus had finished these sayings* . . . It also marks His last departure from Galilee for Jerusalem. Every step taken now is toward the Cross. The healings continue (2), for His compassion never diminishes.

This section of chapter 19 opens with a test question put to Jesus by the Pharisees concerning marriage and divorce. The problem was never more acute than today!

1. *Marriage is defended.* Citing the Genesis record, Jesus insists that union between husband and wife should be indissoluble. What God has joined man is not to sever.

Appealing to Mosaic legislation which permitted divorce (Deut. 24:1), the Pharisees challenged the stringent standard of permanent, monogamous union which Jesus has enunciated as the original intention of God. Why would Moses permit what God did not will? Jesus' reply is blunt. Divorce was permitted as a concession (not approval!) to the hardness of men's hearts. In the Kingdom, where love is primary and obedience is radical, divorce should be invalid and God's creative intention honored.

Jewish society permitted husbands to divorce their wives for any trivial reason, though some rabbis issued strong protest against the liberal practice. The "indecency" clause in Deut. 24:1 was interpreted as sexual immorality by some, but as a blanket provision for anything that displeased a husband by others.

Divorce, then, is a heart ailment. Where hardness of heart has given way to a forgiving spirit (as c. 18 inculcates), divorce is unthinkable. The one exception is unchastity (v. 9), but even this breach of fidelity is no insuperable barrier to love.

The teaching is clear in its emphasis. If you marry, stay married, and avoid unchastity in order to preserve your union.

2. *An alternative to marriage is discussed.* The disciples also reacted to the stringency of Jesus' teaching. Better not to marry if divorce is prohibited!

While marriage is the normal situation, there is an alternative for those *to whom it is given*. Both marriage and celibacy can be the gift of divine grace, and God's power can enable holy living in either situation.

Some are celibate because of physical disability, but others because of spiritual dedication. To devote a maximum of time, energy, and resources to the work of the Kingdom some forego the married state. This is viewed as a worthy (but not worthier) alternative to marriage, and is nowhere urged upon a majority of believers, even among the clergy.

Christian love will not deprecate marriage. We serve One who healed a mother-in-law and attended wedding feasts! Neither will Christian love belittle the alternative. We serve One who did not marry! But the alternative to marriage which Christianity should recognize is chaste celibacy, not "practicing marriage without a license."

3. *The fruitage of marriage is blessed.* He who taught the sacredness of marriage welcomes and blesses children. The parents who brought them were rebuked by the disciples, who were mistakenly jealous of the time and strength of their busy Master. But Jesus said, *"Let the children come to me; do not try to stop them; for the kingdom of Heaven belongs to such as these"* (14, NEB). The children and the childlike who trust in Jesus are members of the Kingdom.

In one of the loveliest scenes in the Bible, Jesus puts His hands upon the children and prays for them! Those hands were often placed in healing love upon the diseased and crippled. As health is better than healing, how wonderful it is when the touch of His grace upon children prevents the damaging careers of evil from which He rescues believing adults! What incentive this passage affords for parents to bring their children to Jesus! How tragic that children are deprived of His blessings because parents will not serve Him!

The Possessed Possessor

Matthew 19:16-22

16 And, behold, one came and said unto him, Good Master, what good thing shall I do, that I may have eternal life?

17 And he said unto him, Why callest thou me good? there is none good but one, that is, God: but if thou wilt enter into life, keep the commandments.

18 He saith unto him, Which? Jesus said, Thou shalt do no murder, Thou shalt not commit adultery, Thou shalt not steal, Thou shalt not bear false witness,

19 Honour thy father and thy mother: and, Thou shalt love thy neighbour as thyself.

20 The young man saith unto him, All these things have I kept from my youth up: what lack I yet?

21 Jesus said unto him, If thou wilt be perfect, go and sell that thou hast, and give to the poor, and thou shalt have treasure in heaven: and come and follow me.

22 But when the young man heard that saying, he went away sorrowful: for he had great possessions.

The story of this encounter between Jesus and the rich young ruler forms a contrast to the preceding context. The humble and obedient, the childlike, enter the Kingdom; but this seeker fails, as the rich often do, because he is possessed by his possessions.

1. *Here is a young man with an old question.* He is concerned about *eternal life,* the life of the age to come, the life of the kingdom of God. Even in youth men sense the transitoriness of this present life and discover its incapacity to satisfy the deepest longings of the heart. The soul's disquiet cannot be hushed by things or people. Something more is demanded, life with God. Men have always felt this need, whatever difficulty they may have had in articulating the question or discovering the answer.

This unnamed man raises the question of eternal life at the choicest time in temporal life, during the days of youth. The quest for life cannot be initiated or satisfied too soon, for this eternal life is all that really matters.

2. *Here is a "good" man with a bad theology.* His understanding of Jesus is deficient. If Jesus is no more than *Teacher* (RSV), just another rabbi, the question is out of court. No human teacher has authority to fix the conditions of eternal life.

Jesus did not labor the questioner's "Christology." God is the good One, as He is the one Good. He alone can establish the conditions for life in His kingdom. Therefore, Jesus cites the commandments to the young man.

The specific commandments which Jesus cites relate

to the man-to-man laws of the Decalogue, capped with the summary commandment which fulfills them all, *Love thy neighbour as thyself.*

His reply is, *All these things have I kept from my youth up.* The answer shows that, just as he underrated Jesus, so he overrated himself. He may have abstained from outward sins, but his response to the next demand of Jesus will show that he neither loves God supremely nor his neighbor unselfishly. His heart is turned in upon itself.

Jesus puts His finger on the real trouble, saying, *"Go, sell what you possess and give to the poor, and you will have treasure in heaven; and come, follow me"* (21, RSV). No mere teacher has the right to impose such an absolute claim on another's life. Unless the young man will acknowledge the lordship of Jesus, renouncing his wealth at Jesus' word and trusting his life to Jesus' care, he cannot enter into life.

The Lord did not make this specific demand of all who were called to follow Him. Some retained property. The one thing He requires of all is radical obedience, submission to His absolute lordship.

3. *Here is a rich man with a poor future. He went away sorrowful: for he had great possessions.* In truth, the possessions had him. He was a possessed possessor. He was joined to his idol; his god was mammon (cf. 6:24).

We do not know what happened to him, whether or not his foolish decision was ever reversed. If not, he had put a mortgage on his future that no measure of wealth could redeem. Last seen, he had his back to Jesus and sorrow clouded his face. The farther from Jesus one goes, the sadder life gets.

Jesus did not call him back, did not run after him. He respects the freedom which God has given men, and Ho will not coerce anyone into discipleship. Neither will He reduce His terms to gain a follower.

The Enriched Sacrificers

Matthew 19:23-30

23 Then said Jesus unto his disciples, Verily I say unto you, That a rich man shall hardly enter into the kingdom of heaven.

24 And again I say unto you, It is easier for a camel to go through the eye of a needle, than for a rich man to enter into the kingdom of God.
25 When his disciples heard it, they were exceedingly amazed, saying, Who then can be saved?
26 But Jesus beheld them, and said unto them, With men this is impossible; but with God all things are possible.
27 Then answered Peter and said unto him, Behold, we have forsaken all, and followed thee; what shall we have therefore?
28 And Jesus said unto them, Verily I say unto you, That ye which have followed me, in the regeneration when the Son of man shall sit in the throne of his glory, ye also shall sit upon twelve thrones, judging the twelve tribes of Israel.
29 And every one that hath forsaken houses, or brethren, or sisters, or father, or mother, or wife, or children, or lands, for my name's sake, shall receive an hundredfold, and shall inherit everlasting life.
30 But many that are first shall be last; and the last shall be first.

1. *The kingdom of heaven costs.* This is the plain force of Jesus' demand upon the rich young ruler, and of His comment upon watching the young man retreat from the demand in sorrow. *"It will be hard for a rich man to enter the kingdom of heaven"* (RSV). The saying is introduced by the solemn formula, *"Truly, I say to you"* (RSV), and is reinforced by the graphic imagery of the camel and the needle's eye. We must not allow the truth of salvation by grace to obscure the cost of discipleship. No man can purchase God's forgiveness with money or work. But no man can follow Jesus without sacrifice and self-denial.

On the authority of Jesus, it is hard for the rich to be saved. Their possessions so possess them, their privileged status so inflates them, that few of them are willing to humble themselves, admit their need for Him, and become His disciples. The attempt of the largest beast known to Him to pass through the smallest opening is Jesus' vivid, hyperbolic way of underscoring the difficulty.

To the amazement of the disciples, it is hard for the rich to be saved. Jesus' words *exceedingly amazed* them. Like most of their contemporaries (and ours), they regarded material wealth as an evidence of God's favor. By philanthropic gestures that favor could be increased. If a rich man can scarcely be saved, *who then can be saved?*

If it is hard for the rich to be saved, is it not hard for the saved to be rich? If men are called to leave riches to follow Jesus, are they not called to give riches to serve men? Our Lord continually willed bread for the hungry and healing for the sick. Does anyone really honor His name who amasses wealth and lives in ease while suffering and hunger abound in the world He died to save?

To the astonished outburst of the disciples Jesus gave a penetrating reply: *With men this is impossible; but with God all things are possible.* By human power no man can be saved, not the poorest. By divine power any man can be saved, even the richest. But this power is persuasive, not coercive. Jesus reserves to those whom He calls the freedom to refuse, as the case of the rich young ruler has just shown.

2. *The kingdom of heaven pays.* This is the plain force of Jesus' reply to Peter's question, *What shall we have?* Peter says, in effect, We have done what the young man refused to do. What are we gaining by our sacrifice? His question sounds crass and mercenary on the surface, but Jesus responds with promise, not with rebuke.

Those who have suffered with Jesus shall reign with Him. A new social order for humanity is coming (cf. 2 Pet. 3:13; Rom. 8:18-25; Rev. 21:1-7; 22:1-5). Those who have followed Jesus will help to administer that Kingdom. The *thrones* which He mentioned need not be literalized, neither the number *twelve* (cf. 1 Cor. 6:2; 2 Tim. 2:11-12; 3:6-8). The reward for discipleship is to share the ministry of Jesus to the world, both now and in the age to come.

Verse 29 recognizes that real sacrifices are made for Jesus' sake. Lands and houses and families may be forsaken in order to answer His call to discipleship. But no sacrifice goes unrewarded. Rather, it is compensated *an hundredfold,* not materially, but spiritually. The reward which pales all sacrifice to insignificance is God's gift of eternal life. The one qualification is *for my name's sake.* To respond for the reward's sake is not discipleship but barter. To give in order to get does not honor Jesus as Lord, but attempts to use Him as a servant. Such effort to bargain with God for life would be reprehensible.

Verse 30 is a warning. While rewards are sure, Peter and the other disciples must not think that they are more important or more deserving because they were first to follow Jesus. All service is privilege and all rewards are gracious. A merit system cannot be smuggled into the situation. *Many that are first shall be last; and the last shall be first.*

MATTHEW 20

The Generous Employer

Matthew 20:1-16

> 1 For the kingdom of heaven is like unto a man that is an householder, which went out early in the morning to hire labourers into his vineyard.
> 2 And when he had agreed with the labourers for a penny a day, he sent them into his vineyard.
> 3 And he went out about the third hour, and saw others standing idle in the marketplace,
> 4 And said unto them; Go ye also into the vineyard, and whatsoever is right I will give you. And they went their way.
> 5 Again he went out about the sixth and ninth hour, and did likewise.
> 6 And about the eleventh hour he went out, and found others standing idle, and saith unto them, Why stand ye here all the day idle?
> 7 They say unto him, Because no man hath hired us. He saith unto them, Go ye also into the vineyard; and whatsoever is right, that shall ye receive.
> 8 So when even was come, the lord of the vineyard saith unto his steward, Call the labourers, and give them their hire, beginning from the last unto the first.
> 9 And when they came that were hired about the eleventh hour, they received every man a penny.
> 10 But when the first came, they supposed that they should have received more; and they likewise received every man a penny.
> 11 And when they had received it, they murmured against the goodman of the house,
> 12 Saying, These last have wrought but one hour, and thou hast made them equal unto us, which have borne the burden and heat of the day.
> 13 But he answered one of them, and said, Friend, I do thee no wrong: didst not thou agree with me for a penny?
> 14 Take that thine is, and go thy way: I will give unto this last, even as unto thee.
> 15 Is it not lawful for me to do what I will with mine own? Is thine eye evil, because I am good?
> 16 So the last shall be first, and the first last: for many be called, but few chosen.

The parable of the laborers in the vineyard occurs only in Matthew, and is obviously placed here to illustrate the saying, *Many that are first shall be last; and the last shall be first.*

This parable troubles interpreters greatly. We must begin by recognizing that Jesus is talking about how things are in *the kingdom of heaven,* and not how things should be in a modern industry or business. And the Householder for whom we labor in the Kingdom has placed His love and justice beyond cavil by the Cross! Whatever our deficiency of understanding, we can trust our Lord to be always kind and fair.

The parable speaks to two issues, one relating to job opportunity and the other to work remuneration.

1. *The parable shows how Kingdom service is determined.* It is determined by the needs of the vineyard. No one in the story is given work for his own sake, as an ego satisfaction. Each laborer is sent into the vineyard because the vineyard needs attention. As we observed, on 5:13-14, the Church is not self-contained. Disciples serve the world, not the world the disciples. Those who attempt Christ's work from self-oriented motives invariably fail. To pastor a church, for example, in order to satisfy an ego need for status, or power, or publicity is a doomed experiment. The pulpit is not a stage, and a church is not a retinue of servants for the minister.

Kingdom service is determined by the call of the Householder. None of the workers entered the vineyard at his own initiative. The Divine Householder determines when and where men shall be set to work in His vineyard (cf. *the Lord of the harvest,* 9:37-38). Whether they shall begin early or late, and how long they shall continue in their labors is His decision, not theirs. This is what discipleship means in the kingdom of heaven, submission to lordship.

2. *The parable shows how Kingdom service is rewarded.* It is rewarded sovereignly. This is the note struck throughout the parable. Just as workers are sovereignly called and sent to the task (cf. 10:1, 5), so they are sovereignly rewarded for their work. *"Am I not allowed to do what I choose with what belongs to me?"* (15, RSV). That "sovereignly" does not mean arbitrarily or capriciously is clear from the words, *I am good,* in v. 15. When we talk about the sovereignty of God, we need to remember what kind of God He is, and our fears and grumblings will cease. His

self-disclosure in Jesus Christ assures us that He seeks the highest good of His creatures. What He gives us will be generous and just. If it does not seem so, the defect lies not in His dealings with us, but in our warped self-estimates. If our eyes are evil (15), His actions will seem scandalous. Sovereign love and justice, not mere sovereign power, rewards Kingdom service.

Kingdom service is rewarded equally. Each laborer received a denarius. Some expected less, some expected more, but all got the same. There are differences of position in the Kingdom, but not of reward.

This equality must be understood in light of the fact that each laborer entered the vineyard as soon as he was called by *the lord* (Gk., *kurios*) *of the vineyard.* The hours varied, but there is one constant, namely, faithfulness to opportunity. Those standing in the marketplace at the eleventh hour were not idlers; no man had hired them. There is not a loafer in the story (cf. the remarks on 4:18-22). Kingdom rewards are equal in that they are based on faithfulness to opportunity, not upon the size or length or importance (by human criteria) of the task assigned. The disciple who dies at 30 may serve as faithfully as one who lives until 90. The man who reaps in a village parish may serve as faithfully as the man who reaps in huge urban crusades. The person who works unnoticed may be as faithful as one who gets maximum publicity.

The Lord of the vineyard is good. The work of the vineyard is urgent. The laborers in the vineyard are brothers. To share this Kingdom service anytime, anywhere is such privilege that all rewards are graciously bestowed. No one deserves them.

The Suffering Servant

Matthew 20:17-28

> 17 And Jesus going up to Jerusalem took the twelve disciples apart in the way, and said unto them,
> 18 Behold, we go up to Jerusalem: and the Son of man shall be betrayed unto the chief priests and unto the scribes, and they shall condemn him to death,
> 19 And shall deliver him to the Gentiles to mock, and to scourge, and to crucify him: and the third day he shall rise again.
> 20 Then came to him the mother of Zebedee's children with her sons, worshipping him, and desiring a certain thing of him.

21 And he said unto her, What wilt thou? She saith unto him, Grant that these my two sons may sit, the one on thy right hand, and the other on the left, in thy kingdom.

22 But Jesus answered and said, Ye know not what ye ask. Are ye able to drink of the cup that I shall drink of, and to be baptized with the baptism that I am baptized with? They say unto him, We are able.

23 And he saith unto them, Ye shall drink indeed of my cup, and be baptized with the baptism that I am baptized with: but to sit on my right hand, and on my left, is not mine to give, but it shall be given to them for whom it is prepared of my Father.

24 And when the ten heard it, they were moved with indignation against the two brethren.

25 But Jesus called them unto him, and said, Ye know that the princes of the Gentiles exercise dominion over them, and they that are great exercise authority upon them.

26 But it shall not be so among you: but whosoever will be great among you, let him be your minister;

27 And whosoever will be chief among you, let him be your servant:

28 Even as the Son of man came not to be ministered unto, but to minister, and to give his life a ransom for many.

Jesus is en route to Jerusalem to attend the Passover feast and to become the Passover Lamb. In company with Him are many others making the annual pilgrimage. He draws the Twelve apart from the crowd and speaks out the burden of His mind. For the third time a clear and detailed prediction of His death and resurrection is given. New elements are added, chief among them the fact that Gentile authorities will actually carry out the execution to which Jewish leaders will condemn Him.

The incident which follows reveals the persistent misunderstanding of His disciples. They simply cannot grasp the concept of a King who conquers by suffering torture and death at the hands of His enemies. There can be no Cross in their minds when there are thrones in their eyes. They are not too hard for us to identify with, are they? The personnel of this drama are full of lessons for every age.

1. *The ambitious two.* James and John seek privileged position through their mother. That need not surprise us, when millions have been taught that Jesus can be influenced through His mother! The earlier mention of thrones (19:28) may have sparked this request. Antennae were up when crowns were mentioned, but switches were off when He spoke of crosses. No one had volunteered to share His suffering, but all of them wanted to share His reign. The

sons of Zebedee want places of honor on either side of what they envision as a throne of earthly empire.

To His challenge of the *cup* and *baptism,* both figures of speech for His death, they confidently affirm, *We are able.* Their confidence is spawned of ignorance. Jesus does not give them an outright refusal. He implies that their one concern should be the Father's will, as was His.

The words of Jesus, *"What do you want?"* (21, RSV), suggest a certain risk in our desires and prayers. Think where James and John would have been when Jesus died if He had granted their petition!

His words, *"You do not know what you are asking"* (22, RSV), are often true of our own requests. There is frequent ignorance in prayer.

2. *The indignant ten.* The reaction of *the ten* did not stem from moral rectitude but from carnal jealousy. What incensed them was not the ambition of James and John, but their strategy! The sons of Zebedee had outmaneuvered them, but they had the same selfish ambition for places of power.

Jesus rebuked them all for thinking and acting like pagan politicians. How modern this ancient story sounds. In the kingdom of God, values are reversed. The great are those who serve, not those who *lord it over* others (25, RSV).

3. *The unselfish One.* Jesus demonstrated the principle He advocated for them: *Even as the Son of man came not to be ministered unto, but to minister, and to give his life a ransom for many* (28).

This saying tells us who Jesus is. *Son of man* in the Old Testament was a synonym for man (Ps. 8:4), God's title of address for a prophet (Ezek. 2:1), and the title of a heavenly ruler who received a kingdom from God (Dan. 7:13). By Jesus' time, *Son of man* was popularly conceived as a power figure, but He merged the ruler concept with a sufferer role. He is the King whose rule and conquest are by suffering love.

This saying tells us how Jesus lived. He filled His days with service to human need. His power was exercised to confer benefits, not to exact them. He lived for what He could give, not for what He could get.

This saying tells us why Jesus died. His life was not taken but given, and given as a ransom, a price paid to redeem captives. Here, for the first time, He adds the element of vicarious substitution to an announcement of His coming death. He will ransom the slaves of sin, purchasing their freedom by His death in their stead.

His solemn rebuke hushes the ambitious, jealous disciples, at least for a while. It rather shames us to silence, too, doesn't it?

The Compassionate Healer

Matthew 20:29-34

> 29 And as they departed from Jericho, a great multitude followed him.
> 30 And, behold, two blind men sitting by the way side, when they heard that Jesus passed by, cried out, saying, Have mercy on us, O Lord, thou son of David.
> 31 And the multitude rebuked them, because they should hold their peace: but they cried the more, saying, Have mercy on us, O Lord, thou son of David.
> 32 And Jesus stood still, and called them, and said, What will ye that I shall do unto you?
> 33 They say unto him, Lord, that our eyes may be opened.
> 34 So Jesus had compassion on them, and touched their eyes: and immediately their eyes received sight, and they followed him.

In this pericope Matthew has *two blind men,* where Mark and Luke mention only one (cf. 8:28-34). These physically blind men form an interesting contrast to the two spiritually blind men, James and John, in the previous section. Jesus responded to both pairs in pity. In pity He grants the request of these blind men at Jericho. In pity He refused the request of James and John. His mercy is displayed alike in what He gives and in what He withholds.

1. *Behold the wisdom of the blind.* They had no sight but they had good sense. Their place shows wisdom. They were *sitting by the roadside* (RSV). Dependent on the mercy of men, they sat where crowds were passing on religious pilgrimage, where help was likeliest to be found. By contrast, masses who need God's mercy never sit in His house or before His Word.

The prayer of the blind men shows wisdom. *They*

heard that Jesus was passing by (30, RSV), and cried out earnestly for mercy. Passing by! Opportunity is never static, always dynamic, always passing. The wise meet opportunity with importunity.

Their persistence shows wisdom. They were not intimidated by the crowd's rebuke, but *cried the more.* Theirs was a desperate case and a fleeting chance, and they refused to lose it by yielding to the pressure of the unconcerned. Let anyone get serious about seeking God and there are always some who would discourage their attempts. The rebukers must be ignored if Christ is to be found.

2. *Behold the folly of the crowd.* They were too interested in themselves to be concerned for others. En route to the royal city for a great celebration, and looking for some personal benefits from this enigmatic Bread-Maker, they had no time and patience for a couple of insignificant beggars in Jericho. Quite sure that they mattered to Jesus, and that He was on His way to something spectacular and revolutionary, they could not believe that these ragged beggars were worth the briefest interruption. The world is full of persons who are so busy with their own plans, to which they would make God party, that they feel only irritation at troubled lives about them.

They were too excited about the future to appreciate the present. Next week in Jerusalem, not today in Jericho, was the time and place of important action. Passover was a red-letter day on the calendar, but today was just another day to be hurried through with eyes fixed on the feast day. Christians can live like that, so bent on heaven's glory that they miss every earthly good.

3. *Behold the pity of the Lord. Jesus stood still!* He has time for everyone who wants His help.

> *The cry of a beggar can stop*
> *God as He marches by,*
> *If a crowd's indifference cannot stop*
> *That beggar's cry!*

Once again Matthew notes the *compassion* of Jesus. No other emotion was more characteristic of the Lord.

He *called them*. The question he put to them, *"What do you want?"* (32, RSV), appears also in v. 21. This time the reply is wiser: *That our eyes may be opened* (33).

He healed them. On this occasion He healed with a touch. In similar cases He employed other methods, a word, and even a mudpack! He cannot be locked in to any one method of doing His work, a lesson His Church has been slow to learn.

He led them. Upon receiving sight *they followed him*. And He was leading them to the place of His rejection and crucifixion. Disciples who really get their eyes open tread the way of self-giving service, for they know that Jesus is the Suffering Servant.

MATTHEW 21

Jesus Enters Jerusalem

Matthew 21:1-11

> 1 And when they drew nigh unto Jerusalem, and were come to Bethphage, unto the mount of Olives, then sent Jesus two disciples,
> 2 Saying unto them, Go into the village over against you, and straightway ye shall find an ass tied, and a colt with her: loose them, and bring them unto me.
> 3 And if any man say ought unto you, ye shall say, The Lord hath need of them; and straightway he will send them.
> 4 All this was done, that it might be fulfilled which was spoken by the prophet, saying,
> 5 Tell ye the daughter of Sion, Behold, thy King cometh unto thee, meek, and sitting upon an ass, and a colt the foal of an ass.
> 6 And the disciples went, and did as Jesus commanded them,
> 7 And brought the ass, and the colt, and put on them their clothes, and they set him thereon.
> 8 And a very great multitude spread their garments in the way; others cut down branches from the trees, and strawed them in the way.
> 9 And the multitudes that went before, and that followed, cried, saying, Hosanna to the son of David: Blessed is he that cometh in the name of the Lord; Hosanna in the highest.
> 10 And when he was come into Jerusalem, all the city was moved, saying, Who is this?
> 11 And the multitude said, This is Jesus the prophet of Nazareth of Galilee.

The entry of Jesus into Jerusalem for His final week of ministry, followed by His torture and death, is commonly referred to as the Triumphal Entry. There were crowds and shouts of acclamation and demonstrations of allegiance to Him as Messiah. But when He turned out to be the wrong kind of Messiah, fulfilling God's will, not man's expectations, the issue was a lonely gallows. This was really the tragic entry.

1. *Of particular interest to Matthew was the prophecy Jesus fulfilled* (1-7). The prophecy, a collation of passages from Isaiah and Zechariah, is prefaced with the introductory formula common to Matthew. Like all his quotations, these are not proof texts, arbitrarily chosen without regard to context in order to support a theological position. They are intended to recall the contexts of each brief citation, which are distinctly messianic. Matthew makes it clear that Jesus deliberately staged His entry into the city in a manner that would designate Him as the Messiah— but Messiah on His terms, not those of mistaken men.

He came as an uncommon King. He does not ride in an ornate chariot, nor is He mounted on a war steed. He rides a donkey. Royal vestments are not flung upon His mount or in His path, but the homespun cloaks of peasants. He is meek and His mission is peaceful. He offers himself as One who will conquer, not by force of arms, but by love. The advance guard and rear guard shouted, *Hosanna,* meaning, "Lord, save!" They did not know that He would save, not by inflicting suffering on His foes, but by enduring suffering for His foes.

He came using common things. *The Lord hath need of them* is spoken of an ass and its colt! If He ever invades our cities it will be through the instrumentality of ordinary people doing common deeds of love in His name.

2. *Of general interest was the excitement Jesus kindled* (8-11). *All the city was moved* (10). The RSV reads *stirred.* The Greek is even stronger, for the term is elsewhere used of an earthquake! Messianic fever was at a high pitch. *Who is this?* The question was flung from person to person, from group to group, in mounting excitement. The *multitude* answered, but popular opinion is seldom right.

Their concept of Jesus was inadequate. *This is Jesus the prophet* (11). But no prophet can be the answer to

Hosanna. No prophet can be the Saviour. Prophets can denounce sin and promise salvation, but they cannot be atoning sacrifices, they cannot effect reconciliation between God and men.

The first activity of Jesus in the city underscores the fact that He is no mere prophet, but the Lord of the Temple (cf. 12). Prophets, as Jeremiah, could stand at the door of the Temple and rebuke the sins of its functionaries, but no prophet had ever "cleansed" the Temple as did Jesus.

The crowd's enthusiasm for Jesus was short-lived. Before a week had ended, He would be crucified by His enemies, deserted by His followers, and mocked by the bystanders. When He marshals no troops, smashes no Roman armies, creates no independent Jewish government, He will be dropped like a hot potato by multitudes who feverishly acclaimed Him as the Son of David short days before.

The city was moved, but it was not saved, The salvation the people wanted was political and material. That which He offered was spiritual. Men in bondage to Satan do not really solve their problems by exchanging one set of power-mad rulers for another. Revolutions invariably fail where regeneration does not occur. But men will not have it so, and crosses still await those who are advocates of a suffering-servant Messiah.

Jesus Cleanses the Temple

Matthew 21:12-17

> 12 And Jesus went into the temple of God, and cast out all them that sold and bought in the temple, and overthrew the tables of the money-changers, and the seats of them that sold doves,
> 13 And said unto them, It is written, My house shall be called the house of prayer; but ye have made it a den of thieves.
> 14 And the blind and the lame came to him in the temple; and he healed them.
> 15 And when the chief priests and scribes saw the wonderful things that he did, and the children crying in the temple, and saying, Hosanna to the son of David; they were sore displeased,
> 16 And said unto him, Hearest thou what these say? And Jesus saith unto them, Yea; have ye never read, Out of the mouth of babes and sucklings thou hast perfected praise?
> 17 And he left them, and went out of the city into Bethany; and he lodged there.

Jesus went into the temple of God, and said and did things that cannot be squared with the familiar prayer-words "Gentle Jesus, meek and mild." He was aggressive and severe in bringing this cleansing judgment upon the house of God.

1. *"The temple of God" is seen as a place of racketeering.* For the convenience of those who came to worship, doves were sold for sacrifice, and other monies could be exchanged for the Tyrian coins in which the Temple tax was to be paid. The price of doves and the rate of exchange permitted these religious merchants to rake off a handsome profit. Doves were legitimate substitutes for lambs in the case of the poor, so that those who could afford it least were bearing the greatest hardship.

The Court of the Gentiles was the scene of this odious commerce, which made bad matters worse. The time was drawing near for the fulfillment of Isaiah's prophecy, when Jews and Gentiles would be gathered into God's kingdom (Isa. 56:6-8). The noisy and greedy merchandising that angered Jesus was contradicting the very saving truth which God's house should have symbolized.

The traffic, therefore, represented the vested interest of wealthy and powerful men, but this was no deterrent to Jesus' moral indignation and action. He cast out sellers and buyers alike, the sellers for their avarice which created the wretched business, and the buyers for their acquiescence which perpetuated it. The unprotesting share the guilt of those who commit injustices and crimes.

The actions and words of Jesus in this incident bring under indictment every attempt to hide or excuse materialism by a religious facade.

2. *"The temple of God" is seen here as a place of healing.* Following the purging action of Jesus, *the blind and the lame came to him in the temple; and he healed them* (14). Here the true purpose of the Temple is realized. The gifts of vision and strength are sovereignly and graciously bestowed.

The lesson is too plain to miss. The house of God becomes a source for vision and strength only when the

Lord is present. And He is present in the place of worship to heal and save, to illumine and empower, only when He can bring all the programs and practices of that house under His judging and correcting words.

3. *"The temple of God" is seen here as a place of praise.* There were children in the Temple crying, *Hosanna to the Son of David* (15). These boys had heard the shout raised by the crowds who accompanied Jesus at His entry into the city. Now the authority with which He evicted the money changers and healed the blind and lame reinforced the conviction that He was the Messiah. They gave vent to the conviction with that enthusiasm typical of youth.

The priests and scribes objected. They *saw the wonderful things that he did* (15): He purged the Temple, healed the afflicted, and inspired the children. Instead of rejoicing they complained. He was costing them money and popularity. To their objection Jesus gave a sharp rejoinder, quoting Ps. 8:2. If you knew and believed your Bibles, He was saying in effect, you would know what was going on and join the praise.

Then *he left them.* (17). In Matthew's Gospel it is instructive and sobering to see how frequently the conflict situations end on the note of Jesus' withdrawal. Forfeiture of His presence is the direst of judgments.

In the three aspects under which the Temple is viewed in this section we have three aspects of religion which speak with relevance to our times: (1) religion as exploitation; (2) religion as restoration; (3) religion as celebration.

Jesus Withers a Tree

Matthew 21:18-22

18 Now in the morning as he returned into the city, he hungered.
19 And when he saw a fig tree in the way, he came to it, and found nothing thereon, but leaves only, and said unto it, Let no fruit grow on thee henceforward for ever. And presently the fig tree withered away.
20 And when the disciples saw it, they marvelled, saying, How soon is the fig tree withered away!
21 Jesus answered and said unto them, Verily I say unto you, If ye have faith, and doubt not, ye sall not only do this which is done to the fig tree, but also if ye shall say unto this mountain, Be thou removed, and be thou cast into the sea; it shall be done.
22 And all things, whatsoever ye shall ask in prayer, believing, ye shall receive.

This miracle is certainly different from the others. Some scholars will not admit it as genuine, for they do not see how it served as a sign of the Kingdom's coming or as a means to its coming. Having no authority, and feeling no compulsion to dismiss as inauthentic what is difficult to understand, we are content to accept and value the incident for what it can tell us about Jesus.

1. *The incident witnesses to the genuine humanity of Jesus.* Matthew says little about the human emotions of Jesus, compared to Mark. Yet his Christ is not docetic—no sham human—for here Jesus experiences real hunger on this hike through the rugged terrain. Attracted to this fig tree whose foliage would normally betoken fruit, He experienced real disappointment in finding nothing on it but leaves. To resort to theories of pretended hunger, pretended surprise, and pretended letdown, as some commentators have done, is both witless and pointless. The Incarnation was real. The human mind of Jesus was subject to the necessity of growth, and some areas of ignorance attended every stage of His development. For us He became truly one of us.

2. *The incident witnesses to the unique power of Jesus.* He could confidently speak a word of judgment against the tree, for He was conscious of lordship over nature. Men without such authority, uttering such "curses" (cf. Mark 11:21), would be mocked by the next crop of figs! But by the following morning this tree was withered from the roots.

The temerity of some men in questioning the moral rectitude of Jesus for withering this tree is amusing and pathetic. A fellow will sit before a fireplace and raise no moral issue about trees that have been killed for his comfort, to supply furniture and fuel, and then question the morality of Jesus in sacrificing a single fig tree to the service of truth! If we object that it was sacrificed to His anger we add libel to inanity. Not a thing is said about anger in this whole incident. The sole use to which the incident is put makes the withered tree a symbol of faith's removal of hindrances to Kingdom objectives.

Destruction of unproductive trees is a fact of life in every orchard and grove in the world. No one impugns the motives of those who cut down such trees. That Jesus does with a word what other men can do only with an axe raises no valid moral questions, but serves to make conspicuous His authority.

3. *The incident witnesses to the great faith of Jesus.* The disciples marveled because the tree was so immediately withered. In response, Jesus gave a promise to faith. If they really believe, they can tell the Mount of Olives to be cast into the Mediterranean Sea, and it will happen! Those who take Jesus' words here literally have imaginations withered from the root. He is not suggesting that God willed the relocation of the mountain. He is saying that every barrier to the accomplishment of the apostolic mission can be removed by faith. Such faith as He has evidenced they can exercise also.

The promise to faith is implemented through the prayer of faith. The scope of the promise is adequate incentive for the prayer: *And all things, whatsoever ye shall ask in prayer, believing, ye shall receive.* The promise is not totally unconditioned. *All things* is qualified by *believing.* We cannot believe for what God neither wills nor promises. And we cannot believe for what God condemns or forbids. Otherwise, however, the sky is the limit.

To put a dead tree in service as a symbol of such achieving faith is one of the best uses ever made of wood!

Jesus Defends His Authority

Matthew 21:23-32

> 23 And when he was come into the temple, the chief priests and the elders of the people came unto him as he was teaching, and said, By what authority doest thou these things? and who gave thee this authority?
> 24 And Jesus answered and said unto them, I also will ask you one thing, which if ye tell me, I in like wise will tell you by what authority I do these things.
> 25 The baptism of John, whence was it? from heaven, or of men? And they reasoned with themselves, saying, If we shall say, From heaven; he will say unto us, Why did ye not then believe him?
> 26 But if we shall say, Of men; we fear the people; for all hold John as a prophet.
> 27 And they answered Jesus, and said, We cannot tell. And he said unto them, Neither tell I you by what authority I do these things.

28 But what think ye? A certain man had two sons; and he came to the first, and said, Son, go work to day in my vineyard.
29 He answered and said, I will not: but afterward he repented, and went.
30 And he came to the second, and said likewise. And he answered and said, I go, sir: and went not.
31 Whether of them twain did the will of his father? They say unto him, The first. Jesus saith unto them, Verily I say unto you, That the publicans and the harlots go into the kingdom of God before you.
32 For John came unto you in the way of righteousness, and ye believed him not; but the publicans and the harlots believed him: and ye, when ye had seen it, repented not afterward, that ye might believe him.

While Jesus was teaching in the Temple, members of the Sanhedrin came bristling with challenge to His authority. We know that sin and guilt are the parents of fear, but they can also breed a strange boldness. Imagine these religious impotents daring to question the authority of One who had healed the sick, raised the dead, cast out demons, cleansed the Temple, and taught with unprecedented authority! But He is Challenger as well as challenged, as this section of Matthew clearly shows.

1. *The authority of Jesus is challenged. "By what authority are you doing these things, and who gave you this authority?"* (23, RSV). The implication of their question is obvious. They regard Him as an impostor, arrogating to himself an authority He did not truly possess. Self-styled prophets with self-assumed rights are part of the history of religion. To them, Jesus is one more such fanatic.

These things refers to what they had recently observed, His acceptance of messianic praise, His cleansing of the Temple, His healings and teaching in the house of God. These activities alone should have made them cautious of crossing blades with Him, but "fools rush in where angels fear to tread."

The devastation of His answer was awesome. Jesus had a discomforting way at times of replying to questions with questions. *The baptism of John, whence was it? from heaven, or of men?* Was John the Baptist a man sent from God, or was he self-sent? They held a quick *ad hoc* committee meeting and voted not to trade answers with Him (24), since trading questions had already proved embarrassing. They replied evasively, *We cannot tell.* As they could not answer Him, He would not answer them.

Of course, both Jesus and His challengers knew that He had answered. His authority was authenticated at John's baptism. There He was identified by the forerunner as the Mightier One whom the Baptist was sent to proclaim. There He was anointed by the Spirit for His ministry as beloved Son and chosen Servant of God. Once admit that John was God-sent and their hostility to Jesus was emptied of logic and defense.

2. *The sincerity of Jesus' critics is challenged.* The parable of the two sons exposed their hypocrisy (28-32).

The first son repented. His initial revolt against the father's will was followed by a reversal of attitude and action. Jesus likens him to *the publicans and the harlots* who turned from their sins and prepared to enter the Kingdom under John's preaching.

The second son obeyed with his lips but not with his life. He represents these Jewish leaders who witnessed the dramatic converting effect of John's ministry but refused to believe his preaching and enter the kingdom of God. "Publicans and harlots," as a phrase, carried something of the force of "scum of the earth." To be told that persons regarded as the lowest and vilest in society were Kingdom-insiders while these Jewish leaders were outsiders was a sledgehammer blow to the pride of these self-righteous scribes and priests. Jesus flunked the Dale Carnegie course then and there. But it has been observed that there is often no difference between a good diplomat and a big liar!

Jesus left them no alibi on the grounds of John's character or preaching. He came *in the way of righteousness.* Both his behavior and his message marked John as a man of God, leaving these Jewish leaders no excuse for their unbelief and rejection.

The Murderous Tenants

Matthew 21:33-46

> 33 Hear another parable: There was a certain householder, which planted a vineyard, and hedged it round about, and digged a winepress in it, and built a tower, and let it out to husbandmen, and went into a far country:

34 And when the time of the fruit drew near, he sent his servants to the husbandmen, that they might receive the fruits of it.
35 And the husbandmen took his servants, and beat one, and killed another, and stoned another.
36 Again, he sent other servants more than the first: and they did unto them likewise.
37 But last of all he sent unto them his son, saying, They will reverence my son.
38 But when the husbandmen saw the son, they said among themselves, This is the heir; come, let us kill him, and let us seize on his inheritance.
39 And they caught him, and cast him out of the vineyard, and slew him.
40 When the Lord therefore of the vineyard cometh, what will he do unto those husbandmen?
41 They say unto him, He will miserably destroy those wicked men, and will let out his vineyard unto other husbandmen, which shall render him the fruits in their seasons.
42 Jesus saith unto them, Did ye never read in the scriptures, The stone which the builders rejected, the same is become the head of the corner: this is the Lord's doing, and it is marvellous in our eyes?
43 Therefore say I unto you, The kingdom of God shall be taken from you, and given to a nation bringing forth the fruits thereof.
44 And whosoever shall fall on this stone shall be broken: but on whomsoever it shall fall, it will grind him to powder.
45 And when the chief priests and Pharisees had heard his parables, they perceived that he spake of them.
46 But when they sought to lay hands on him, they feared the multitude, because they took him for a prophet.

A friend of mine is fond of saying, "Life is one thing and then two." The critics of Jesus must have felt that way. He has just seared the priests and elders with one parable, and now He follows it with two more, equally blunt and hard-hitting. The second in this trilogy of indictments is the story of the murderous tenants.

1. *The elements of the story.* There are allegorical elements to be carefully considered. To deny any allegorical features in Jesus' parables is an unwarranted over-reaction to the wholesale allegorization which was common before modern parables-study turned in a healthier direction under Jülicher.

This story has an Old Testament background (cf. Isa. 5:1 f.). The *vineyard* is a familiar symbol for Israel as a theocratic nation. The *tenants,* reprehended for the wanton beating and slaying of the householder's servants, were apostate leaders of Israel throughout her history, who disposed of prophet after prophet when these men of God demanded fruits of righteousness from the nation. The history of this God-rejecting leadership is now encapsulated into the priests and elders hearing the parable, who will be responsible for slaying the householder's son. This is precisely how *the chief priests and Pharisees* perceived this parable. They got the point! Jesus had placed them in the story (45).

There are autobiographical elements in the story, also. Jesus not only *spake of them;* he spoke of himself. He is *the son . . . the heir,* who represents the householder's final appeal to the rebellious tenants.

Jesus expresses here His consciousness of standing in a different relationship to God than did the prophets. Like them, He is a Servant of God; but in a way which they were not, He is the Son of God. His rejection, therefore, represents more than another item in a series. God has no other or greater to send, and with His rejection the judgment of the tenants is inevitable.

Thus the wrath of *the lord . . . of the vineyard* is nothing less than the righteous judgment of God, by which the nation is to be set aside and the Kingdom given to another nation which produces its fruits. This other nation is the true Israel, the messianic community of which Jesus had earlier spoken, His *ekklesia* (cf. 16:16-18).

The rejected-stone saying from Psalm 118 is applied by Jesus to himself. His rejection will be vindicated when He is seen as the Foundation of the new Israel. Thus the slaying of Jesus, to officialdom the removal of an impostor, *is the Lord's doing,* and marvelous to those who can discern the divine action.

Matthew reverses the slaying-casting out sequence in Mark, perhaps reflecting a growing interest in the theological significance of Jesus' crucifixion outside of Jerusalem (cf. Heb. 13:12 f.).

2. *The effect of the story.* The Jewish leaders, stung by the parable, wanted to arrest Jesus. They would still His accusing, probing voice as Herod had John's. When men will not yield to the truth, they seek to rid themselves of those who proclaim it.

The arrest was foiled because these leaders *feared the multitude,* who regarded Jesus as a prophet. Had they feared God more and men less they could have spared themselves the guilt of casting His Son out of the vineyard and killing Him.

MATTHEW 22

The Marriage Feast

Matthew 22:1-14

1 And Jesus answered and spake unto them again by parables, and said,
2 The kingdom of heaven is like unto a certain king, which made a marriage for his son,
3 And sent forth his servants to call them that were bidden to the wedding: and they would not come.
4 Again, he sent forth other servants, saying, Tell them which are bidden, Behold, I have prepared my dinner: my oxen and my fatlings are killed, and all things are ready: come unto the marriage.
5 But they made light of it, and went their ways, one to his farm, another to his merchandise:
6 And the remnant took his servants, and entreated them spitefully, and slew them.
7 But when the king heard thereof, he was wroth: and he sent forth his armies, and destroyed those murderers, and burned up their city.
8 Then saith he to his servants, The wedding is ready, but they which were bidden were not worthy.
9 Go ye therefore into the highways, and as many as ye shall find, bid to the marriage.
10 So those servants went out into the highways, and gathered together all as many as they found, both bad and good: and the wedding was furnished with guests.
11 And when the king came in to see the guests, he saw there a man which had not on a wedding garment:
12 And he saith unto him, Friend, how camest thou in hither not having a wedding garment? And he was speechless.
13 Then said the king to the servants, Bind him hand and foot, and take him away, and cast him into outer darkness; there shall be weeping and gnashing of teeth.
14 For many are called, but few are chosen.

This is the third parable by which Jesus indicted the Jewish leaders for their hostility to His ministry, and for their responsibility for His approaching death. The figures are changed, but the theme is constant. Those who refuse the Kingdom offered in His person and preaching are severely judged, while another group, those deemed unlikely by Pharisaical criteria, are welcomed into the Kingdom and become God's people.

1. *The kingdom is a feast.* In the Gospels the messianic Kingdom is often set forth under the imagery of banqueting; here as a marriage feast for the king's son.

The figure employed accents the feature of joy. Feasts are fun. Jesus, no ascetic himself, does not impose killjoy rules upon His followers. The satisfaction of good food with good friends for good reasons was part of His life and should be part of ours. The joy of the consummated Kingdom is brought forward into the present age. For those who believe, the eschatological banquet is anticipated in every eucharistic celebration, and even in common daily meals.

The figure of feasting also accents the feature of fellowship. The highest joy of a feast is not in the food but in the friendship expressed and enhanced. Again, the eschatological fellowship pictured is partially realized in the community of faith here and now. The apostles thought of fellowship as a goal of gospel proclamation (cf. 1 John 1:3; 1 Cor. 1:9-10).

The church at Corinth proved that feasting and fellowship can degenerate into an unspiritual orgy of gluttony and drunkenness (1 Cor. 11:17-34). But abuses cannot destroy the blessed truth that the kingdom of heaven means joy and fellowship, banqueting with Jesus and His disciples.

2. *The gospel is an invitation.* Its essence is *Come unto the marriage!* It announces the King's actions. He makes the marriage, prepares the dinner, and sends His servants to say, *All things are ready: come* (4). Everything results from the prior decisions and actions of the King.

The gospel admits of but two options. An invitation can be accepted or rejected, and nothing else. There is no neutral ground, no possibility of evasion, no escape from decision.

The gospel is addressed to all sorts of people, *both bad and good.* Goodness doesn't merit the invitation; badness doesn't prevent the invitation.

3. *God is a Sovereign.* He is a King, not a president. He does not act by the sufferance of an electorate. He cannot be deposed and He will not be ignored. The note of sover-

eignty needs to be sounded strongly, as Jesus does here.

Sovereignly, God gives the feast.

Sovereignly, God calls the invitees.

Sovereignly, God judges the rejectors of that invitation. This truth has special force in the parable. The invitation is not rejected for legitimate reasons but with trifling excuses. *They made light of it, and went their ways* (5). They attempted the age-old myth of the autonomous man, which denies that God is sovereign. The spiting and slaying of the servants make clear the hatred of these rejectors for the King (cf. Rom. 8:7). The inexcusable reaction meets with terrible judgment; the murderers are slain and their city burned. The passage has been read in the light of Jerusalem's overthrow in A.D. 70 by subsequent generations of Christians.

The rejection of those who were first bidden does not cancel the feast. Others are invited who accept (cf. 21:31-32, 41). The sinners and commoners of Israel, and those who responded to the apostolic mission, are found in this reference.

Sovereignly, God inspects the guests. The second part of the story is difficult, but probably looks to the same future judgment as the cleansing of the Kingdom in 13:47-50. Failure of the guest to appear in the wedding garment is to be understood as rebellion, again man's effort at moral autonomy. He felt that his own attire was acceptable; he did not need what the king provided.

Sovereignly, God condemns the rebel. He is cast into *outer darkness,* where pain and rage persist, a vivid image of the eschatological punishment. What is missing in hell is precisely the joy and fellowship of the banquet. Sartre said, "Hell is other people," and that is true where there is no fellowship.

Crooked Questions, Straight Answers

Matthew 22:15-46

15 Then went the Pharisees, and took counsel how they might entangle him in his talk.
16 And they sent out unto him their disciples with the Herodians, saying, Master, we know that thou art true, and teachest the way of God in truth, neither carest thou for any man: for thou regardest not the person of men.

17 Tell us therefore, What thinkest thou? Is it lawful to give tribute unto Caesar, or not?

18 But Jesus perceived their wickedness, and said, Why tempt ye me, ye hypocrites?

19 Shew me the tribute money. And they brought unto him a penny.

20 And he saith unto them, Whose is this image and superscription?

21 They say unto him, Caesar's. Then saith he unto them, Render therefore unto Ceasar the things which are Caesar's; and unto God the things that are God's.

22 When they had heard these words, they marvelled, and left him, and went their way.

23 The same day came to him the Sadducees, which say that there is no resurrection, and asked him,

24 Saying, Master, Moses said, If a man die, having no children, his brother shall marry his wife, and raise up seed unto his brother.

25 Now there were with us seven brethren: and the first, when he had married a wife, deceased, and, having no issue, left his wife unto his brother:

26 Likewise the second also, and the third, unto the seventh.

27 And last of all the woman died also.

28 Therefore in the resurrection whose wife shall she be of the seven? for they all had her.

29 Jesus answered and said unto them, Ye do err, not knowing the scriptures, nor the power of God.

30 For in the resurrection they neither marry, nor are given in marriage, but are as the angels of God in heaven.

31 But as touching the resurrection of the dead, have ye not read that which was spoken unto you by God, saying,

32 I am the God of Abraham, and the God of Isaac, and the God of Jacob? God is not the God of the dead, but of the living.

33 And when the multitude heard this, they were astonished at his doctrine.

34 But when the Pharisees had heard that he had put the Sadducees to silence, they were gathered together.

35 Then one of them, which was a lawyer, asked him a question, tempting him, and saying,

36 Master, which is the great commandment in the law?

37 Jesus said unto him, Thou shalt love the Lord thy God with all thy heart, and with all thy soul, and with all thy mind.

38 This is the first and great commandment.

39 And the second is like unto it, Thou shalt love thy neighbour as thyself.

40 On these two commandments hang all the law and the prophets.

41 While the Pharisees were gathered together, Jesus asked them,

42 Saying, What think ye of Christ? whose son is he? They say unto him, The son of David.

43 He saith unto them, How then doth David in spirit call him Lord, saying,

44 The Lord said unto my Lord, Sit thou on my right hand, till I make thine enemies thy footstool?

45 If David then call him Lord, how is he his son?

46 And no man was able to answer him a word, neither durst any man from that day forth ask him any more questions.

The three parables directed against the Jewish leaders are followed by three questions directed to Jesus by these leaders. The quizzers' motives are bad. They do not seek to learn but to trap Jesus into answers that will discredit Him with the crowds.

1. *The question about taxes* (15-22). The Pharisees put a loaded question to Jesus. "Yes" will be interpreted as traitorous, for the Jews hate to give tax support to the Romans. "No" will be translated as seditious, a precipitate of rebellion against Rome. They have Jesus in a dilemma, so they think.

The loaded question receives a brilliant answer. Calling for a Roman coin, Jesus asks, *"Whose likeness and inscription is this?"* (20, RSV). The answer is, *Caesar's.* Very well, then: *Render therefore unto Caesar the things which are Caesar's; and unto God the things that are God's* (21).

The answer recognized Caesar's rights. Benefits and services from government should be paid for by taxation. But the answer also delimited Caesar's authority. Man is stamped with God's likeness (cf. Gen. 1:27 f.). Human life, therefore, is to be governed by God's will. If God and Caesar issue counter commands, men should obey God, whatever the cost (cf. Acts 5:29).

At His answer they marveled—and retreated!

2. *The question about the resurrection* (23-33). The Sadducees ask a phony question. They do not believe in the resurrection, but they ask whose wife a woman will be in the resurrection who had been married to seven brothers successively. It was a stock question for testing the competence of novice teachers.

Jesus gives the insincere question a scorching reply. He flatly charges these proud and powerful leaders with ignorance. They do not know the Scriptures and they do not know the power of God. The power of God assures, and the Scriptures teach, the resurrection. The word of God to Moses was not, I was the God of the patriarchs, as though they had perished finally, but *I am the God of Abraham, and the God of Isaac, and the God of Jacob. God is not the God of the dead, but of the living* (32).

In the resurrection, however, there will be no marriages and no married living. Here men and women are incomplete without each other. Male and female are one flesh (cf. 19:4-6). But in the eternal order each person will be complete, as are the angels. Marriage is for the temporal order only. Some think of this saying as a promise!

3. *The question about the great commandment* (34-40). The lawyer's question seems to be more sincere, though it does intend to test Jesus. *Which is the great commandment in the law?* With so many commandments in the law, and so many more added in the oral tradition which purported to interpret the law, the quest for a basic command, a summarizing concept, was practical.

There is no severity in the reply of Jesus. Unhesitatingly, He declares that the command to love God wholeheartedly is *first and great*. Alongside it He placed the command to love the neighbor as oneself. All other commandments derive from these two. As A. B. Bruce wrote, "The moral drift of the whole Old Testament is love." Law and love are not incompatible. The various laws were intended as expressions of love to God and men.

The order is significant. One cannot love God without loving men. Life is triangular (God—others—self), not horizontal (self—others), not vertical (self—God). Unless the whole complex of relationships is held intact by love, life is subverted, unreal, and dissatisfying.

The answers of Jesus astonished the crowds, not because they deftly got Him off the hook, but because they were insightful and helpful. They marveled at His *doctrine*, not His dodging. His words are not evasive but pervasive, penetrating and incisive, going to the heart of the issues and providing wisdom for living.

4. *The question about the Messiah* (41-46). Jesus turns the table and becomes the Questioner. From the Pharisees, He extracts the popular concept of the Messiah, *the Son of David.* Quoting Ps. 110:1, regarded as messianic by the Jews until the Middle Ages, Jesus shows that Messiah can be no ordinary man, no temporal ruler. He is David's *Lord,* who shares the reign of Yahweh in the putting down of all His foes.

With this the interviews are closed, never to be reopened. The critics are silenced but not converted. They will answer Him next with whips and nails.

MATTHEW 23

Preaching Without Practice Condemned

Matthew 23:1-12

> 1 Then spake Jesus to the multitude, and to his disciples,
> 2 Saying, The scribes and the Pharisees sit in Moses' seat:
> 3 All therefore whatsoever they bid you observe, that observe and do; but do not ye after their works: for they say, and do not.
> 4 For they bind heavy burdens and grievous to be borne, and lay them on men's shoulders; but they themselves will not move them with one of their fingers.
> 5 But all their works they do for to be seen of men: they make broad their phylacteries, and enlarge the borders of their garments,
> 6 And love the uppermost rooms at feasts, and the chief seats in the synagogues,
> 7 And greetings in the markets, and to be called of men, Rabbi, Rabbi.
> 8 But be not ye called Rabbi: for one is your Master, even Christ; and all ye are brethren.
> 9 And call no man your father upon the earth: for one is your Father, which is in heaven.
> 10 Neither be ye called masters: for one is your Master, even Christ.
> 11 But he that is greatest among you shall be your servant.
> 12 And whosoever shall exalt himself shall be abased; and he that shall humble himself shall be exalted.

The scribes and Pharisees will not dare to question Jesus again (22:46). But they will continue to harass the disciples and influence the crowds. Jesus feels a responsibility for counteracting this influence, so He gives a warning to the crowds, and delivers *woes* to the scribes and Pharisees.

1. *He commends the preaching of the scribes and Pharisees.* "Practice and observe whatever they tell you" (3, RSV). Insofar as they occupy *Moses' seat,* i.e., insofar as they honestly interpret and apply the Mosaic law, they are to be obeyed.

The law is of God though the devil himself should teach it. False teachers do not invalidate the claims of truth. Jesus is guarding against a common mistake, that of equating the messenger with the message and rejecting both uncritically. The problem is twofold. Some imbibe heresy because they are attracted to its exponents: Surely they cannot be wrong in what they say, for they are so right in what they do! Others disown truth because they are repulsed by its bearers: How can the teaching be true if the teacher is false? Both responses are gullible. Jesus warns against the fallacy of *ad hominem* argument. God's law must be honored though insincere or misguided men teach it.

2. *He condemns the practice of the scribes and Pharisees.* *"They preach, but do not practice"* (3, RSV). They say one thing but do another. The continued discussion indicts these false teachers on two counts.

They are loveless (4). They burden men but do not help them. The *heavy burdens* mentioned here are the multiplicity of rules imposed by scribal tradition which left the average person confused and bound. Law became legalism. Religion bore men down when it should have borne them up. They would not lift a finger to ease the burden, for they equated their traditions with divine revelation (cf. 15:3-9).

And they are proud. They seek honor from men, not from God. *They do all their deeds to be seen by men* (5, RSV). Jesus scorns the enlarged phylacteries fashionable with the Pharisees. These were little containers fastened around the head and on the arms with leather thongs, in which copies of certain scripture passages were carried, literalizing Deut. 6:8. These, with the enlarged tassels at the corners of their robes, were advertisements of superior piety! See how holy we are! These same men scrambled for conspicuous seats at the feasts and in the synagogues, and they thrived on the deferential greetings from men in public places.

By contrast, our Lord's followers are to be *brethren* (8), avoiding distinctions of class and seeking no honors from men. Titles that have become terms of flattery and adulation, such as *rabbi, father,* and *master,* they are to shun. The authority of the one Father in heaven and the one Master on earth is not to be arrogated by or conferred upon men.

The sins of pride and self-seeking which Jesus condemns have been sadly repeated throughout the history of the Church. Within the institution that bears the name of Christ there have been many with a "big I and little you" attitude. As these Pharisees did not represent the true meaning of the law, so ecclesiastical bureaucrats with bloated egos do not represent the genius of the gospel. And if the loveless pride of the Pharisees did not excuse men from the claims of the law, neither does the disgusting place-seeking of Christians exempt men from the claims of the gospel.

In Christ's kingdom greatness is measured by service, and the way up is down (11-12). God exalts the humble and abases the proud. The Church has no Father but God, no Master but Jesus. And its only meaningful title for men is *brother*. To "brother" a man, after all, is much harder than to "doctor" him!

The Seven Woes

Matthew 23:13-36

13 But woe unto you, scribes and Pharisees, hypocrites! for ye shut up the kingdom of heaven against men: for ye neither go in yourselves, neither suffer ye them that are entering to go in.
14 Woe unto you, scribes and Pharisees, hypocrites! for ye devour widows' houses, and for a pretence make long prayer: therefore ye shall receive the greater damnation.
15 Woe unto you, scribes and Pharisees, hypocrites! for ye compass sea and land to make one proselyte, and when he is made, ye make him twofold more the child of hell than yourselves.
16 Woe unto you, ye blind guides, which say, Whosoever shall swear by the temple, it is nothing; but whosoever shall swear by the gold of the temple, he is a debtor!
17 Ye fools and blind: for whether is greater, the gold, or the temple that sanctifieth the gold?
18 And, Whosoever shall swear by the altar, it is nothing; but whosoever sweareth by the gift that is upon it, he is guilty.
19 Ye fools and blind: for whether is greater, the gift, or the altar that sanctifieth the gift?
20 Whoso therefore shall swear by the altar, sweareth by it, and by all things thereon.
21 And whoso shall swear by the temple, sweareth by it, and by him that dwelleth therein.
22 And he that shall swear by heaven, sweareth by the throne of God, and by him that sitteth thereon.
23 Woe unto you, scribes and Pharisees, hypocrites! for ye pay tithe of mint and anise and cummin, and have omitted the weightier matters of the law, judgment, mercy, and faith: these ought ye to have done, and not to leave the other undone.
24 Ye blind guides, which strain at a gnat, and swallow a camel.

25 Woe unto you, scribes and Pharisees, hypocrites! for ye make clean the outside of the cup and of the platter, but within they are full of extortion and excess.

26 Thou blind Pharisee, cleanse first that which is within the cup and platter, that the outside of them may be clean also.

27 Woe unto you, scribes and Pharisees, hypocrites! for ye are like unto whited sepulchres, which indeed appear beautiful outward, but are within full of dead men's bones, and of all uncleanness.

28 Even so ye also outwardly appear righteous unto men, but within ye are full of hypocrisy and iniquity.

29 Woe unto you, scribes and Pharisees, hypocrites! because ye build the tombs of the prophets, and garnish the sepulchres of the righteous,

30 And say, If we had been in the days of our fathers, we would not have been partakers with them in the blood of the prophets.

31 Wherefore ye be witnesses unto yourselves, that ye are the children of them which killed the prophets.

32 Fill ye up then the measure of your fathers.

33 Ye serpents, ye generation of vipers, how can ye escape the damnation of hell?

34 Wherefore, behold, I send unto you prophets, and wise men, and scribes: and some of them ye shall kill and crucify; and some of them shall ye scourge in your synagogues, and persecute them from city to city:

35 That upon you may come all the righteous blood shed upon the earth, from the blood of righteous Abel unto the blood of Zacharias son of Barachias, whom ye slew between the temple and the altar.

36 Verily I say unto you, All these things shall come upon this generation.

Jesus taught His disciples to respect the office of the scribes and Pharisees even when they could not respect the lives of the officeholders. Now He makes it clear that the dignity of the office does not immunize the insincere professors from judgment. He who taught, *Blessed are ye* (5:1-12), now as often repeats, *Woe unto you!*

1. *The description of the scribes and Pharisees.* Seven terms are used in this withering reproof of religious leaders who preached but did not practice. Jesus' speech is as colorful as His mood was indignant.

He called them *hypocrites* again and again. The term does not imply a conscious effort to deceive. Indeed, they were blind to their own faults. But it does mark a deep chasm between profession of loyalty to the law and practice of the law. The dichotomy is always present when love is extracted from righteousness, allowing law to become legalism.

Child of hell (15, lit., Gehenna) is the second term of

reproach. By nature they were suited for the place of ultimate punishment symbolized by the city's burning garbage dump.

Jesus calls them *blind guides* and *fools*. Purporting to be leaders, they have missed the way themselves. Not having a "single eye" (cf. 6:22-24), they have become spiritually darkened. Fools, in Hebrew wisdom literature, are set in contrast to the wise. These leaders do not possess that fear of God which is the beginning of wisdom.

Whitewashed tombs (27, RSV) is graphic and strong. The outward appearance of piety covers a heart filled with the moral putrefaction of hate, greed, ambition, and self-exaltation.

They are murderers, *sons of those who murdered the prophets* (31, RSV). Sonship is not biological descent but moral resemblance (cf. John 8:39-47; Matt. 5:43-48). Like father, like son! They evidence the same hostility to truth that prompted their ancestors to kill the prophets.

Finally, they are *serpents* (33), a traditional figure for the deadly and deceptive influences which oppose God and destroy men.

2. *The denunciation of the scribes and Pharisees.* The vigorous language employed was suited to the character and conduct of these religious leaders. The severity of Jesus' denunciations, therefore, need not surprise us.

He employs the ancient prophetic "woe" form of reproof (cf. Isa. 5:8-23). The solemn "woe" does not indicate petulant anger but holy wrath. God cannot be passive toward sin. Where repentance is refused, forgiveness is impossible, and judgment becomes inevitable. The impressive bill of charges vindicates the awful severity of punishment.

The woes are provoked by a damning influence (13-15). With a "dog in the manger" attitude the Pharisees refused to enter the Kingdom, and by their hostility they intimidated others from entering. They blocked the way to salvation and opened the way to damnation, making their proselytes sons of Gehenna.

The woes are provoked by a trifling religion (16-23).

These Pharisees distinguished between binding and non-binding oaths. Thus, if one swore *by the gold of the temple, he is a debtor!* But the same vows could be supported by swearing *by the temple,* and then *it is nothing,* i.e., non-obligatory. If a man was careful in phrasing his oaths he would not have to keep them. In similar vein, the scribes and Pharisees tithed even the garden herbs, but they felt no obligation to *justice and mercy and faith* (23, RSV). "They magnified trifles and trifled with magnitudes," straining out gnats and swallowing down camels!

The woes are provoked by a pretended righteousness (24-28). Like dishes clean on the outside, like tombs splashed with whitewash, these leaders were inwardly corrupt, rapaciously extorting for themselves what should have been others'. Their meticulously washed utensils held food dishonestly obtained. To avoid accidental defiling contact with a grave, the tombs were conspicuously marked, the fair exterior a contrast to the decay within. So the outward life of scrupulous piety concealed an inner deadness toward God.

The woes are provoked by the murdered prophets (29-36). These hypocrites praise the prophets who are dead and reject those who are living. They will fill the cup of iniquity to overflowing, surpassing the guilt of their fathers, by killing Jesus and those whom He will send with His gospel. The awesome judgment that will befall the city and nation avenges every martyr mentioned in the Old Testament, from Abel, the first, to Zechariah, the last. God permits His messengers to be slain, but their deaths are not to remain forever unvindicated.

Still today the choice before each of us what it was to the contemporaries of Jesus. We choose the "blesseds" or we choose the "woes."

Ownership Transferred, Property Doomed

Matthew 23:37—24:2

> 37 O Jerusalem, Jerusalem, thou that killest the prophets, and stonest them which are sent unto thee, how often would I have gathered thy children together, even as a hen gathereth her chickens under her wings, and ye would not!
> 38 Behold, your house is left unto you desolate.

39 For I say unto you, Ye shall not see me henceforth, till ye shall say, Blessed is he that cometh in the name of the Lord.

1 And Jesus went out, and departed from the temple: and his disciples came to him for to shew him the buildings of the temple.
2 And Jesus said unto them, See ye not all these things? verily I say unto you, There shall not be left here one stone upon another, that shall not be thrown down.

The denunciation of the impenitent leaders is followed by a lamentation over the city of Jerusalem, the civil and religious heart of a nation that had repeatedly stoned and killed God's messengers, and soon would execute His Son.

The glory of the city is its vast and magnificent Temple, bustling with religious life that belies its spiritual death. Soon it will be *desolate,* an inexorable fate that breaks the heart of Jesus. No more pathetic and sobering eloquence can be found in literature.

1. *Ownership is transferred.* When Jesus cleansed the Temple, He said, *My house shall be called the house of prayer* (21:13). Now He says, closing His public ministry, *Behold, your house is forsaken and desolate* (38, RSV). "My house . . . your house"! How terrible! Between these sayings lay the rejection of His authority as rightful Lord of the Temple (21:23-27). They insisted upon having their own way. They will run city and Temple in defiance of His cleansing protest. And He gives it to them!

The conflict which produced this judgment has been accumulating in intensity since the first "conflict story" in chapter 9. The entire clash is here summed up in His words, *"How often would I have gathered your children together as a hen gathers her brood under her wings, and you would not!"* (37, RSV). "I would . . . you would not!" The compassionate will of Jesus opposed by the obstinate will of men; He longing to save, they refusing to repent. And now He withdraws, sadly leaving them to the judgment necessitated by their abuse of freedom.

2. *Property is doomed.* The house will be *forsaken and desolate* (38, RSV), i.e., abandoned by God. Then it will be *thrown down* (24:2), i.e., destroyed by men. A few years later this prophecy of doom was bloodily fulfilled.

What God deserts, men can destroy. The security of the city did not rest in the money of the Sadducees or the piety of the Pharisees, but in a right response to the ministry of Jesus. That rejected, and nothing can avert doom, not the wealth of its commerce, not the zeal of its religion.

The words of Jesus deeply disturbed His own followers, and they pointed out to Him the ornate and impressive architecture of the Temple complex. But artifacts of human culture, however elaborate, costly, and enduring, cannot be fetishes to ward off the righteous judgments of God. *"Truly, I say to you, there will not be left here one stone upon another"* (2, RSV).

The language is not woodenly literal, but vividly true. Some parts of the foundation of that Temple exist today, and that little patch of stones, so dear to pious Jews, called the Wailing Wall. These insignificant remains bear mute testimony to His words, whom the nation that was His own will continue to reject until His *parousia*.

Christian, this passage has a searching message for you. The author of Hebrews declared that God's house is His people, over whom Christ is the High Priest (Heb. 3:1-6). And Paul insists that the temple of God is the Church (Eph. 3:19-22) and the believer's body (1 Cor. 6:19-20). Where the lordship of Jesus is rejected, His house can become your house! With transfer of ownership there is condemnation of property.

Fifth Teaching Section:
The Eschatological Discourse
Matthew 24:3—25:46

The Signs of the End

Matthew 24:3-35

3 And as he sat upon the mount of Olives, the disciples came unto him privately, saying, Tell us, when shall these things be? and what shall be the sign of thy coming, and of the end of the world?

4 And Jesus answered and said unto them, Take heed that no man deceive you.

5 For many shall come in my name, saying, I am Christ; and shall deceive many.

6 And ye shall hear of wars and rumours of wars: see that ye be not troubled: for all these things must come to pass, but the end is not yet.

7 For nation shall rise against nation, and kingdom against kingdom: and there shall be famines, and pestilences, and earthquakes, in divers places.

8 All these are the beginning of sorrows.

9 Then shall they deliver you up to be afflicted, and shall kill you: and ye shall be hated of all nations for my name's sake.

10 And then shall many be offended, and shall betray one another, and shall hate one another.

11 And many false prophets shall rise, and shall deceive many.

12 And because iniquity shall abound, the love of many shall wax cold.

13 But he that shall endure unto the end, the same shall be saved.

14 And this gospel of the kingdom shall be preached in all the world for a witness unto all nations; and then shall the end come.

15 When ye therefore shall see the abomination of desolation, spoken of by Daniel the prophet, stand in the holy place, (whoso readeth, let him understand:)

16 Then let them which be in Judaea flee into the mountains:

17 Let him which is on the housetop not come down to take any thing out of his house:

18 Neither let him which is in the field return back to take his clothes.

19 And woe unto them that are with child, and to them that give suck in those days!

20 But pray ye that your flight be not in the winter, neither on the sabbath day:

21 For then shall be great tribulation, such as was not since the beginning of the world to this time, no, nor ever shall be.

22 And except those days should be shortened, there should no flesh be saved: but for the elect's sake those days shall be shortened.

23 Then if any man shall say unto you, Lo, here is Christ, or there; believe it not.

24 For there shall arise false Christs, and false prophets, and shall

shew great signs and wonders; insomuch that, if it were possible, they shall deceive the very elect.

25 Behold, I have told you before.

26 Wherefore if they shall say unto you, Behold, he is in the desert; go not forth: behold, he is in the secret chambers; believe it not.

27 For as the lightning cometh out of the east, and shineth even unto the west; so shall also the coming of the Son of man be.

28 For wheresoever the carcase is, there will the eagles be gathered together.

29 Immediately after the tribulation of those days shall the sun be darkened, and the moon shall not give her light, and the stars shall fall from heaven, and the powers of the heavens shall be shaken:

30 And then shall appear the sign of the Son of man in heaven: and then shall all the tribes of the earth mourn, and they shall see the Son of man coming in the clouds of heaven with power and great glory.

31 And he shall send his angels with a great sound of a trumpet, and they shall gather together his elect from the four winds, from one end of heaven to the other.

32 Now learn a parable of the fig tree; When his branch is yet tender, and putteth forth leaves, ye know that summer is nigh:

33 So likewise ye, when ye shall see all these things, know that it is near, even at the doors.

34 Verily I say unto you, This generation shall not pass, till all these things be fulfilled.

35 Heaven and earth shall pass away, but my words shall not pass away.

Jesus departed from the Temple, never to enter it again. From this point what teaching remains to be done will involve only His disciples. The crowds and the critics are no longer in class!

Troubled by His severe denunciation of the Jewish leaders, and by His sorrowful lamentation over Jerusalem, the disciples ask about the signs which will betoken the fall of the city and the coming of the Lord. His reply constitutes the "Olivet Discourse," which is the last of the five blocks of teaching material forming the vertebrae of Matthew's Gospel (cc. 24—25).

This section is an extremely difficult one for exegesis. The task is not simplified by those who are cocksure of its detailed meaning, and in their zeal for a particular tradition of interpretation have sometimes made their tradition a test of orthodoxy, and even of fellowship. Consult the commentaries; but here, as perhaps nowhere else, the caveat of A. M. Hunter is wise: "Don't expect too much of commentaries."

This section is concerned with signs, warnings, and promises.

1. *Signs.* The sign *par excellence* is *the sign of the Son of man in heaven* (30). The Greek construction may indicate that the Son of Man is himself the Sign. The *end of the world* (3), i.e., the close of the age, will be signified by the visible return of Christ. He who came as a Servant and was slain will come in power and glory as our final Judge, an event that will occasion both rejoicing and mourning (30-31).

Meanwhile, there will be false signs wrought by false messiahs and false prophets: *"For false Christs and false prophets will arise and show great signs and wonders, so as to lead astray, if possible, even the elect"* (24, RSV). This passage is calculated to give us pause today, with the proliferation of gurus, witches, astrologers, and political messiahs that plague our nation and the world. Whether this section relates to the fall of Jerusalem or to the yet future end is of little consequence. False messiahs and prophets with deceptive wonders have been a continuing element of history.

Before the end, and along with the false signs, will be other signs, legitimate pointers and indicators of the approaching *eschaton.* These pointers seem to include (1) false messiahs; (2) world evangelism (14); and (3) great tribulation (21).

2. *Warnings.* Because enemies of Christ and the gospel will be busy until the end, warnings are in order for His disciples.

Disciples are warned against (1) deception (4-5, 11, 24-25); (2) apostasy (10); and (3) coldness (12-13). These are not unrelated. Falling away takes place only when the heart grows cold, and nothing cools Christian ardor more effectively than heretical teachings.

3. *Promises.* Threatened disciples, throughout the age between the advents, are sustained by precious promises.

There is a promise of unfailing grace. This is not stated but certainly implied in v. 13: *"But he who endures to the end will be saved"* (RSV). Christians can endure because Christ continually ministers grace to them, enabling them to press on in the face of deception, threats, wars, persecution, and abounding iniquity.

There is also a promise of unfailing truth: *Heaven and earth shall pass away, but my words shall not pass away* (35). As sure as the budding of the fig tree is a harbinger of summer, the fulfillment of the signs heralds the nearness of the Son of Man's coming. History moves toward a God-appointed goal. Soon or late, the divine purpose will be consummated. His word is a sufficient guarantee.

And when He comes, we will know. The glory of His presence will be as impossible to conceal as the brilliance of lightning (27).

The Wisdom of Watching

Matthew 24:36-51

36 But of that day and hour knoweth no man, no, not the angels of heaven, but my Father only.
37 But as the days of Noe were, so shall also the coming of the Son of man be.
38 For as in the days that were before the flood they were eating and drinking, marrying and giving in marriage, until the day that Noe entered into the ark,
39 And knew not until the flood came, and took them all away; so shall also the coming of the Son of man be.
40 Then shall two be in the field; the one shall be taken, and the other left.
41 Two women shall be grinding at the mill; the one shall be taken, and the other left.
42 Watch therefore: for ye know not what hour your Lord doth come.
43 But know this, that if the goodman of the house had known in what watch the thief would come, he would have watched, and would not have suffered his house to be broken up.
44 Therefore be ye also ready: for in such an hour as ye think not the Son of man cometh.
45 Who then is a faithful and wise servant, whom his lord hath made ruler over his household, to give them meat in due season?
46 Blessed is that servant, whom his lord when he cometh shall find so doing.
47 Verily I say unto you, That he shall make him ruler over all his goods.
48 But and if that evil servant shall say in his heart, My lord delayeth his coming;
49 And shall begin to smite his fellowservants, and to eat and drink with the drunken;
50 The lord of that servant shall come in a day when he looketh not for him, and in an hour that he is not aware of,
51 And shall cut him asunder, and appoint him his portion with the hypocrites: there shall be weeping and gnashing of teeth.

One Person, and one only, knows the *day and hour* of Christ's coming. Some have pretended to know and have caused embarrassment and grief to their followers. Others pretend to know at least the year or the decade within which the Lord will return. They may survive as "prophets" if their readers have short memories and soft brains.

The day is unknown but the event is certain. The scriptures are too explicit on this subject for efforts to explain away the Second Advent to be convincing. The only rational attitude for the believer, therefore, is to *watch*, to be spiritually alert and constantly prepared for the denouement of history.

1. *The coming of the Son of Man will be sudden* (36-39). It will interrupt normal events. The references to eating, drinking, marrying, working in fields, and grinding at mills do not suggest that these activities are wrong. The point is simply that his coming will interrupt "business as usual." The only wrong is in being so exclusively devoted to secular activities that spiritual affairs are ignored. This, of course, results from unbelieving rejection of God's messengers, as Noah's contemporaries scorned his preaching and were caught in helpless exposure to the judgment of the Flood.

But the event which interrupts normal routines of life will bring salvation to those who believe. Reference to the ark accents the availability of deliverance from the judgment upon evil.

2. *The coming of the Son of Man will be separative* (40-51). As those in the ark were saved, and others were swept away, so division will occur at the end. Noah's family was saved, but the references to *two* in the field, and *two* at the mill, with one *taken* and *the other left* in each case, point to separations occurring within family groups (cf. 10:34-39).

The element of division is continued in the parable of the *wise* and *evil* servants. The wise servant faithfully discharges the responsibilities assigned him by his master. The wicked servant, assuming the master's return to be remote, mistreats his fellows and disgraces his master. The sudden return of the master brings reward to the wise servant, punishment to the wicked servant.

The reward is promotion to greater responsibilities, not the imposition of forced retirement! Life beyond the Lord's return will not be dull and static! The punishment is expressed in awesome language. The wicked servant is cut in two (Gk., *dichotomesei*). Parallels in Psalm 37, and in the Qumran literature, support the meaning of exclusion from the covenant people of God, with all the pain and rage this produces.

The thrust of the passage is clear. Life must go on, with attention to routine necessities, such as plowing, grinding, feeding, etc. But life should be lived in readiness for the Lord's coming, not in indolence, carelessness, or unbelief. For His coming means salvation for those who live in obedience to His Word, and destruction for those who ignore and reject His Word.

As a thief plunders a home without announcing his visit, so the coming of the Son of Man will be sudden, surprising, and separating. *Watch therefore!* And watching means faithful, obedient service to His will.

MATTHEW 25

The Ten Virgins

Matthew 25:1-13

> 1 Then shall the kingdom of heaven be likened unto ten virgins, which took their lamps, and went forth to meet the bridegroom.
> 2 And five of them were wise, and five were foolish.
> 3 They that were foolish took their lamps, and took no oil with them:
> 4 But the wise took oil in their vessels with their lamps.
> 5 While the bridegroom tarried, they all slumbered and slept.
> 6 And at midnight there was a cry made, Behold, the bridegroom cometh; go ye out to meet him.
> 7 Then all those virgins arose, and trimmed their lamps.
> 8 And the foolish said unto the wise, Give us of your oil; for our lamps are gone out.
> 9 But the wise answered, saying, Not so; lest there be not enough for us and you: but go ye rather to them that sell, and buy for yourselves.
> 10 And while they went to buy, the bridegroom came; and they that were ready went in with him to the marriage: and the door was shut.
> 11 Afterward came also the other virgins, saying, Lord, Lord, open to us.
> 12 But he answered and said, Verily I say unto you, I know you not.
> 13 Watch therefore, for ye know neither the day nor the hour wherein the Son of man cometh.

The importance of constant readiness for the Son of Man's coming is underlined by a second parable. Here the contrast is not between wise and wicked, but between *wise* and *foolish.* The Anchor Bible uses the predicate adjectives "sensible" and "silly." The foolish bridesmaids are not indicted for gross sins, as was the wicked servant (24: 49), but for imprudence, for failure to be adequately prepared in the situation. Three factors stand out.

1. *The unexpected delay. The bridegroom tarried.* No reason is given. All kinds of things occasion delay in wedding plans! Precisely because delays were common in such situations, unpreparedness was inexcusable.

The coming of Christ is delayed in the estimate of every succeeding generation of Christians. Despairing of man's efforts to produce a just society, and believing that His return to reign is the world's only hope, we are eager for the *parousia.* Our very eagerness makes the interval seem to drag past.

In this case the anticipation of a joyful wedding feast makes the delay seem interminable. The joy of Christ's presence and reign stands in such contrast with the woes and wars of this age, who would not be eager for His appearing?

The unexpected delay becomes a test of faith. Not to lose hope, not to dismiss the promise, but to continue in readiness *to meet him* at the midnight cry is our challenge.

2. *The unprepared maidens.* The stress of the parable is negative, on the *foolish* virgins, rather than on the *wise.* The wise meet the bridegroom and enter into the wedding feast. The foolish miss out for two reasons.

The first reason is insufficient oil. Their lamps were going out. They did not think ahead and provide themselves with an adequate supply in the event of a delay. The wise refuse to share their own supply, an attitude that on the surface appears selfish and churlish. But a significant point is made: One cannot prepare for Christ's coming by proxy!

The second reason is insufficient time. The improvident maidens rush away to procure oil, but they arrive back too late to share the festivities. This is the focal point of the story: We must be prepared, for a time comes when it is too late to get prepared!

3. *The unopened door. The door was shut.* There is a chilling finality to those simple words.

In the pleas of the foolish virgins, *Lord* is vainly used. *Lord, Lord, open to us,* is a hollow address when His lordship has been repudiated by the very failure to be prepared as He commanded. Here, as everywhere in Matthew, there can be no substitute for obedience to His words (cf. 7:21-23).

In the reply of the bridegroom, lordship is seriously exercised. The saying is prefaced with that solemn formula which evidences the unique, divine authority of Jesus (cf. 5:18f.): *Amen, I say to you* (lit.). The saying is brief, *I know you not,* but never have such short and simple words been more heavily freighted with destiny. To have been known here, even by applauding throngs, will mean nothing if He does not know us then!

The story is closed with the admonition to *watch,* which in this section of Matthew is synonymous with being ready. To watch, in this immediate context, is to be prepared for whatever "delay" may happen, to be adequately prepared while there is yet time for getting ready. The urgency of decision now cannot be exaggerated.

The Parable of the Talents

Matthew 25:14-30

> 14 For the kingdom of heaven is as a man travelling into a far country, who called his own servants, and delivered unto them his goods.
> 15 And unto one he gave five talents, to another two, and to another one; to every man according to his several ability; and straightway took his journey.
> 16 Then he that had received the five talents went and traded with the same, and made them other five talents.
> 17 And likewise he that had received two, he also gained other two.
> 18 But he that had received one went and digged in the earth, and hid his lord's money.
> 19 After a long time the lord of those servants cometh, and reckoneth with them.
> 20 And so he that had received five talents came and brought other five talents, saying, Lord, thou deliveredst unto me five talents: behold, I have gained beside them five talents more.
> 21 His lord said unto him, Well done, thou good and faithful servant: thou hast been faithful over a few things, I will make thee ruler over many things: enter thou into the joy of thy lord.
> 22 He also that had received two talents came and said, Lord, thou deliveredst unto me two talents: behold, I have gained two other talents beside them.
> 23 His lord said unto him, Well done, good and faithful servant; thou

> hast been faithful over a few things, I will make thee ruler over many things: enter thou into the joy of thy lord.
>
> 24 Then he which had received the one talent came and said, Lord, I knew thee that thou art an hard man, reaping where thou hast not sown, and gathering where thou hast not strawed:
>
> 25 And I was afraid, and went and hid thy talent in the earth: lo, there thou hast that is thine.
>
> 26 His lord answered and said unto him, Thou wicked and slothful servant, thou knewest that I reap where I sowed not, and gather where I have not strawed:
>
> 27 Thou oughtest therefore to have put my money to the exchangers, and then at my coming I should have received mine own with usury.
>
> 28 Take therefore the talent from him, and give it unto him which hath ten talents.
>
> 29 For unto every one that hath shall be given, and he shall have abundance: but from him that hath not shall be taken away even that which he hath.
>
> 30 And cast ye the unprofitable servant into outer darkness: there shall be weeping and gnashing of teeth.

This parable continues the theme of readiness for the coming of the Son of Man. The emphasis now is placed on the accounting that must be made to Him by His disciples upon His return. Two features dominate the story, the distribution of resources and the settling of accounts.

1. *The Lord distributes resources* (14-18). Prior to leaving, the lord calls his servants and provides them with money for conducting business in his interest during his absence. The amounts vary because they are given to each *according to his several ability* (15). The talents represent the gifts and opportunities for service which Christ gives His followers, on the basis of their ability to use and improve them in the work of the Kingdom.

The distribution of resources does two things: (1) It creates opportunity, and (2) It imposes obligation. As the abilities and resources are varied, so the opportunities are varied. But each servant is given something to invest. The impossible is not demanded, but the unattempted will not be excused.

2. *The Lord settles accounts* (19-30). The second movement in the story makes three points.

a. First, the return is delayed. The Lord comes *after a long time.* To see in such phrases an invention of the Early Church to deal with the embarrassment created by a continuing interval between the Cross and the *parousia* is gratuitous. That Jesus expected the eschatological Kingdom, and died disappointed, has its source in the imagination of critics, not in the text. An unknown date would have to raise two possibilities, an imminent end or a delayed end. Wisdom would dictate the necessity of constant readiness and continuing faithfulness. The delay, by human reckoning, was an occasion for scoffing in the first century of church history, and has been ever since. But the Son of Man will come, and judgment will ensue (2 Peter 3).

b. Second, the faithful are rewarded. Two of the servants doubled their investment, and each is commended in the same terms: *Well done, thou good and faithful servant* (21). Here goodness and faithfulness are virtually synonymous. Standing in this Gospel, where Jesus is heard frequently opposing legalism, the statement speaks volumes to our common notion of being good. Goodness is not adherence to a list of rules; it is faithfulness in the performance of Kingdom service. Being faithful is good; goodness is being faithful.

The rewards are twofold. (1) They take the form of increased responsibility. *"You have been faithful over a little, I will set you over much"* (21, 23 RSV). Service to the Lord continues beyond the time of reckoning (cf. 19:27-29; 24:45-47). The eternal order is not one of inactivity and boredom! (2) They take the form of superlative joy. *"Enter into the joy of your master"* (RSV). The joy of the consummated kingdom of God is alike the experience of Master and servants (cf. Heb. 12:2). It is a fellowship that no present delight can approach.

c. Third, the unfaithful is punished. The last servant forms a vivid contrast to the others. He has made no investment, reaped no profit, and feels vindicated because he can return the talent entrusted to him.

He excuses his failure on the ground of fear; *I was afraid* (25). And he rationalizes his fear by slandering his lord's character, accusing him of being an austere man who seized the produce of other men's toil. Because he could not keep the profits, this servant would not make the investment. He is rebuked for being *wicked and slothful* (26). Like *good and faithful,* the terms are interchangeable. To be wicked is not merely a matter of gross misconduct, as in 21:48-49. It is a matter of indolence in the face of Kingdom-service opportunities. Hell is also for those who do nothing!

As the rewards were twofold, so is the punishment. (1) The wicked servant is punished with the loss of further opportunity: *Take therefore the talent from him* (28). (2) The wicked servant is punished with the loss of the Lord's presence: *Cast ye the unprofitable servant into outer darkness* (30). Exclusion from the joy of the consummated kingdom of God is indescribably horrible. *Weeping and gnashing of teeth* only weakly conveys the horror of the reality.

The Final Judgment

Matthew 25:31-46

> 31 When the Son of man shall come in his glory, and all the holy angels with him, then shall he sit upon the throne of his glory:
> 32 And before him shall be gathered all nations: and he shall separate them one from another, as a shepherd divideth his sheep from the goats:
> 33 And he shall set the sheep on his right hand, but the goats on the left.
> 34 Then shall the King say unto them on his right hand, Come, ye blessed of my Father, inherit the kingdom prepared for you from the foundation of the world:
> 35 For I was an hungred, and ye gave me meat: I was thirsty, and ye gave me drink: I was a stranger, and ye took me in:
> 36 Naked, and ye clothed me: I was sick, and ye visited me: I was in prison, and ye came unto me.
> 37 Then shall the righteous answer him, saying, Lord, when saw we thee an hungred, and fed thee? or thirsty, and gave thee drink?
> 38 When saw we thee a stranger, and took thee in? or naked, and clothed thee?
> 39 Or when saw we thee sick, or in prison, and came unto thee?
> 40 And the King shall answer and say unto them, Verily I say unto you, Inasmuch as ye have done it unto one of the least of these my brethren, ye have done it unto me.
> 41 Then shall he say also unto them on the left hand, Depart from me, ye cursed, into everlasting fire, prepared for the devil and his angels:
> 42 For I was an hungred, and ye gave me no meat: I was thirsty, and ye gave me no drink:
> 43 I was a stranger, and ye took me not in: naked, and ye clothed me not: sick, and in prison, and ye visited me not.
> 44 Then shall they also answer him, saying, Lord, when saw we thee an hungred, or athirst, or a stranger, or naked, or sick, or in prison, and did not minister unto thee?
> 45 Then shall he answer them, saying, Verily I say unto you, Inasmuch as ye did it not to one of the least of these, ye did it not to me.
> 46 And these shall go away into everlasting punishment: but the righteous into life eternal.

Then (1) becomes *when* (31). However long the delay, the Son of Man will come *in his glory.* He came in deep humility, and occupied a cross. He will come in glorious majesty and occupy a *throne.* His throne of grace is now accessible to all who seek His mercy (Heb. 4:14-16). His *throne of . . . glory* will be the scene of judgment.

A time and title change occurs at verse 34. *Then shall the King say . . .* Some understand the references in Matthew to the coming of the Son of Man to mean His coming to God, namely, in the event of His crucifixion-exaltation, and not to mean His coming in a Second Advent. The division in vv. 32-33 would take place as the result of right or wrong responses to the ministry of Jesus as the Son of Man, which is climaxed at the Crucifixion-Exaltation. *Then* would refer to the eschatological judgment, of which the present divisions are proleptic, and which carries these divisions to their final consequences. The traditional understanding, however, regards *then* as a simple connective which carries forward the action. *When* He comes, *then* He will say. By either interpretation the reality of the *eschaton* and the depiction of a final judgment are upheld.

Three issues in this judgment scene call for consideration.

1. *The separation effected.* A note of inclusiveness is sounded: *Before him shall be gathered all nations* (32). The Son of Man is not King of the Jews only, but of all the earth. To Him every nation and person is ultimately accountable.

A note of exclusiveness is also sounded: *"He will separate them one from another as a shepherd separates the sheep from the goats"* (32, RSV). Jesus is already a Divider of men (cf. 10:34-39). The end-time division is not to be anticipated by men who would usurp His prerogative of judgment (13:24-30). Nevertheless, the final separation only confirms the division now being effected by the differing responses of men to His gospel of the kingdom of God.

2. *The sentences announced.* To those on the right an invitation is given. *"Come . . . inherit the kingdom prepared for you"* (34, RSV). The *kingdom* of God, in its final mani-

festation, is the inheritance of those who belong to the King. These are designated as *the righteous,* and their inheritance as *life eternal,* in v. 46.

The sheep, the righteous, are those who have committed themselves to follow Jesus, and to express that commitment by a service to human need which extends the ministry He himself began among men.

Eternal life is the endless and boundless fellowship which the righteous shall have with God and one another.

For those on the left a rejection is voiced. *Depart . . . into everlasting fire* (41). There is no ground for fellowship between Him who is identified with the needy of earth and these who have lived in selfish disregard of others.

The *kingdom* was prepared for those who enter it, but not so the *fire!* God did not prepare hell for men or men for hell. Hell is the self-chosen fate of those who refuse the Kingdom. The whole ministry of the Messiah is represented as the conflict of God's kingdom with Satan's kingdom. To remain in the devil's kingdom is to share the devil's fate.

3. *The surprises registered.* The *righteous* are surprised to learn that their spontaneous love-response to human need was service to Christ himself. The *cursed* are surprised to learn that selfish neglect of the homeless, hungry, and hurting about them was neglect of Christ himself. The source of surprise is the solidarity of Christ with His people, a blessed and serious truth of scripture fraught with implications for salvation or damnation.

The whole dialogue has been surprising to many religious people because of the materiality of the actions the King approves. Food, water, clothes, shelter, medicine, friendship! Why, we thought the judgment would turn on "spiritual" issues, such as fasting, tithing, Bible reading, tract distribution, and Sunday school going!

Sixth Narrative Section:
The Passion Story
Matthew 26:1—28:20

MATTHEW 26

Poured-out Love

Matthew 26:1-16

1 And it came to pass, when Jesus had finished all these sayings, he said unto his disciples,
2 Ye know that after two days is the feast of the passover, and the Son of man is betrayed to be crucified.
3 Then assembled together the chief priests, and the scribes, and the elders of the people, unto the palace of the high priest, who was called Caiaphas,
4 And consulted that they might take Jesus by subtilty, and kill him.
5 But they said, Not on the feast day, lest there be an uproar among the people.
6 Now when Jesus was in Bethany, in the house of Simon the leper,
7 There came unto him a woman having an alabaster box of very precious ointment, and poured it on his head, as he sat at meat.
8 But when his disciples saw it, they had indignation, saying, To what purpose is this waste?
9 For this ointment might have been sold for much, and given to the poor.
10 When Jesus understood it, he said unto them, Why trouble ye the woman? for she hath wrought a good work upon me.
11 For ye have the poor always with you; but me ye have not always.
12 For in that she hath poured this ointment on my body, she did it for my burial.
13 Verily I say unto you, Wheresoever this gospel shall be preached in the whole world, there shall also this, that this woman hath done, be told for a memorial of her.
14 Then one of the twelve, called Judas Iscariot, went unto the chief priests,
15 And said unto them, What will ye give me, and I will deliver him unto you? And they covenanted with him for thirty pieces of silver.
16 And from that time he sought opportunity to betray him.

Chapter 26 opens with Matthew's formula for marking the transition from a block of teaching to resumed narrative: *When Jesus had finished all these sayings.*

The Passover is at hand, and Jesus' mind is occupied with His coming death, a sacrifice that will result in a new Exodus, purchasing redemption for the slaves of sin and death. His passion-prediction once more contains the mystery so troubling to His disciples (then and now!), namely, that the Son of Man is a suffering Figure, not merely a ruling Figure.

This section contains references to the murderous counsel of the chief priests and the elders, to the treacherous bargain of Judas Iscariot, and to the anointing of Jesus by Mary of Bethany (not named in Matthew). Both love and hate are prominent in the passage.

1. *The outpouring of love* (6-13). While Jesus was dining as the Guest of a healed leper, Mary poured expensive ointment upon His head. John's Gospel tells us that His feet, too, were anointed.

The outpouring of love enacted by the woman was protested by the disciples: *They were indignant, saying, "Why this waste?"* (8, RSV). They justified *waste* by remarking aloud that the ointment could have been sold and the money *given to the poor.*

What they protested, Jesus defended. What they called *waste,* He called *a beautiful thing* (RSV). If they were concerned for the poor, they would never lack opportunity to help them. There would always be poor folks to serve, but Jesus would soon be taken away. Possibly the disciples were influenced by the parable of judgment in 25:36-46. But service to the needy is not the only way of ministering to Jesus, and as Broadus remarked, "Extraordinary occasions may justify extraordinary expenditures."

Jesus relates the anointing to His death, as a burial preparation. Whether this is what Mary intended we cannot say, but it is how He received it. This made it appropriate, for His death was an outpouring of love.

Jesus also related it to the preaching of the gospel throughout the world, for the gospel, too, is an outpouring of love. The story of the anointing, repeated throughout the centuries, is a *memorial* to Mary's gesture of love.

Whom they "troubled," He immortalized, and in so doing He reminds us that only what is done in love will last.

2. *The outpouring of hate* (14-16). This act of generous love is bracketed by two incidents of hate.

It is prefaced by the priestly plot to secretly arrest and kill Jesus (3-5). *Stealth* (4, RSV) is needed to prevent an uproar among the crowds who have but recently hailed Him as Messiah.

The anointing is followed by an account of Judas Iscariot's infamous bargain with the priests. Who can measure the pathos of that phrase, *one of the twelve!* One of the inner circle, who had benefited from Jesus the most, now treats Him the worst. His shame is compounded by the fact that he took the initiative. He *went unto the chief priests*. They did not seek him out and apply pressure on him. The betrayal was his idea.

Every attempt to analyze the motive of Judas has failed. All we really know is what is written. *"What will you give me if I deliver him to you?"* (15, RSV). On the face of it, greed seems to prompt him (cf. John 12:6). Did more complex motives lurk beneath the surface? We do not know. The mystery of iniquity defies understanding as well as the mystery of redeeming love.

Poor Judas! What he really set a price on was his own soul! And he sold himself too cheaply.

An Old Meal, a New Meaning

Matthew 26:17-29

17 Now the first day of the feast of unleavened bread the disciples came to Jesus, saying unto him, Where wilt thou that we prepare for thee to eat the passover?
18 And he said, Go into the city to such a man, and say unto him, The Master saith, My time is at hand; I will keep the passover at thy house with my disciples.
19 And the disciples did as Jesus had appointed them; and they made ready the passover.
20 Now when the even was come, he sat down with the twelve.
21 And as they did eat, he said, Verily I say unto you, that one of you shall betray me.
22 And they were exceeding sorrowful, and began every one of them to say unto him, Lord, is it I?
23 And he answered and said, He that dippeth his hand with me in the dish, the same shall betray me.
24 The Son of man goeth as it is written of him: but woe unto that man

by whom the Son of man is betrayed! it had been good for that man if he had not been born.
25 Then Judas, which betrayed him, answered and said, Master, is it I? He said unto him, Thou hast said.
26 And as they were eating, Jesus took bread, and blessed it, and brake it, and gave it to the disciples, and said, Take, eat; this is my body.
27 And he took the cup, and gave thanks, and gave it to them, saying, Drink ye all of it;
28 For this is my blood of the new testament, which is shed for many for the remission of sins.
29 But I say unto you, I will not drink henceforth of this fruit of the vine, until that day when I drink it new with you in my Father's kingdom.

Table fellowship played a significant part in Jesus' ministry. Now He will share a final meal with the Twelve before going to His death, and it will turn out to be the most significant meal in all history.

The supper took place in the borrowed room of an unnamed disciple, "Mr. X," to use Filson's designation. Whoever he was, he accepted Jesus' authority without question. *"The Teacher says"* (18, RSV) had for him the force of the prophet's formula, "Thus says the Lord."

The Passover was prepared and Jesus dined that evening with His inner circle. Two factors dominate the account in Matthew.

1. *The disciples' sorrow.* As they were eating, Jesus announced that one of them would betray him. The solemn formula, *Verily I say unto you,* indicates the deep pathos with which the betrayal was mentioned.

The reaction of the disciples is caught up in one terse phrase, *exceeding sorrowful.* Because He would be so ill-treated who deserved to be loyally loved? Because He could think for a moment that one of them would stoop to such treachery? One by one they ask, *Lord, is it I?* The question, in the Greek construction, anticipates a negative answer.

Jesus replies, *He that dippeth his hand with me in the dish* (23), which is another way of saying, *One of you,* since all had. But it emphasizes the tragic note. One who had enjoyed such intimate fellowship would be the traitor. A solemn *woe* (cf. 23:13 f.) is pronounced upon the betrayer, though his act will fulfill scripture. God works within the framework of man's freedom so that man remains responsible for all his deeds.

The reaction of Judas is evasive and revealing: *Master, is it I?* Not *Lord*, but Rabbi, Teacher, is his title for Jesus. Nowhere in the Gospels does Judas ever call Him Lord. The uncommitted life made possible the awful sellout. Jesus' words, *Thou hast said*, are an idiom with the force of a simple "yes."

2. *The Lord's Supper.* Taking bread and wine, Jesus instituted the new covenant. Jeremiah had predicted it, in a memorable passage highlighted by the promise of an intimate knowledge of God grounded upon the forgiveness of sin (Jer. 33:31-34).

The bread, blessed and broken, became a symbol of His body, soon to be broken at Calvary. The cup of wine became a symbol of His blood, to be *shed for many for the remission of sins* (28). This statement recalls Isa. 53:12, where the Suffering Servant dies to justify many.

How the death of Jesus can provide the forgiveness of sins, He does not explain. That it does, millions have testified. Experienced forgiveness is vastly more important than theological understanding. No theory of atonement has proven fully satisfying (the various theories have destroyed table fellowship because exponents were more zealous for logic than for love!), for there are unfathomable depths of mystery in any truly unique event, since man's knowledge is analogical.

The words of Jesus in v. 29 make the Lord's Supper an anticipation of the messianic banquet, the glorious fellowship of the fully manifested kingdom of God. Thus the Eucharist celebrated by the Church brings His death into the present from the past, and brings the kingdom of the Father into the present from the future. The sacrament is a visible word proclaiming the same gospel set forth in the audible word of preaching.

How ironic and tragic that what Jesus established in a setting of fellowship has become so divisive in the history of the Church!

A Place Called Gethsemane

Matthew 26:30-46

30   And when they had sung an hymn, they went out into the mount of Olives.
31   Then saith Jesus unto them, All ye shall be offended because of me this night: for it is written, I will smite the shepherd, and the sheep of the flock shall be scattered abroad.
32   But after I am risen again, I will go before you into Galilee.
33   Peter answered and said unto him, Though all men shall be offended because of thee, yet will I never be offended.
34   Jesus said unto him, Verily I say unto thee, That this night, before the cock crow, thou shalt deny me thrice.
35   Peter said unto him, Though I should die with thee, yet will I not deny thee. Likewise also said all the disciples.
36   Then cometh Jesus with them unto a place called Gethsemane, and saith unto the disciples, Sit ye here, while I go and pray yonder.
37   And he took with him Peter and the two sons of Zebedee, and began to be sorrowful and very heavy.
38   Then saith he unto them, My soul is exceeding sorrowful, even unto death: tarry ye here, and watch with me.
39   And he went a little farther, and fell on his face, and prayed, saying, O my Father, if it be possible, let this cup pass from me: nevertheless not as I will, but as thou wilt.
40   And he cometh unto the disciples, and findeth them asleep, and saith unto Peter, What, could ye not watch with me one hour?
41   Watch and pray, that ye enter not into temptation: the spirit indeed is willing, but the flesh is weak.
42   He went away again the second time, and prayed, saying, O my Father, if this cup may not pass away from me, except I drink it, thy will be done.
43   And he came and found them asleep again: for their eyes were heavy.
44   And he left them, and went away again, and prayed the third time, saying the same words.
45   Then cometh he to his disciples, and saith unto them, Sleep on now, and take your rest: behold, the hour is at hand, and the Son of man is betrayed into the hands of sinners.
46   Rise, let us be going: behold, he is at hand that doth betray me.

The supper ended with singing, probably the Hallel Psalms (113—118). Jesus then retired with His disciples to the Mount of Olives. He had predicted His betrayal, and now He predicts His denial. All of them will be scattered when He is smitten, but will be gathered and strengthened after His resurrection. One of them, and he the leader, the confessor (cf. 16:16), would three times over deny Him. Peter was unsure of the others, but confident of his own loyalty and courage: *"Though they all fall away because of you, I will never fall away"* (33, RSV). He insists that he will die with Jesus before he will deny Him. Peter was sincere. He meant every word of it. He was soon to find out what we all need to know, that sin and fear will drive men, in unguarded moments, to great depths of failure.

Following these sad predictions and vain protestations Matthew records the Gethsemane struggle. Against the backdrop of their weakness we view the testing and triumph of Christ's strength. Two features are salient, the sorrow of Jesus and the sleep of His disciples.

1. *The sorrowing Christ.* As He approached the place of prayer Jesus said, *My soul is exceeding sorrowful, even unto death* (38). The depth of that sorrow no human imagination can plumb. Sorrow so great that it threatens death wrings from the distressed Christ an appeal for sympathetic companionship: *Watch with me!* Loneliness augments the burdens of life.

Two elements mark His three prayers: recoil and resolution. He recoils from His approaching death: *O my Father, if it be possible, let this cup pass from me* (39). All that this means we cannot know. Jesus was no less brave than others have been who faced death without flinching. What He recoils from is the kind of death He faces. He will bear man's sin, and His immaculate soul is repulsed by the hideous burden. We have no capacity for gauging that kind of sorrow, for we have known too well and too comfortably the defilement of sin, without the experience of perfect moral purity.

His resolution is greater than His recoil. Every prayer closes with uncompromised commitment to the path chosen for Him by the Father. *Nevertheless . . . thy will be done* (39, 42). Never was temptation stronger; never was consecration costlier. He will drink the cup of death so that His followers may drink the cup of life (cf. 27-28).

2. *The sleeping disciples.* Three times the troubled Saviour returns to Peter, James, and John, and each time finds them sleeping. What awful loneliness He felt, unsupported by even a sympathetic spectator to His anguish.

These three had been more highly favored than all His followers (cf. Mark 5:37; Matt. 17:1). *To whom much is given, of him will much be required* (Luke 12:48, RSV). *Watch with me* was not an unreasonable requirement, but they could not measure up. They really wanted to. In *spirit* they were willing. But as *flesh*—as men sinful, fallen, and weak—they found the assignment too much for them.

When He rouses them the third time, it is too late. The opportunity to lend Him comfort in His trial has passed. Already the mob is approaching the Garden to arrest Him. The betrayer is *at hand*. The one disciple who was wide-awake was Judas. He would never sleep soundly again! What a contrast: Jesus on His face praying, Judas on his feet betraying!

We are frequently told that every Christian life must have its Gethsemane. In a sense this is true. At some point we must take up the cross, consent to the death of self-centeredness, and abandon our lives totally to the will of God. Even so, our struggles are tempered by the account of His victory. And no sorrow that we pass through reaches the depth of His anguish in Gethsemane.

Jesus Under Arrest

Matthew 26:47-56

47 And while he yet spake, lo, Judas, one of the twelve, came, and with him a great multitude with swords and staves, from the chief priests and elders of the people.
48 Now he that betrayed him gave them a sign, saying, Whomsoever I shall kiss, that same is he: hold him fast.
49 And forthwith he came to Jesus, and said, Hail, master; and kissed him.
50 And Jesus said unto him, Friend, wherefore art thou come? Then came they, and laid hands on Jesus, and took him.
51 And, behold, one of them which were with Jesus stretched out his hand, and drew his sword, and struck a servant of the high priest's, and smote off his ear.
52 Then said Jesus unto him, Put up again thy sword into his place: for all they that take the sword shall perish with the sword.
53 Thinkest thou that I cannot now pray to my Father, and he shall presently give me more than twelve legions of angels?
54 But how then shall the scriptures be fulfilled, that thus it must be?
55 In that same hour said Jesus to the multitudes, Are ye come out as against a thief with swords and staves for to take me? I sat daily with you teaching in the temple, and ye laid no hold on me.
56 But all this was done, that the scriptures of the prophets might be fulfilled. Then all the disciples forsook him, and fled.

Why so large a posse for so kind a Man? Doubtless they feared that His friends would intervene to prevent the arrest. One did try, but the disciples as a whole were readier for flight than fight. The reinforced Temple guard easily took charge of the nonresisting Christ and led Him away for trial. This record of His arrest brings into focus three actions.

1. *The first is the seizure of Jesus* (47-50). The traitor's kiss appalls us. That a symbol of affection should be the *sign* by which Jesus was betrayed deepens the perfidy of the act. He *kissed him* can be laid beside *one of the twelve* as a phrase of infinite sadness and shame. Between these phrases occurs the greeting, *Hail, master* (Rabbi). As previously pointed out, Judas never called Him Lord; but even Rabbi was an empty title, for Judas had not really learned the lessons Jesus taught.

The Lord's kindness contrasts sharply with the traitor's kiss. Jesus calls him, *Friend,* not as a description of what Judas was, but certainly an implied offer of a love that could even yet save Judas if he would respond. Jesus' question, *"Why are you here?"* (50, RSV), is the *et tu Brute* of the gospel story. Our discipleship under the love-commandment is certainly challenged by the example of One who would react as a Friend to a betrayer!

2. *The second important action is the swordplay of Peter* (51-54). As soon as the guards seized Jesus, Peter drew a sword and slashed out at them. Matthew keeps him anonymous, but John identifies the brave, awkward defender. He struck off the ear of the high priest's slave. Peter was a fisherman, not a swordsman. His target was not the ear. He intended to lop off the man's head!

The show of resistance was halted by the renunciation of force. Jesus ordered Peter to sheath the sword, and restored the ear, a detail supplied by Luke. The command, *Put up . . . thy sword,* followed by the statement that all who use the sword will die by it, forbids to the disciples of Jesus the use of violence and arms to achieve Kingdom objectives. Unfortunately, the Church has often disobeyed, and its march through history has left a trail-mark of one-eared men.

He who could have summoned legions of angels to His defense, and would not, does not sanction the employment of force in His name. Nothing is more damaging, less defensible, than the Church's resort to arms, torture, and execution to silence those whom it branded as heretics and enemies. "The blood of martyrs was the seed of the Church." A suffering Church proved undefeatable. But when the Church does the martyring, the blood of heretics can become a force to retard its growth. Satan cannot cast out Satan. Violence only breeds further violence. The only approved weaponry for the Church of Jesus Christ is suffering and forgiving love.

3. *The third significant action is the shaming of the crowd* (55-56). The farce of their size and arms was rebuked. The cowardice represented by their swords and clubs was scorned. For days Jesus had taught openly in the Temple and they did not seize Him. Now they ambush Him, as though He was a dangerous criminal. How little they knew Him! How little had they profited from His teachings! How easily they were influenced against Him by His enemies! Implicitly and explicitly Jesus made them aware of the contempt and cowardice of their actions. He was under arrest, but they were being indicted.

Jesus gathers courage from the fact that this sordid scheme is fulfilling the prophetic word in which He had traced the lineaments of His career as Messiah. He quietly goes with His captors, and the disciples scurry away for safety. Jesus giving himself, His disciples trying to save themselves! Does that say anything to us?

Jesus on Trial—the Sanhedrin

Matthew 26:57-68

> 57 And they that had laid hold on Jesus led him away to Caiaphas the high priest, where the scribes and the elders were assembled.
> 58 But Peter followed him afar off unto the high priest's palace, and went in, and sat with the servants, to see the end.
> 59 Now the chief priests, and elders, and all the council, sought false witness against Jesus, to put him to death;
> 60 But found none: yea, though many false witnesses came, yet found they none. At the last came two false witnesses,
> 61 And said, This fellow said, I am able to destroy the temple of God, and to build it in three days.
> 62 And the high priest arose, and said unto him, Answerest thou nothing? what is it which these witness against thee?
> 63 But Jesus held his peace. And the high priest answered and said unto him, I adjure thee by the living God, that thou tell us whether thou be the Christ, the Son of God.

64 Jesus saith unto him, Thou hast said: nevertheless I say unto you, Hereafter shall ye see the Son of man sitting on the right hand of power, and coming in the clouds of heaven.

65 Then the high priest rent his clothes, saying, He hath spoken blasphemy; what further need have we of witnesses? behold, now ye have heard his blasphemy.

66 What think ye? They answered and said, He is guilty of death.

67 Then did they spit in his face, and buffeted him; and others smote him with the palms of their hands,

68 Saying, Prophesy unto us, thou Christ, Who is he that smote thee?

Jesus was taken to the palace of Caiaphas for a hearing before the Sanhedrin. The Son of Man was homeless (8:20); the high priest had a palace. Things have not changed much since. Religious bureaucrats live at ease while God's true servants often barely get by.

Peter followed him afar off (58). Well that he did; preachers have needed the text so badly! We sometimes forget that even afar off he was closer than the other disciples (cf. 56).

As the hearing proceeded, two items stood out, the testimony given and the torment endured.

1. *The testimony.* Testimony was given falsely against Him. The council *sought false witness,* and those who do so never have to look far. But it is one thing to engage liars; it is quite another to find competent liars. *Many false witnesses came* but did not produce testimony upon which a death sentence could be framed. These bungling liars must have been a sore disappointment to the bloodthirsty kangaroo court. Finally, however, two came forward to charge Jesus with having claimed power to destroy the Temple and rebuild it in three days.

Testimony was given truly by Jesus. At first He refused to dignify the farce with any response to the accusations. *Jesus was silent* (63, RSV). The angry high priest placed Him under oath and demanded to know whether He was the Messiah, the Son of God. Jesus gave an affirmative reply, indirectly but unmistakably affirmative. He went on to say that the Son of Man will be seated at God's right hand and be seen coming on the clouds of heaven, further claim to be the Messiah (64).

The admission to messiahship prompted an accusation of blasphemy. Preferring custom to law, the high priest tore his robes (cf. Lev. 21:10). Pretending a grief he did not feel, Caiaphas called for the death sentence and the council readily assented.

The Sanhedrin had what they desired. Before Pilate they could interpret the claim to messiahship as political and revolutionary. Rome was swift to move against such threats. Their mission accomplished, the council released its tensions by abusing its Prisoner.

2. *The torment.* Two phrases sum it up. *They spat in his face,* and they *struck him* (67, RSV). The spitting was ultimate insult, and the slapping added injury to insult. In cruel mockery of His supernatural powers, which they had denied or attributed to demons, they blindfolded Him, then challenged Him to identify the ones who amused themselves by striking Him.

In this section we have a threefold perspective on Christ. In v. 63, the *silent Christ,* so poised and unafraid that He can ignore the lies and threats swirling about Him. In v. 64, the *seated Christ,* invested with the power of God, and destined to come to consummate the kingdom of God. Their Prisoner will be their Judge! In v. 67, the *smitten Christ,* meekly bearing insult and injury in order to be the Saviour of undeserving men.

Had the council been able to grasp the significance of these concepts, they would have dismissed the case and spared themselves from history's most heinous crime. But sin binds and blinds, driving men to irrational and suicidal courses of action.

History mocks their verdict. *"He deserves death"* (66, RSV), they cried. No, He is the one Man in the long history of a fallen race who did not deserve death, for death is the issue of sin—and He was sinless. But He consents to receive what He does not deserve—death—in order that we might receive what we do not deserve—life (cf. 2 Cor. 5:21).

The Denial of Peter

Matthew 26:69-75

69 Now Peter sat without in the palace: and a damsel came unto him, saying, Thou also wast with Jesus of Galilee.

70　But he denied before them all, saying, I know not what thou sayest.
71　And when he was gone out into the porch, another maid saw him, and said unto them that were there, This fellow was also with Jesus of Nazareth.
72　And again he denied with an oath, I do not know the man.
73　And after a while came unto him they that stood by, and said to Peter, Surely thou also art one of them; for thy speech bewrayeth thee.
74　Then began he to curse and to swear, saying, I know not the man. And immediately the cock crew.
75　And Peter remembered the word of Jesus, which said unto him, Before the cock crow, thou shalt deny me thrice. And he went out, and wept bitterly.

Briefly and painfully the denial of Jesus by His first disciple (cf. 10:2) is related. Scripture does not idealize the disciples. They are painted "warts and all." Their sins and failures are not glossed over, are not alibied. The truth emerges clearly that they are men who can live only by the renewed forgiveness of God.

Here Peter, the Rock, crumbles. Pentecost will weld the diffuse and fragile elements of the broken leader into a tower of strength. But for now, he comes bitterly to know his weakness.

1. *Peter's fears.* Three times he is pointed out as a follower of Jesus. Three times he vehemently denies it. The first time he pretends to be confused by the accusation, as though he has not so much as heard of Jesus. The second time he disclaims knowing *the man,* and bolsters the disclaimer with an oath. The third time he keeps taking an oath and repeating, *I know not the man.* He will not even use the name of Jesus! In the progression of these denials we can sense the mounting panic which seized him. The efforts to convince his accusers become so desperate that he sounds increasingly unconvincing.

What brought him to this pitiful descent into dishonesty? Fear. With Jesus on trial in the palace it was dangerous to confess Him in the courtyard. At his strongest point, his courage, he is assaulted and capitulates. For Peter has a fear of the Cross that he cannot control. Examine the record: Every time Jesus talked about the Cross, Peter tried to change the subject (cf. 16:21-22; Luke 9:30-33). This obsessive fear of a horrible and shameful death drove him to deny Jesus. He was afraid for Jesus, and even more afraid for himself.

2. *Peter's tears.* *"He went out, and wept bitterly"* (75). Filled with shame and regret at his failure, he sobbed out the brokenness of his heart. He was a great sinner, but he was a great repenter, and his capacity for regretting sin kept him from total spiritual collapse.

Remembered words started the flow of tears. He remembered the prediction of his denial, and the proud boast that he would die rather than fail Jesus. Perhaps he remembered, also, the promise of Jesus about the building of the Church (16:18) and wept for its ruined foundation. Perhaps he recalled the solemn warning that those who denied Jesus before men would be denied before the Father (10:32-33), and wept in fear of being disavowed and disinherited. There were so many words of Jesus that applied to this tragic situation.

But he must have remembered words that awakened hope and promised comfort, too. Did not the Lord advocate unlimited forgiveness for a sinning brother (18:21-22)? Had He not taught His disciples to pray, "Forgive us our sins" (6:12)? Through his tears the stricken disciple must have seen some rainbow of hope.

The next section gives us a final glimpse of Judas. Like Peter, he was filled with regret. But unlike Peter, he had no tears and no rainbows.

MATTHEW 27

The Remorse of Judas

Matthew 27:1-10

> 1 When the morning was come, all the chief priests and elders of the people took counsel against Jesus to put him to death:
> 2 And when they had bound him, they led him away, and delivered him to Pontius Pilate the governor.
> 3 Then Judas, which had betrayed him, when he saw that he was condemned, repented himself, and brought again the thirty pieces of silver to the chief priests and elders,
> 4 Saying, I have sinned in that I have betrayed the innocent blood. And they said, What is that to us? see thou to that.

5 And he cast down the pieces of silver in the temple, and departed, and went and hanged himself.

6 And the chief priests took the silver pieces, and said, It is not lawful for to put them into the treasury, because it is the price of blood.

7 And they took counsel, and bought with them the potter's field, to bury strangers in.

8 Wherefore that field was called, The field of blood, unto this day.

9 Then was fulfilled that which was spoken by Jeremy the prophet, saying, And they took the thirty pieces of silver, the price of him that was valued, whom they of the children of Israel did value;

10 And gave them for the potter's field, as the Lord appointed me.

Judas *repented.* He had second thoughts (the Greek word means "regretted"). Jesus was condemned to die, and the infamy of his betrayal hit Judas like a blow to the stomach. He tried to make amends by returning the money. Now the whole affair had been a nonprofit venture. What the betrayal cost him proved to be infinitely more than what it had paid him. Nonprofit? Worse. He suffered deep, irreparable loss.

1. *Betrayal cost him self-respect.* Deep inside, beyond whatever twisted reasons and confused motives caused him to perpetrate the perfidious act, he found a self he could not love and would not forgive. He had been unwilling to live for Jesus, and now he could not live with himself.

2. *Betrayal cost him friendship.* Jesus had been his best Friend, and remained a Friend to the end (26:50). Now that Friend was on His way to the gallows, and Judas had abetted the miscarriage of justice. He pays Jesus the only tribute which the situation permits: *I have sinned . . . I have betrayed the innocent blood* (4).

The disciples had been his friends. He had belonged to the group, sharing their life and work. But they are scattered in fear. And remembering the swordplay at the Garden, would he dare to seek them out and hope for understanding and forgiveness?

The priests who bargained with him would not be his friends. They were so unmoved by the torture of his lonely soul that they flung his confession back in his face with contempt. That is your problem!

3. *Betrayal cost him life.* He flung down the blood money

as if the coins seared his palms, and then he *hanged himself.*

> *Out in the night*
> > *Clutching a rope,*
> *No glimmer of light,*
> > *No gleaming of hope!*
> *The last action taken,*
> > *Betrayer! he cried,*
> *And friendless, forsaken,*
> > *Iscariot died.*

Peter went out and wept bitterly. Judas went out and hanged himself. Both sinned, both regretted their actions. But one found hope, comfort, forgiveness, and restoration. The other found despair and oblivion.

The priests, who could murder an innocent Man without flinching, were scrupulous about keeping the law! Blood money could not be placed in the Temple treasury (Deut. 23:18), nor will they defile themselves by keeping it. They bought a potter's field which became a cemetery for unclaimed bodies of aliens. *The field of blood* becomes the memorial of Judas Iscariot. A memorial to treachery. A memorial to hypocrisy. A memorial to futility.

Judas had branded Mary's anointing of Jesus "waste." Was there ever a greater waste in history than the life and death of Judas, *one of the twelve, the betrayer?*

Jesus on Trial—Pilate

Matthew 27:11-26

11 And Jesus stood before the governor: and the governor asked him, saying, Art thou the King of the Jews? And Jesus said unto him, Thou sayest.
12 And when he was accused of the chief priests and elders, he answered nothing.
13 Then said Pilate unto him, Hearest thou not how many things they witness against thee?
14 And he answered him to never a word; insomuch that the governor marvelled greatly.
15 Now at that feast the governor was wont to release unto the people a prisoner, whom they would.
16 And they had been a notable prisoner, called Barabbas.
17 Therefore when they were gathered together, Pilate said unto them, Whom will ye that I release unto you? Barabbas, or Jesus which is called Christ?
18 For he knew that for envy they had delivered him.
19 When he was set down on the judgment seat, his wife sent unto

him, saying, Have thou nothing to do with that just man: for I have suffered many things this day in a dream because of him.

20 But the chief priests and elders persuaded the multitude that they should ask Barabbas, and destroy Jesus.

21 The governor answered and said unto them, Whether of the twain will ye that I release unto you? They said, Barabbas.

22 Pilate saith unto them, What shall I do then with Jesus which is called Christ? They all say unto him, Let him be crucified.

23 And the governor said, Why, what evil hath he done? But they cried out the more, saying, Let him be crucified.

24 When Pilate saw that he could prevail nothing, but that rather a tumult was made, he took water, and washed his hands before the multitude, saying, I am innocent of the blood of this just person: see ye to it.

25 Then answered all the people, and said, His blood be on us, and on our children.

26 Then released he Barabbas unto them: and when he had scourged Jesus, he delivered him to be crucified.

Pontius Pilate, procurator of Palestine, was placed in a bad spot. Only a strong man, committed to justice at any cost, even the loss of career, could escape the problem with integrity intact. But Pilate was a weak man, for whom the politically expedient took precedent over the morally right. He was the civil counterpart of the priests and elders. He was caught in a crunch and must have set a new Roman record for perspiration on the day of Jesus' formal trial.

1. *Pilate had a Prisoner he could not figure out* (11-14). The governor was troubled by the silence of Jesus. The Man was accused of sedition by His own nation's leaders. He surely knew what Rome did with "kings" who plotted revolution! And yet, to the barrage of accusing voices Jesus gave no reply, made no defense. He just stood there, serene, unafraid, master of himself, the one unagitated Figure in the whole proceedings. Pilate *marvelled greatly.* Prisoners with their lives at stake usually raged or whined, but this Man was the calm at the center of the hurricane.

The governor was also troubled by the speech of his wife (19). She had sent him a message, urging a hasty acquittal, for in a troubled dream she saw Jesus as a just Man. Pilate evidently put stock in such messages.

2. *Pilate faced a crowd he could not calm down* (15-23). He was outwitted by the priests. Convinced of Jesus' innocence and anxious to free Him, Pilate resorted to a current political maneuver. At Passover time, to cool the fever of

nationalism, he would release a Jewish prisoner. He offered the crowd a choice, Jesus or Barabbas, *a notorious prisoner* (RSV), robber, murderer, and insurrectionist (cf. John 18: 40; Mark 15:7; Luke 23:19). But the crafty priests had foreseen the ploy and had persuaded the crowd to ask for the release of Barabbas. To Pilate's famous question, *What shall I do then with Jesus?* the crowd chanted, *Crucify him.* Every man to whom the gospel comes faces that question. Barabbas is the world's alternative to Jesus.

Pilate was overwhelmed by the mob. In response to his, *Why?* and public statement of Jesus' innocence, they did not debate. Their method was less refined but more effective. Louder and louder they roared, *Let him be crucified.* The mood was ugly and verging on riot, so Pilate caved in.

3. *Pilate contracted a stain he could not wash off* (24-26). An empty symbolism was enacted. Pilate washed his hands to demonstrate his innocence of Jesus' blood. It was a pitiful spectacle of cowardice. What honesty and courage failed to prevent, no ritual of washing could amend.

A spineless surrender was made. Barabbas was released. Jesus was cruelly beaten, and then He was handed over to soldiers for execution. Barabbas became what every Christian is, a man who lived because Jesus died. Did Pilate ever learn that the stain of guilt he vainly tried to wash with water could be removed only by the blood of Jesus?

The priests and the procurator, joined in unholy alliance to effect the death of Jesus, gained a negative immortality in history. Power politics and institutional religion, fearful for their vested interests, have often conspired in crimes against truth, justice, and freedom. But priests and politicians would not succeed without the people they persuade to put the weight of numbers behind a tissue of lies. No one is exonerated from the death of Jesus.

The Death of Jesus

Matthew 27:27-54

27 Then the soldiers of the governor took Jesus into the common hall, and gathered unto him the whole band of soldiers.

28 And they stripped him, and put on him a scarlet robe.

29 And when they had platted a crown of thorns, they put it upon his head, and a reed in his right hand: and they bowed the knee before him, and mocked him, saying, Hail, King of the Jews!

30 And they spit upon him, and took the reed, and smote him on the head.

31 And after that they had mocked him, they took the robe off from him, and put his own raiment on him, and led him away to crucify him.

32 And as they came out, they found a man of Cyrene, Simon by name: him they compelled to bear his cross.

33 And when they were come unto a place called Golgotha, that is to say, a place of a skull,

34 They gave him vinegar to drink mingled with gall: and when he had tasted thereof, he would not drink.

35 And they crucified him, and parted his garments, casting lots: that it might be fulfilled which was spoken by the prophet, They parted my garments among them, and upon my vesture did they cast lots.

36 And sitting down they watched him there;

37 And set up over his head his accusation written, THIS IS JESUS THE KING OF THE JEWS.

38 Then were there two thieves crucified with him, one on the right hand, and another on the left.

39 And they that passed by reviled him, wagging their heads,

40 And saying, Thou that destroyest the temple, and buildest it in three days, save thyself. If thou be the Son of God, come down from the cross.

41 Likewise also the chief priests mocking him, with the scribes and elders, said,

42 He saved others; himself he cannot save. If he be the King of Israel, let him now come down from the cross, and we will believe him.

43 He trusted in God; let him deliver him now, if he will have him: for he said, I am the Son of God.

44 The thieves also, which were crucified with him, cast the same in his teeth.

45 Now from the sixth hour there was darkness over all the land unto the ninth hour.

46 And about the ninth hour Jesus cried with a loud voice, saying, Eli, Eli, lama sabachthani? that is to say, My God, my God, why hast thou forsaken me?

47 Some of them that stood there, when they heard that, said, This man calleth for Elias.

48 And straightway one of them ran, and took a spunge, and filled it with vinegar, and put it on a reed, and gave him to drink.

49 The rest said, Let be, let us see whether Elias will come to save him.

50 Jesus, when he had cried again with a loud voice, yielded up the ghost.

51 And, behold, the vail of the temple was rent in twain from the top to the bottom; and the earth did quake, and the rocks rent;

52 And the graves were opened; and many bodies of the saints which slept arose,

53 And came out of the graves after his resurrection, and went into the holy city, and appeared unto many.

54 Now when the centurion, and they that were with him, watching Jesus, saw the earthquake, and those things that were done, they feared greatly, saying, Truly this was the Son of God.

The mockery which Jesus endured at the hands of brutal soldiers is a vivid commentary on the power of sin to dry the springs of sympathy. They amused themselves with the helpless Victim in the way a cat plays with a mouse before killing it. But the One they crowned with thorns is now crowned with honor and glory (Heb. 2:9). The One before whom they knelt in mock homage will have the entire world on its knees before God's purposes are concluded (Phil. 2:9-11). They hailed Him in jest as King of the Jews, but He is in truth Lord of the universe (Eph. 1:20-21; Rev. 1:5). Their cruel fun could only delay by minutes His march to the throne, for His route to that throne lay by way of the Cross.

Tired of their sport, they led the blood-and-spittle-smeared Prisoner to His gallows. Simon of Cyrene was *compelled to bear his cross,* and learned that some of life's compulsions are enriching. Arriving at the *place of a skull* they offered Him the customary sedative, which He refused. Then *they crucified him.* So simply can profound events be recorded!

One way to view the death of Jesus is to listen to the voices raised on the occasion.

1. *There was a cry of derision* (39-44). It arose from the passersby, repeating the false testimony given at His trial, and challenging Him, *Save thyself!* The voice of the tempter is echoed by the crowd, *"If you are the Son of God, come down from the cross"* (40, RSV). The obedience He affirmed in the wilderness He now demonstrates on the Cross. What can spectators know of real issues? Mere onlookers soon imbibe and repeat the counsels of the devil.

The cry of derision was flung, also, from the mouths of leaders: the priests, scribes, and elders who hounded Jesus to His death. They mocked His apparent helplessness: *He saved others; himself he cannot save* (42). Blind fools, He had called them, and they were never so blind as now. Just when He seemed the most passive He was the most active. In suffering love which would not spare himself, He was lifting with nailed hands the weight of a world's sin and guilt! *Let him now come down from the cross, and we will believe him.* The adulterous generation still sought a sign, and still could not read the transcript of the kingdom of God being fulfilled before their eyes. He claimed to be the Son of God, they taunted; let God have Him if God wants Him! That is precisely what happened. The One rejected by men was accepted by God, and our only hope of acceptance lies in that prior acceptance of Jesus in our stead.

Even the criminals crucified with Him joined the derisive chorus (44). The burden of His loneliness was to become even heavier as He split the darkened sky with His own cry.

2. *There was a cry of dereliction* (45-50). A terrible cry of forsakenness was wrung from the tortured heart and throat of Jesus: *My God, my God, why hast thou forsaken me?* Who can measure the depths of alienation that His words attest? This is the only time that Jesus ever called on God without addressing Him as Father. He was not merely quoting a psalm; He was experiencing it. Debates among theologians as to whether God actually forsook Him, even for a moment, are fruitless. To Jesus it was real!

And yet it was a cry of faith. He cries, *My* God! He clings to God when He loses consciousness of being held by God. Loss of nerve? No, the profoundest act of faith in all of history!

He experienced that utter forsakenness in order that we might be joined to God forever. That is as close to an answer to His *why* as the Church has come, and it is sufficient. My trust, and not my understanding, brings to my needy life the benefits of His atoning death.

3. *There was a cry of confession* (51-54). When Jesus died, strange portents occurred (51-53). The veil that hung between the two rooms of the sanctuary was torn from top to bottom. Nature sickened and convulsed, and the earthquake opened tombs. We can assign meaning to these events, but Matthew does not; he is content to record them.

But he also tells us that the Roman officer and his men, awed by the quaking earth, exclaimed, *Truly this was the Son of God.* Just what he meant is debatable.

Certainly he was not voicing the theological content of later Christian creeds. After all, we are hard pressed to explicate what we mean by the same confession today! Matthew closes the death scene on this note of confession in order to say, No man ever lived, taught, or died as Jesus did. He was no ordinary man. He was *the Christ, the Son of the living God.*

The Burial of Jesus

Matthew 27:55-66

55 And many women were there beholding afar off, which followed Jesus from Galilee, ministering unto him:

56 Among which was Mary Magdalene, and Mary the mother of James and Joses, and the mother of Zebedee's children.

57 When the even was come, there came a rich man of Arimathaea, named Joseph, who also himself was Jesus' disciple:

58 He went to Pilate, and begged the body of Jesus. Then Pilate commanded the body to be delivered.

59 And when Joseph had taken the body, he wrapped it in a clean linen cloth,

60 And laid it in his own new tomb, which he had hewn out in the rock: and he rolled a great stone to the door of the sepulchre, and departed.

61 And there was Mary Magdalene, and the other Mary, sitting over against the sepulchre.

62 Now the next day, that followed the day of the preparation, the chief priests and Pharisees came together unto Pilate,

63 Saying, Sir, we remember that that deceiver said, while he was yet alive, After three days I will rise again.

64 Command therefore that the sepulchre be made sure until the third day, lest his disciples come by night, and steal him away, and say unto the people, He is risen from the dead: so the last error shall be worse than the first.

65 Pilate said unto them, Ye have a watch: go your way, make it as sure as ye can.

66 So they went, and made the sepulchre sure, sealing the stone, and setting a watch.

The Crucifixion story closes on a note of deep pathos, but these final verses of chapter 27 are richly laden for those who join the vigil at the Cross and the tomb, though their treasures of truth are seen through tears.

1. *The women represent an exercise in loyalty.* They were watching from a distance when Jesus died, and some of them observed more closely His entombment. Three of them are named, and the others remain anonymous, but all wear a badge of distinction. They are identified as women who *followed Jesus.* They were not spectators but

participants in His work, for they followed Jesus, *ministering unto him.*

Their previous service is caught up in the one word *ministering.* The precise forms of that ministry were varied. Luke 8:3 suggests gifts of food and money, likely accompanied by the cooking and serving of meals. Some served as living demonstrations of His healing power, and all served as trophies of His redeeming love.

Their present service is one of *beholding.* That is all they can do now, but done in love and loyalty such beholding was a ministry also. The Church is learning to value the ministry of presence. In situations which preclude activity or speech, just being present in sympathy and caring has great value.

2. *Joseph of Arimathaea represents an exercise in bravery.* When hatred for Jesus crackled like lightning from the eyes and lips of His crucifiers, it took real courage for this man to step forward and rescue the body of the Crucified one from being flung on the garbage dump and left for the vultures.

Identification with Jesus has always been costly. John tells us that Joseph had been a disciple *secretly* (John 19: 38). Now the death of Jesus shames him from the fear of Jesus' enemies and he openly ministers the burial rites.

Evaluation of Jesus is involved, also, in this act of courage. By executing Jesus as a criminal and with criminals, the enemies of Jesus had said, He is worthless. Now by his tender ministrations, as this *rich man* lays the body *in his own new tomb,* he is affirming the worthiness of Jesus to receive the kind of honor Jewish society reserved for its wealthiest and most respected citizens. This contradiction of the leaders, of his own peer group, was a splendid gesture of courage. It challenges all of us who follow Jesus today to openly affirm our love for Him.

3. *The priests and Pharisees represent an exercise in futility.* They came to Pilate, defaming Jesus as an impostor and His disciples as predators. They urged the posting of a guard at the tomb to prevent body-snatching as a means of inciting riot. Soon they will bribe the guards

to say that the body was stolen. Poor, frantic men! They try to prevent what could not happen, and then are forced to invent what did not happen.

The tomb was sealed. The seal emblemized the authority of Rome, and threatened dire punishment to any who dared to intrude into the tomb. And a guard of soldiers was posted to scare away any not intimidated by the seal. There is something pathetic in Pilate's words, *"Make it as secure as you can"* (65, RSV). No security was needed against the terrified disciples, and none was possible against Almighty God! No stone, no seal, no soldiers could keep death from losing its grip upon Him who is "the resurrection, and the life." It was well that He lay in a borrowed tomb, for His would be a brief sleep!

MATTHEW 28

The Resurrection

Matthew 28:1-15

1 In the end of the sabbath, as it began to dawn toward the first day of the week, came Mary Magdalene and the other Mary to see the sepulchre.
2 And, behold, there was a great earthquake: for the angel of the Lord descended from heaven, and came and rolled back the stone from the door, and sat upon it.
3 His countenance was like lightning, and his raiment white as snow:
4 And for fear of him the keepers did shake, and became as dead men.
5 And the angel answered and said unto the women, Fear not ye: for I know that ye seek Jesus, which was crucified.
6 He is not here: for he is risen, as he said. Come, see the place where the Lord lay.
7 And go quickly, and tell his disciples that he is risen from the dead; and, behold, he goeth before you into Galilee; there shall ye see him: lo, I have told you.
8 And they departed quickly from the sepulchre with fear and great joy; and did run to bring his disciples word.
9 And as they went to tell his disciples, behold, Jesus met them, saying, All hail. And they came and held him by the feet, and worshipped him.
10 Then said Jesus unto them, Be not afraid: go tell my brethren that they go into Galilee, and there shall they see me.
11 Now when they were going, behold, some of the watch came into the city, and shewed unto the chief priests all the things that were done.
12 And when they were assembled with the elders, and had taken counsel, they gave large money unto the soldiers,

13 Saying, Say ye, His disciples came by night, and stole him away while we slept.
14 And if this come to the governor's ears, we will persuade him, and secure you.
15 So they took the money, and did as they were taught: and this saying is commonly reported among the Jews until this day.

As it began to dawn (happy phrase, for such a light was about to burst upon history as all the darkness of unbelief and evil could not put out!), two women, bearing a common name and joined in a common purpose, approached the tomb of Jesus. There they found that everything was changed. Instead of a sacred corpse, a shining angel! Instead of tragic death, triumphant life! Instead of despair, hope! Instead of mourning, joy! Nothing can ever be the same again—not sin, not death, not history, not eternity, not man, and not God, because Jesus was risen from the dead.

Matthew associates two great quakes with this climactic event, the quaking ground and the quaking guards. The same Greek root is used to describe both. The ground shook as the mighty energies of nature's awakening Lord vibrated through the Garden. The guards shook as the radiant presence of the angel chased specters of guilt from the depths of their depraved hearts. And neither earth nor man has ever been at peace since, nor can they be until He who came from the grave comes again from the heavens.

What claims our attention, primarily, is neither trembling earth or trembling men, but the message of the angel to the women, soon to be theirs to the disciples, and soon to be the Church's to all nations: *"He is not here; for he has risen, as he said. Come, see the place where he lay. Then go quickly and tell his disciples"* (6-7, RSV).

1. *How magnificent the declaration of the angel! "He has risen"* (6, RSV). He who said, *Rise . . . and walk,* to the paralytic, delivering him from a bed of illness, has heard the same command of God delivering Him from *the place where he lay* (RSV). The Crucified is now the Resurrected. Men said no to His claims, divine claims, as He forgave sins. Men said no to His words, divine words, as He taught in their midst. Men said no to His deeds, divine deeds, as

He healed the sick. The resurrection is God's mighty yes to all that Jesus claimed, taught, and did. It reverses the verdict of the Cross, exposes the guilt of men, and heralds the ultimate triumph of the kingdom of God.

2. *How eloquent the demonstration of the empty tomb! Come, see the place where the Lord lay* (6). Critics have charged with dreary monotony that the empty tomb is inadmissible as evidence and irrelevant for faith. But the very ones who saw the tomb filled (27:61) now see it vacant. The body is gone. Any explanation that radically divorces the "Jesus of history" from "the Christ of faith" and posits a psychological or metaphysical resurrection, instead of a bodily resurrection, does rank injustice to the facts. The psychological transformation of the disciples could not have occurred apart from the vacancy of that tomb.

The angel said, *Ye seek Jesus. . . . He is not here* (5-6). Where is He now to be found? Verse 9 tells us: *Jesus met them and said, "Hail!"* (RSV). The risen Christ is found in a living encounter which He initiates by His grace and mediates through His word.

3. *How urgent the deputation of the women! "Go quickly, and tell his disciples"* (7). Come and see; go and tell! First, tell His disciples; then tell all others (19). Church and world alike need to hear the message, first proclaimed by the angel, and soon transferred as the responsibility of people. Men defeated and doomed by sin need to know that sin itself has been conquered and death itself has been vanquished. *Quickly,* for good news cannot travel too fast when it is needed so urgently.

Even as the women hastened away, it was "go and tell" time for some others. The guards reported to the priests the empty tomb (11-15). And religious leaders bribed too willing accomplices to tell people that the disciples of Jesus had stolen the body. Incidentally, the Greek terms used show that the bribe given to the guards exceeded that paid to Judas for the betrayal. The cost of opposing Jesus always gets higher as time passes.

Thus began the denial of the Resurrection which

persists *to this day* (15, RSV). And every new theory propounded to explain it away partakes of the insincerity and incredulity of the original lie. Falsehood is not improved by changing its clothes.

If the guards hurried to circulate a lie, the disciples would speed to proclaim the truth. Wesley once preached from his father's tombstone. From the empty tomb of Jesus the gospel has radiated to the ends of the earth!

The Great Commission

Matthew 28:16-20

> 16 Then the eleven disciples went away into Galilee, into a mountain where Jesus had appointed them.
> 17 And when they saw him, they worshipped him: but some doubted.
> 18 And Jesus came and spake unto them, saying, All power is given unto me in heaven and in earth.
> 19 Go ye therefore, and teach all nations, baptizing them in the name of the Father, and of the Son, and of the Holy Ghost:
> 20 Teaching them to observe all things whatsoever I have commanded you: and, lo, I am with you alway, even unto the end of the world. Amen.

With this story, which only he records, Matthew fittingly draws his account of the earthly ministry of Jesus to its close.

A note of sadness tinges the opening phrase of this passage: *Then the eleven disciples.* There should have been 12. One fell and died disgraced. But the circle will be endlessly widened, despite the occasional failures, for the 11 are commissioned to *make disciples of all nations* (19, RSV). We should mourn the losses, but they must never paralyze our efforts to gain others for the Lord.

The passage is highlighted by inclusive phrases, *all power . . . all nations . . . all the days* (lit.).

1. *The power which Jesus claims is absolute. All power* (Gk. *exousia,* authority) *is given unto me in heaven and in earth* (18). Not simply the highest power, but *all power.* This means that Jesus is Lord of all, and every authority exercised by men is at His sufferance and under His judgment. No king, dictator, president, coalition, congress, or court has ultimate authority over men or control of history. Jesus is *ruler of the kings of the earth* (Rev. 1:5, NEB).

Verse 19 speaks of *the name of the Father and of the*

Son and of the Holy Spirit (19, RSV). The singular is employed—*the name,* not the names. Jesus possesses absolute power because He participates equally with the Father and the Spirit in the one name of God. His authority is divine, hence universal. Matthew identifies Him as the *son of David,* but He possesses such power as His illustrious ancestor could never have imagined. Under the aegis of that power, the Church can face the herculean task which He has assigned it without dismay.

2. *The program which Jesus outlines is universal. "Go therefore and make disciples of all nations"* (19, RSV). As none are omitted from the authority He exercises, so none are excluded from the salvation He offers. Matthew began by establishing Jesus as the *son of Abraham.* Jesus fulfills the covenant which God made with Abraham, a covenant terminating upon all nations (Gen. 12:1-3). The fulfillment was to be actualized historically by the discipling ministry of His followers, beginning with the 11 who first received the Great Commission.

The discipling ministry has two parts: (1) *baptizing,* and (2) *teaching.* The Church has a reaching ministry; it must convert men to Christ and admit them into His body. Therefore the risen Lord scatters the Church for witness. But the Church has also a teaching ministry; it must instruct the converts in the way of life which Jesus has commanded. Therefore the risen Lord gathers the Church for worship. Such gathering and worshiping is viewed in this passage. The disciples go to the mountain which Jesus *appointed,* and there they worship Him. He comes to them and speaks to them. Then He sends them out to speak for Him. This is what the Church essentially is, a people who live under the lordship of Jesus, worshiping and witnessing at His command.

3. *The promise which Christ extends is sufficient. "Lo, I am with you always"* (20, RSV). He is no rear-line commander. He shares the field with His troops.

He will be present when they worship, and His presence will evaporate their doubts. *They worshipped him; but some doubted,* the record says. And the next words are, *And Jesus came.* Our doubts are seldom dissolved by intellectual arguments, but by His reassuring presence!

He will be present when they witness, and His presence will guarantee the sustenance of those who undertake the task. But only those! The *lo* is linked inseparably to the *go*.

On this high note, Jesus then, Jesus now, Jesus coming, the first Gospel ends.

A Selected Bibliography

Albright, W. F., and Mann, C. S. "Matthew," *The Anchor Bible.* Garden City, N.Y.: Doubleday and Company, Inc., 1971.

Allen, W. C. "A Critical and Exegetical Commentary on the Gospel According to S. Matthew," *The International Critical Commentary.* New York: Charles Scribner's Sons, 1907.

Broadus, J. A. "The Gospel of Matthew," *An American Commentary on the New Testament.* Philadelphia: The American Baptist Publication Society, 1886.

Buttrick, George A. "The Gospel According to St. Matthew" (Exposition), *Interpreter's Bible.* New York: Abingdon-Cokesbury Press, 1951, Vol. VII.

Daube, David. *The New Testament and Rabbinic Judaism.* London: Athlone Press, 1956.

Davies, W. D. *The Setting of the Sermon on the Mount.* Cambridge: University Press, 1964.

Earle, Ralph. "The Gospel According to Matthew," *Beacon Bible Commentary.* Kansas City: Beacon Hill Press of Kansas City, 1964, Vol. 6.

Filson, Floyd V. "The Gospel According to St. Matthew," *Harper's New Testament Commentaries.* New York: Harper and Bros., 1960.

Guthrie, Donald. *New Testament Introduction.* Chicago: Inter-Varsity Press, 1966.

Jeremias, J. *The Parables of Jesus.* New York: Charles Scribner's Sons, 1953.

Kingsbury, Jack D. *The Parables of Jesus in Matthew 13.* Richmond, Va.: John Knox Press, 1969.

Ladd, George Eldon. *A Theology of the New Testament.* Grand Rapids, Mich.: William B. Eerdmans Publishing Company, 1974.

Plummer, Alfred. *An Exegetical Commentary on the Gospel According to S. Matthew.* New York: Charles Scribner's Sons, 1910.

Selby, Donald J. *Introduction to the New Testament.* New York: The Macmillan Company, 1971.

Stagg, Frank. "Matthew," *The Broadman Bible Commentary.* Nashville: Broadman Press, 1969.

Stendahl, K. *The School of St. Matthew.* London: G. W. K. Gleerup, 1954.